KEN SCHULTZ'S
Field Guide to Freshwater Fish

KEN SCHULTZ'S
Field Guide to Freshwater Fish

by Ken Schultz

WILEY

JOHN WILEY & SONS, INC.

For general information about our other products and services, please contact our
Customer Care Department within the United States at (800) 762-2974, outside the
United States at (317) 572-3993 or fax (317) 572-4002.

Wiley also publishes its books in a variety of electronic formats. Some content that
appears in print may not be available in electronic books. For more information about
Wiley products, visit our web site at www.wiley.com.

ISBN 0–471–44994-6

Printed in the United States of America

10 9 8 7 6 5 4 3 2 1

Contents

Introduction

This guide is derived from the widely praised and award-winning volume *Ken Schultz's Fishing Encyclopedia*. Weighing nearly 10 pounds and containing 1,916 pages of information in an 8.5- by 11-inch format, it is hardly a book that can be taken afield or casually perused.

Among the many virtues of the encyclopedia is its detailed information about prey and predator species worldwide, which many people—including numerous lure designers, scientific researchers, and anglers—find very valuable and which is available nowhere else. To make it easier for people interested in the major North American fish species to reference this subject matter, that portion of the encyclopedia was excerpted into two compact and portable guides, *Ken Schultz's Field Guide to Freshwater Fish* and *Ken Schultz's Field Guide to Saltwater Fish*.

These books are primarily intended for the angler, placing major emphasis on gamefish species (nearly 260) sought in the fresh- and saltwaters of Canada, the United States, and Mexico, and on the prey species that most gamefish use for forage. Although many hundreds of species are included here, such compact books lack room for detailed information about many of the lesser species; however, they are well represented in the information that exists under certain groupings. For example, there are more than 300 species of "minnows" in North America, and much of what is said about them as a group in the freshwater guide pertains to the majority of individuals. Profiles are provided, nonetheless, of some of the more prominent members of this group.

The same is true for some larger, more well-known groups of fish, like sharks. There are at least 370 species of sharks worldwide and dozens in North America. The saltwater guide provides an overview of this group, as well as specific information about the most prominent North American members. And, of course, color illustrations help identify the individual species profiled.

There is a slight but deliberate content overlap in both books, as some species occur in both freshwater and saltwater. This is primarily true for anadromous fish like salmon, shad, and striped bass. However, a few saltwater species, such as snook, mullet, and ladyfish, are known to move into freshwater for part of their lives, even though they are not technically anadromous, and thus are also represented in both volumes. In this sense, certain species were included in both books for practical reasons, as opposed to purely scientific ones.

At the end of the book is a glossary that explains the terms used in the species profiles, and following this introduction are two chapters of information invaluable to anyone who desires to know more about fish in a broad general sense. The Overview and the Fish Anatomy chapters are written in layman's terms and provide concise information about fish that is useful to the angler, the naturalist, and even the aquarium hobbyist—all of whom share a passion and a concern for some of the most remarkable creatures on the planet.

An Overview of Fish

FISH

The term "fish" is applied to a class of animals that includes some 21,000 extremely diverse species. Fish can be roughly defined (and there are a few exceptions) as cold-blooded creatures that have backbones, live in water, and have gills. The gills enable fish to "breathe" underwater, without drawing oxygen from the atmosphere. This is the primary difference between fish and all other vertebrates. Although such vertebrates as whales and turtles live in water, they cannot breathe underwater. No other vertebrate but the fish is able to live without breathing air. One family of fish, the lungfish, is able to breathe air when mature and actually loses its functional gills. Another family of fish, the tuna, is considered warm-blooded by many people, but the tuna is an exception.

Fish are divided into four groups: the hagfish, the lampreys, cartilaginous fish, and bony fish. The hagfish and the lampreys lack jaws, and as such, they form the group called jawless fish; the cartilaginous fish and the bony fish have jaws. The bony fish are by far the most common, making up more than 95 percent of the world's fish species. Cartilaginous fish, including sharks, rays, and skates, are the second largest group, numbering some 700 species. There are 32 species of hagfish and 40 species of lampreys.

Overview

Body of the fish. The body of a fish is particularly adapted to aquatic life. The body is equipped with fins for the purpose of locomotion. Scales and mucus protect the body and keep it streamlined. The skeleton features a long backbone that can produce the side-to-side movements needed for forward propulsion in water. Since water is 800 times more dense than air, fish must be extremely strong to move in their environment. Fish respond to this condition by being mostly muscle. Thus, muscles make up 40 to 65 percent of a fish's body weight. Many fish have air or gas bladders (sometimes called swim bladders), which allow them to float at their desired depth. Fish also have gills, their underwater breathing apparatus, located in the head. Most fish have only one gill cover, although some, like sharks, have gill slits, some as many as seven. The gills are the most fragile part of the fish; anglers should avoid touching the gills on fish that they plan on releasing.

The limbs of fish come in the form of fins. A fin is a membrane that extends from the body of the fish and is supported by spines or rays. Because the number of rays is usually constant within a species, a ray count is often used by scientists to determine the species of a fish. Each of the fins on a fish has a name. Since these names are used in almost all descriptions of fish and are used in this book, it is worthwhile to become familiar with the different fin names.

Moving from the head toward the tail, the first fins are the pectoral fins. The pectoral fins are used for balance and maneuvering in many species and in a few are used for propulsion. Further down the underside of the fish are the pelvic fins, located beneath the belly and used for balance. On the back of the fish is the dorsal fin. Some fish have more than one dorsal fin; in this case the dorsal fins are numbered, with the fin closest to the head called the first dorsal fin. Behind the dorsal fin on the top part of the fish there is occasionally a smaller, fleshy fin called the adipose fin. Back on the underside of the fish, behind the pelvic fins and the anus, is the anal fin. The final fin, usually called the tail, is known scientifically as the caudal fin. The caudal fin is the most important fin for locomotion; by moving it from side to side, a fish is able to gather forward momentum.

The scales of a fish form the main protection for the body. Fish scales are kept for the entire life of a fish; as a fish grows, the scales get larger, rather than growing anew. Scales are divided into several types. Most fish have ctenoid or cycloid scales. Ctenoid scales are serrated on one edge and feel rough when rubbed the wrong way (largemouth bass have such scales). Cycloid scales are entirely smooth, like the scales of trout. More rare types of fish have different types of scales: Sharks have more primitive placoid scales, which are spiny; sturgeon have ganoid scales, which form armor ridges along parts of the body. Some species, like catfish, have no scales at all. Fish scales can be used to determine the age of a fish. A fish scale will develop rings showing annual growth, much like the rings of a tree.

Many fish also have a covering of mucus that gives them a slimy feel. This covering helps streamline their body and prevent infections. The mucus covering will rub off onto a person's hands (this is the slimy substance that you can feel on your hands after handling a fish). Since the loss of mucus is detrimental to the fish, it is better to wet your hands before handling a fish that will be released to minimize the amount of mucus removed, being careful not to harm a fish by holding it too tightly.

The skeletal and muscular systems of fish work together to maximize swimming power. The serially repeated vertebrae and the muscle structure work together to create the shimmering, undulating muscle movements that allow a fish to move forward quickly. This structure is particularly evident in a filleted fish, where the muscles show themselves in their interlocking pattern. The muscular nature of fish is the reason why fish make such good eating and is also a factor in making fish a high-yield food source.

Bony fish have developed an organ called an air bladder, which acts as a kind of flotation device. A fish's body is naturally a bit more dense than water, but the air bladder, filled with gas, increases a fish's ability to float. Fish can change the depth at which they float by varying the amount of gas in their air bladder. This allows a fish to float at any depth it desires without expending any effort. Fish that do not have air bladders, such as sharks, must continually move in order to prevent their sinking.

Like virtually all animals, fish need oxygen to survive. However, a fish can get all the oxygen it needs from water by the use of its gills. Water entering through the mouth of the fish is forced over the gills, and oxygen is removed from the water by the gills. In order to breathe, fish must constantly have water passing over their gills. However, in order to get enough oxygen, certain fish must either move continually or live in water with a strong current.

Although most fish are referred to as cold-blooded creatures, this is mostly but not entirely true. Some species are called warm-blooded, yet they cannot sustain a constant body temperature as humans do. Instead, the body temperature of fish approximates that of their surrounding medium—water. Certain types of fish, such as tuna, by their constant vigorous propulsion through the water, sustain high muscular flexion that creates heat associated with rapid metabolism. Through built-in heat-conservation measures, the fish is capable of maintaining a warmer body temperature than the medium that upholds it; for example, a bluefin tuna's fighting qualities are not impaired physically when it suddenly dives from surface waters where it was hooked down to the colder depths.

Fish Shapes

Fish shapes have also uniquely evolved to suit the needs of their aquatic life. The body shapes of fish fall into general categories: Some fish are narrow, with bodies that are taller than they are thin, like sunfish, largemouth bass, or angelfish. Some are flat, with bodies that are shorter than they are wide, like flounder. Some are torpedo-shaped, like tuna or mackerel. Some are tubular and snakelike, such as eels.

Shapes tend to be related to a fish's habits and habitats. Narrow-bodied fish are extremely maneuverable and tend to live in reefs or densely weeded ponds where the ability to maneuver between rocks or plants is essential. Flatfish tend to live on the bottom, where their low profiles prevent recognition. Torpedo-shaped fish are built for speed and are found either in open water or in strong currents where less-streamlined fish would be swept away. Tubular fish often live in small crevices and areas that are inaccessible to other animals, rather than in wide-open ocean waters.

Fish Color

The amazing variety of colors that fish display clearly demonstrates the importance of color in the fish world. Most fish are colored for purposes of camouflage. When viewed from above, fish tend to be dark in order to blend in with the dark bottom of the water. When viewed from below, they look light in order to blend in with the sky (this is called countershading). Fish have developed a huge variety of colors and markings that allows them to escape detection in their own environments. Color is also used for mating purposes. Certain fish have special breeding colors, usually brighter than normal colors. Many reef fish have brilliant colors year-round. The wide variety of colors of reef fish helps to differentiate between the many species that live on the reef.

Fish Senses

An angler should understand the way a fish's senses work. Knowing what a fish is sensitive to helps an angler approach the fish without scaring it. Although some fish rely more on certain senses than on others, there are statements about senses that apply to all fish.

Fish hear very well. Sound travels five times faster in water than in air, and fish are quite sensitive to loud noise (which is why you should not tap on fish-tank glass). Fish can be scared off by the noise from people banging around in a boat, loud talking, and motors. Although fish do not have external ears, they do have internal ears. These internal ears, set in the bones of the skull, hear very well. The role of sound in the lives of fish is not entirely understood, but many fish are known to be noisy; fish have been recorded grunting, croaking, grinding teeth, and vibrating muscles. The importance of these sounds is not yet fully known; but what is known for certain is that hearing is an important sense for fish.

A fish's sense of smell is often very good, but the importance of this sense varies widely among species and may be subordinate to other senses, especially vision. With olfactory nerves in their nostrils, fish can detect odors in water just as terrestrial animals can detect odors in air. Some fish use their sense of smell to find food, detect danger, and perhaps also to find their way to spawning areas. There is evidence that a salmon's keen sense of smell contributes to its ability to return to its birthplace. Certainly, a salmon's sense of smell must be considered incredible: Salmon can detect one part per billion of odorous material in water. They may refuse to use fish ladders if the water contains the smell of human hands or bear paws. Salmon will panic if placed in a swimming pool with one drop of bear-scented water. With the apparent importance of smell to many fish, removing human scents from fishing tackle is something that anglers should consider, although the extent to which this is useful varies widely with species, and it is considered important by some anglers and irrelevant by many others.

Sight varies in importance for fish. Most fish are nearsighted; although they can see well for short distances, their vision gets blurry past 3 feet or so. Some fish are exceptions to this rule; brown trout, for instance, have excellent vision. An important fact to realize about most fish is that they can see almost 360°; the only space they cannot see is a small patch directly behind them. Fish can also see color. In laboratory experiments, largemouth bass and trout have been able to identify red, green, blue, and yellow. Some fish have demonstrated preferences for certain colors, and red has long been considered a foremost attraction, although this is subject to a host of variables, as well as disagreements among anglers.

The sense of taste does not seem to be as important to fish as are other senses; taste buds are not as well developed, although there are exceptions, especially among bottom-scrounging fish. Some species, like catfish, use taste to find food and utilize this sense much more than do other species of fish. Catfish even have taste buds on their barbels, and certain species have them on the undersides of their bodies.

Fish have an additional sensory organ called the lateral line. Visible as a line running along the length of the bodies of many fish, the lateral line is used to detect low-frequency vibrations. It acts like both a hearing and a touch organ for fish, and it is used to determine the directions of currents, the proximity of objects, and even water temperature. The lateral line is sensitive to water vibrations and helps fish escape predators, locate prey, and stay in schools.

Reproduction

Fish reproduce in many different ways. Most lay eggs, but some bear live young; most eggs are fertilized after they are released from the female's body, but some are fertilized inside the female's body. Since almost all game-fish are egg layers (sharks being the main exception), the reproductive habits of egg-laying fish are the most important to the angler. Mating, called spawning in egg-laying fish, usually occurs once a year at a particular time of year. Each species has its own spawning habits, which have a great influence on behavior. Some fish do not eat when they are in a spawning mode; others are voracious prior to spawning. Some migrate; some build visible nests, and others have no nests; some move to the deep water, and some move to shallow water. Once a site is chosen for spawning by fish, or the time is right, they begin to mate. Sometimes the mating is an elaborate ritual; sometimes it merely amounts to the female scattering the eggs and the male fertilizing them. After the eggs are fertilized, some fish guard and care for the eggs, and some do not. The eggs hatch fairly quickly, at times in as little as 24 hours, although the time is influenced by such factors as water temperature, turbidity, sunlight, salinity, and current. The young fish just out of the eggs are called fry. Fry are usually so much smaller than their parents that they are not recognizably similar. Fry live on microorganisms in the water until they are ready for larger food. In certain species, each spawning pair can produce thousands of fry, but only a few grow to adulthood. Most fall victim to predation; fry are eaten by many predators, including other fish and, in some species, their own parents.

Certain types of fish spawn in habitats other than their normal ones. Some fish that live in the ocean spawn in rivers, and some fish that live in rivers spawn in the sea. Fish that live in the ocean, yet spawn in freshwater, are called anadromous. The most prominent examples of such fish are salmon. Fish that live in freshwater and spawn in the sea are called catadromous. The most prominent examples of such fish are eels.

Fish Food and Feeding

Fish have evolved to fill almost every ecological niche. Many fish are strictly herbivores, eating only plant life. Many are purely plankton eaters. Most are carnivorous (in the sense of eating the flesh of other fish, as well as crustaceans, mollusks, and insects) or at least piscivorous (eating fish), and some—like the great white shark or the piranha—are among the most feared predators in the world by humans, although their danger to humans is oversensationalized. Almost all species that are considered gamefish are predators because their eating habits and aggressive behavior lead them to strike bait or lures that essentially mimic some form of natural food. Many predaceous fish eat other fish, but they also eat insects, worms, and other vertebrates. Some fish will eat almost anything that can fit in their mouths and is alive. Some fish are scavengers and will consume dead fish or parts of fish. Many fish fill only specific niches and have very specific diets. As a result, knowing the natural food of a gamefish can be important for anglers.

Fish Growth

Growth in fish is affected by many factors; especially important are heredity, length of growing season, and food supply. Although each species can be expected to reach a predetermined size, the length of time required to reach this size is extremely variable. The growing season is the time during the year when a fish will actively feed and grow. Generally, fish living in northern latitudes and colder waters have a shorter growing season than do fish living in southern latitudes and warmer waters. If all other growing factors remain the same, the fish with the longer growing season will reach a greater size over a given time period.

In addition, a fish that has optimum food and space conditions will grow more rapidly than one that must compete more heavily for food and space. This in part explains why fish of the same species in the same latitude and growing seasons, but in different bodies of water, may have different rates of growth.

The Diversity of Fish

Fish are the most diverse class of vertebrates. There are more fish species than all other vertebrate species combined. Fish live in almost every aquatic environment in the world, from lakes 14,000 feet above sea level to 36,000 feet beneath the ocean surface. Fish are found in desert pools that are over 100°F and in Antarctic waters that are only 28°F (water freezes at less than 32° there because of the salinity; the fish do not freeze because they have a special biological antifreeze in their bodies). Some fish can survive for entire summers out of water by hibernating; others can glide out of the water for several hundred feet; a few can produce their own electricity or their own light. Some can achieve speeds of 50 or 60 miles an hour, and some live immobile, parasitic lives. In terms of biological and habitat diversity, no group of animals can outdo fish.

Fish Anatomy

ANATOMY (Body, Function, and Relation to Angling)

Size

Fish range widely in size. On the bantam side of the spectrum are tiny Philippine gobies less than half an inch long, the smallest of all animals with backbones. They are so diminutive that it takes literally thousands of them to weigh a pound, yet they are harvested commercially for use in many foods. At the behemoth end of the spectrum are giant whale sharks 65 to 70 feet long. The largest whale sharks can weigh as much as 25 tons, but they are so docile, they may allow inquisitive scientists to pull alongside them with boats and then climb aboard to prod and poke as they give the big plankton-eaters a close examination. Between these extremes are seemingly limitless shapes and sizes among an estimated 21,000 species. This number exceeds the combined numbers of species of all other vertebrate animals— amphibians, reptiles, birds, and mammals.

Another giant of the sea is the mola, or ocean sunfish, which also goes by the name of headfish because its fins are set far to the rear on its broad, almost tailless body. Molas, which have the unusual habit of basking at the surface, lying on their side as though dead, may weigh nearly a ton but are not quarry for anglers. Also in saltwater, such highly prized game species as bluefin tuna, swordfish, and certain sharks and marlin reach weights of more than a thousand pounds, with some shark and marlin specimens weighing considerably more.

The white sturgeon, one of the largest of freshwater fish, formerly reached weights of well over a thousand pounds in the Columbia and Fraser Rivers but is now uncommon over 400 pounds. In the 1800s, monstrous sturgeon of over 2,000 pounds were reported, but fishery workers have not verified such legends. The prehistoric-looking alligator gar of the southeastern United States can attain a weight of 300 pounds.

Fish size is of special interest to anglers. Many anglers aspire to match their skills against the larger specimens of various game species; competitive events often place a premium on large individual catches; and other rewards, both materialistic and intangible, accrue to those who have caught fish deemed to be of large, if not trophy, caliber.

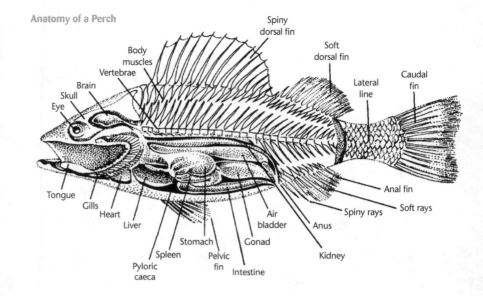

Records for freshwater and saltwater fish caught on rod and reel are maintained by the International Game Fish Association, based upon specific standards and on weight. Yet in many cases, fish are known to grow much larger than sport-caught records indicate. Two all-tackle record tarpon taken on rod and reel, for example, each weighed 283 pounds, which is admittedly sizable but much smaller than the 350-pounders that have reportedly been caught in nets. On the other hand, record rod-and-reel catches greatly exceed the average size of most species. Most brook trout taken by anglers, for example, weigh less than half a pound, but the sport-caught record for the species is 14 pounds, 8 ounces.

Anatomy of a Shark

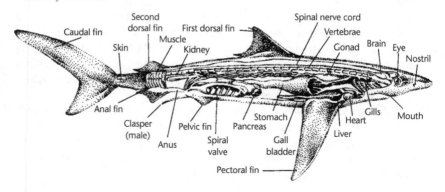

A fish does not have to be gigantic to provide fun, however. In this regard, tackle plays an important role. Anglers, using ultralight tackle in ponds and lakes, find it challenging to catch quarter-pound bluegills, rarely if ever hooking one that approaches a pound in weight, let alone the species' top record of 4 pounds ,12 ounces. Indeed, line-class record categories were long ago established for each species to recognize the angler's fishing skill by virtue of a notable catch for a particular weight of tackle.

Size is a relative issue, both in terms of a fish's fighting ability and in its desirability as a catch. Although most larger fish are more difficult to subdue than smaller ones, that is not always the case. Size is also not necessarily comparable between different species; a 10-pound steelhead, for example, provides far better sport than a 10-pound walleye, and a 10-pound bonefish is much more challenging than a 10-pound barracuda. Growing season and geographic location may be factors as well. A 10-pound largemouth bass in Florida, where a favorable growing season can allow a bass to grow large quickly, is akin to perhaps a 6-pound largemouth bass in Minnesota in terms of age and availability within the bass population, the result being that they are catches of similar accomplishment, despite being of different size.

Form

The typical fish, such as the yellow perch, the largemouth bass, the striped bass, and the grouper, has a compressed body that is flattened from side to side. In others, the body is depressed from top to bottom, as in flounder, rays, and other bottom-hugging types. Still others are spindle-shaped or streamlined, like mackerel, tuna, and trout; and some, such as eels, have an elongated or snakelike body. All fish fit into one of these four categories, but each form in turn may differ with various adaptations in certain portions of its anatomy.

These differences fit the fish for specific environments or particular ways of life. For example, the streamlined tuna is an open-ocean fish that moves constantly, indulges in long migrations, and pursues fast-swimming schools of smaller fish. Its bullet-shaped body is well adapted for such a life. On the other hand, the flounder's depressed body allows it to be completely undetectable as it lies flat on the sandy or muddy bottom, an adaptation that protects it from enemies, as well as allows it to grasp unsuspecting prey. Marlin, sailfish, and swordfish are large fish with long snouts (bills) used as clubs to stun prey or as swords in defense. Eels and cutlassfish have slim, snakelike bodies, enabling them to negotiate seemingly inaccessible areas to hunt for food or to escape enemies.

Among the most unusual fish in shape are those that live in the deep sea. Many have luminous spots or stripes along their bodies, and fins may be reduced to slim filaments, some bearing bulbous and luminous tips. Many have long barbels around their mouths, with lighted tips that serve as lures for attracting smaller prey within reach of their strong jaws. In some, the tails are long and snakelike. Most have very large mouths and an array of long, dagger-sharp teeth that help in holding their catches. The mouth is generally stretchable, as is the stomach. When the fish has the good fortune to capture a meal in the dark depths, where food, as a rule, is scarce, it attempts to devour the prey regardless of size. These deep-sea fish are seldom among the species caught by anglers.

Scales

A typical fish's body is covered with thin scales that overlap each other like the shingles of a roof. They are prominent outgrowths of skin, or epidermis, in which numerous glands secrete a protective coating of slime, often referred to as mucus. The slime is a barrier to the entry of parasites, fungi, and disease organisms that might infest the fish, and it seals in the fish's body fluids so that they are not diluted by the watery surroundings. The slime also reduces friction so that the fish slides through the water with a minimum of resistance; it also makes the fish slippery when predators, including the human variety, try to grab hold. Some fish, such as lampreys and hagfish, give off copious amounts of slime.

As a fish grows, its scales increase in size but not in number. Lost scales may be replaced, however. The ridges and spaces on some types of scales become records of age and growth rate. These can be read or counted like the annual rings in the trunk of a tree to determine a fish's age—the fish's

Fish Shapes

Anatomical differences among fish are most obvious in general body shape but also include body and tail fins.

growth slowing or stopping during winter when food is scarce and becoming much more rapid during the warm months when food is plentiful. Experts in reading scales can tell when a fish first spawned and each spawning period thereafter. They can determine times of migration, periods of food scarcity, illness, and similar facts about the fish's life. The number of scales in a row along the lateral line can be used to identify closely related species, particularly the young. Growth rings occur also in the vertebrae and in other bones of the body, but to study these requires killing the fish. A few scales can be removed without harm to the fish.

Most bony fish have tough, shinglelike scales with a comblike or serrated edge (ctenoid) along their rear margins or with smooth rear margins (cycloid). The scales of garfish are hard and almost bony, fitting one against the other like the bricks on a wall. These are called ganoid scales. Sturgeon also have ganoid scales, some of which form ridges of armor along portions of their sides and backs.

Sharks have placoid scales, which are the most primitive type. These scales are toothlike, each with a central spine coated on the outside with enamel and with an intermediate layer of dentine over a central pulp cavity. The skin of sharks, with the scales still attached, is the shagreen of commerce, widely used in the past and still used today in primitive areas as an abrasive, like sandpaper, or to make nonslip handles for knives and tools.

Scale Types

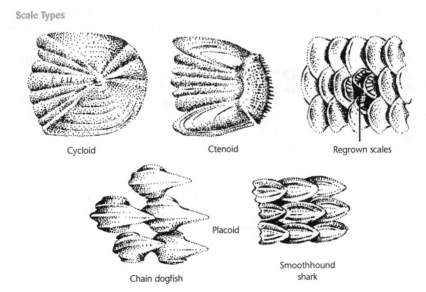

Cycloid

Ctenoid

Regrown scales

Chain dogfish

Placoid

Smoothhound shark

Cycloid scales have smooth rear margins, whereas ctenoid scales have comblike margins; placoid scales, found on sharks, are toothlike. Scales generally are layered, overlapping in rows like roof tiles.

The scales may be variously modified on different species. Some fish do not have scales at all. Most species of catfish, for example, are "naked" or smooth-skinned. Their skin is very slippery, however, and some of the rays in their fins are modified as sharp spines. Paddlefish and sculpin have only a few scales. The scales of mackerel are minute. Trout also have tiny scales. Those of eels are widely separated and buried deep in the skin.

Coloration

The beautiful coloration of fish can be appreciated only when observing them alive, for at death the brilliance and the intensity of color begin to fade immediately. Unquestionably, many fish equal or surpass in appearance the most spectacular colored bird or butterfly, and some of the blends and contrasts of body color are impossible to describe with justice.

The color in fish is primarily produced by skin pigments. Basic or background color is due to underlying tissues and body fluids. Iridescent colors are present in body scales, eyes, and abdominal linings of some fish. The rainbowlike reflecting hues of certain kinds of fish are caused by skin pigmentation fragmenting through the irregular ridges of transparent or translucent scales.

All fish are not highly colored, however; the range extends widely from fish with bright colors to species that are uniformly drab in brown, gray, and even pitch black. In nearly all species, the shades and the acuteness of color are adapted to the particular environment a fish inhabits.

In oceanic fish, basic color may be separated into three kinds: silvery in the upper-water zone, reddish in the middle depths, and violet or black in the great depths. Those that swim primarily in the upper layers of ocean water are typically dark blue or greenish blue on the dorsal portions, grading to silvery sides and white bellies. Fish that live on the bottom, especially those living close to rocks, reefs, and weedbeds, may be busily mottled or striped. The degree of color concentration also varies depending on the character of the fish's surroundings. For example, a striped bass caught from a sandy area will be lighter in general coloration than one captured from deeper water or from around dark rocks.

The same natural rules apply to freshwater fish. A northern pike, a pickerel, or a muskie is patterned in mottled greens because its habitat is primarily aquatic plants, where it is well camouflaged in alternating light and dark shadows. The bottom-dwelling, dark-backed catfish are almost impossible to detect against a muddy background.

Many anglers are bewildered by the color variances in trouts. Often the same species taken from different types of localities in the same stream may differ in coloration to a startling degree. For example, a trout taken from shallow, swiftly running water over sand and pebbles will be bright and silvery in comparison to a relative that lives under a log in a deep, quiet pool. The steelhead, a sea-run rainbow trout, is another good example of color change. When it leaves the ocean to enter western rivers, it is brilliantly silver, but as it remains in freshwater, the characteristic coloration of the rainbow trout develops: a dark greenish-blue back, a crimson lateral band, and profuse black spots over most of the body.

Regardless of the confusing differences under varying conditions, anglers who know the basic color patterns can easily identify any trout. Each species has recognizable characteristics that do not change. The brook trout, *Salvelinus fontinalis,* for example, always has reticulated or wormlike markings on its back, whereas the under edge of the tail fin and the forward edges of the pectoral, ventral, and anal fins are white.

Most types of fish change color during the spawning season; this is especially noticeable among the trout and the salmon tribes. As spawning time approaches, the general coloration becomes darker and more intense. Some examples are surprising, especially in salmon of the U.S. Northwest. All five species are silvery in the ocean, but as they travel upstream to their spawning grounds, they gradually alter to deep reds, browns, and greens—the final colors so drastically different that it seems hardly possible the fish were metallic bright only a short time earlier. Each type of salmon, however, retains its own color characteristics during the amazing transition.

In some types of fish, the coloration intensifies perceptibly when the fish is excited by prey or by predators. Dolphin (mahimahi), a blue-water angler's delight, appear to be almost completely vivid blue when seen from above in

The color exhibited by most fish is adapted to their particular environments, and a wide range of colors exists, as is evident when comparing the brook trout (top), bonefish (middle), and channel catfish (bottom).

a darting school in calm waters. When a dolphin is brought aboard, the unbelievably brilliant golden yellows, blues, and greens undulate and flow magically along the dolphin's body as it thrashes madly about. These changes in shade and degree of color also take place when the dolphin is in varying stages of excitement in the water.

A striped marlin or a blue marlin following a surface-trolled bait is a wondrous spectacle of color to observe. As it eyes its quarry from side to side and maneuvers into position to attack, the deep cobalt-blue dorsal fin and bronze-silver sides are at their zenith. This electrifying display of color is lost almost immediately when the fish is boated.

Fins and Locomotion

Fish are propelled through the water by fins, body movement, or both. In general, the main moving force is the caudal fin, or tail, and the area immediately adjacent to it, known as the caudal peduncle. In swimming, the fins are put into action by muscles attached to the base of the fin spines and rays. Fish with a fairly rigid body, such as the tilefish, the trunkfish, the triggerfish, the manta, and skates, depend mostly on fin action for propulsion. Eels, in contrast, rely on extreme, serpentlike body undulations to swim, with fin movement assisting to a minor extent. Sailfish, marlin, and other big-game fish fold their fins into grooves (lessening water resistance) and rely mainly on their large, rigid tails to go forward. Trout, salmon, catfish, and others are well adapted for sudden turns and short, fast moves. When water is expelled suddenly over the gills in breathing, it acts like a jet stream and aids in a fast start forward.

A fish can swim even if its fins are removed, though it generally has difficulty with direction and balance. In some kinds, however, the fins are highly important in swimming. For example, the pectoral fins of a ray are broad "wings" with which the fish sweeps through the water almost as gracefully as a swallow does in the air. The sharks, which are close relatives of the rays, swim swiftly in a straight line but have great difficulty in stopping or turning because their fins have restricted movement.

Flyingfish glide above the surface of the water with their winglike pectoral fins extended. Sometimes they get additional power surges by dipping their tails into the water and vibrating them vigorously. This may enable them to remain airborne for as long as a quarter of a mile. Needlefish and halfbeaks skitter over the surface for long distances, the front halves of their bodies held stiffly out of the water while their still-submerged tails wag rapidly. An African catfish often swims upside down, and seahorses swim in a "standing up" position.

Many kinds of fish jump regularly. Those that take to the air when hooked give anglers the greatest thrills. Often, however, there is no easy explanation for why a fish jumps, other than the possibility that it derives pleasure from these momentary escapes from its watery world. The jump is made to

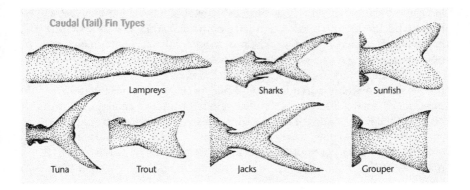

Caudal (Tail) Fin Types

Lampreys

Sharks

Sunfish

Tuna

Trout

Jacks

Grouper

dislodge a hook or to escape a predator in close pursuit, or the fish may try to shake its body free of plaguing parasites. Some species make their jumps by surging at high speed from deep water. Others swim rapidly close to the surface, then suddenly turn their noses skyward and give a powerful thrust with their tails as they take to the air. Sailfish and other high jumpers may leap several feet into the air when hooked, often leaping as many as 20 times before being brought to the boat.

Speed

Fisheries professionals are frequently asked how fast fish swim. This is a difficult question to answer precisely, because fish have a cruising speed, a maximum sustainable speed, and a top speed over relatively short distances.

Statistics for cruising (ordinary travel) speed have been taken mostly from tagged fish released at one point and recaptured at another. For example, some bluefin tuna tagged off Cat Cay, Bahamas, were recaptured in Norwegian waters. Two of these crossed the ocean in less than 3 months. Another completed the trip in the remarkable time of 52 days. These facts, which contradict the belief that all bluefin tuna migrating from the Bahamas spend the summer in western Atlantic coastal waters, indicate that bluefins swim swiftly, but, obviously, we do not know whether the recaptured specimens swam a direct course or indulged in detours. Also, ocean currents can be a help or a hindrance.

Maximum sustainable speed, that is, the speed that a fish can maintain for long periods, is almost impossible to judge unless measured experimentally on small fish by determining the length of time they can swim in approximately the same spot when currents of the same velocity are flowing by. Boats traveling alongside big-game fish have clocked their rate of speed. In addition, some anglers have attempted to gauge the speed of gamefish by improvising speedometers on their fishing reels or by using stopwatches to time the runs of hooked fish. The speed of a sailfish has been estimated to be as high as 100 yards per 3 seconds, or 68 miles per hour. All the speeds indicated by such experiments are approximate at best because many factors have to be considered, including the size of the individual, the temperature of the water, currents, the area of the mouth where the fish was hooked, the physical condition of the particular fish hooked, and so on.

All members of the tunalike fish, such as the bluefin tuna, the bonito, and the albacore, are also extremely fast. Other species having a reputation for great speed are marlin, wahoo, dolphin, and swordfish. Generally, speeds of 40 to 50 miles per hour are attributed to these fish. In freshwater, the top speed of salmon has been estimated at 14 to 30 miles per hour and the cruising speed at 8 miles per hour. The top speed for largemouth bass is about 12 miles per hour.

Air Bladder

The air bladder, located between the stomach and backbone, is also known as the swim bladder, which is misleading because the air bladder has no function in the movement or locomotion of fish in any direction. The mixture of gases that it contains is not normal air, so the correct name should be "gas bladder."

The air bladder is present in most bony fish; it does not appear in lampreys, hagfish, sharks, rays, or skates. The air bladder performs several functions. It may be well supplied with blood vessels, as it is in the tarpon, and may act as a supplementary breathing organ. The tarpon has an open tube that leads from the upper side of its gullet to the air bladder. (The tarpon also has a set of gills.) Some species of fish use the air bladder as a compartment in which to store air for breathing. The fish falls back on this reserve when its usual supply of oxygen may be shut off. The air bladder plays a part in aiding equilibrium of density between the fish and the water. (It has no function of adjustment of pressure to changing levels.) In other words, the volume of water occupied by the fish should weigh about as much as the fish does. The air bladder is a compensator between them. For example, the pickerel is capable of "floating," its body motionless, anticipating its prey. The catfish, on the other hand, has no air bladder; it spends most of its life on the bottom. The saltwater flatfish also has no air bladder, and it dives to the bottom swiftly if it escapes the hook near the surface of the water. (A fish does not raise or lower itself by increasing or decreasing the size of the air bladder.) It has also been definitely established that the air bladder is an efficient hearing aid in many types of fish. It is commonly known that the noises some fish make are produced by the air bladder.

Incidentally, there are some exceptions to the general rule, and that includes the primitive lungfish, which is represented by five living species. These "living fossils" are found in Africa, South America, and Australia. The African lungfish's air bladder is purely respiratory in function; this fish cannot use its gills for breathing. If the African lungfish cannot reach the surface to gulp air, it soon drowns.

Skeleton and Muscles

A fish's skeleton is composed of cartilage or bone. Basically, the skeleton provides a foundation for the body and the fins, encases and protects the brain and the spinal cord, and serves as an attachment for muscles. It contains three principal segments: skull, vertebral column, and fin skeleton.

The meat or flesh covering the fish's muscular system is quite simple. All vertebrates, including fish, have three major types of muscles: smooth (involuntary), cardiac (heart), and striated (skeletal). Functionally, there are two kinds: voluntary and involuntary.

In fish, the smooth muscles are present in the digestive tract, the air bladder, the reproductive and excretory ducts, the eyes, and other organs. The striated muscles run in irregular vertical bands, and various patterns are found in different types of fish. These muscles compose the bulk of the body and are functional in swimming by producing body undulations that propel the fish forward. The muscle segments, called myomeres, are divided into an upper and a lower half by a groove running along the midbody of the fish. The myomeres can be easily seen if the skin is carefully removed from the body or scraped away with a knife after cooking. These broad muscles are the part of the fish that we eat. Striated muscles are also attached to the base of the fin spines and rays, and they maneuver the fins in swimming.

Teeth, Food, and Digestion

A tremendous diversity exists in the form and the size of fish teeth. The character of the dentition is a clue to the fish's feeding habits and the kind of food it consumes. Of all the fish, some sharks display the most awesome arrays of teeth: profuse and well structured for grasping, tearing, and cutting. The barracuda's teeth are different from any shark's, but they also draw attention because of their ferocious appearance. They are flat, triangular, closely set, and extremely sharp. Such teeth are ideally adapted for capturing live fish, the barracuda's main diet. Small victims are usually swallowed whole; the

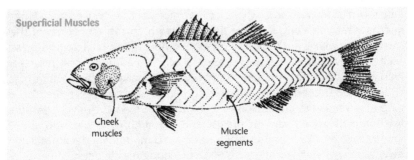

Broad striated muscles make up the bulk of the body of a fish; they run in irregular vertical bands and various patterns, and are functional in swimming.

larger ones may be cut in two and each piece swallowed separately. The bluefish, well known for its ability to chop up a school of baitfish, has teeth of a similar nature but smaller in size.

Some fish possess sharp, conical teeth (called canine, or dog, teeth); pike, pickerel, and muskies are good examples. Such teeth cannot cut but do a good job of grasping and piercing. Fish fortified with canine teeth generally hold a baitfish until its struggles diminish before swallowing it—a fact taken into consideration by anglers before setting the hook. Anglers must exercise extreme caution when removing hooks from sharks, bluefish, barracuda, pikelike fish, and other fish with dangerous dentition.

The yellow perch, the sea bass, the catfish, and other species have multiple rows of numerous short and closely packed teeth that resemble the tips of a stiff brush. Such an arrangement meets the fish's need to grasp a variety of food off the bottom or hold prey in a sandpaperlike grip until ready to be eaten.

Some kinds of fish have sharp-edged cutting teeth called incisors, located in the forward part of the mouth; some are saw-edged, others resemble human teeth, and still others are variously fused into parrotlike beaks. Parrotfish, for example, have such teeth and thrive on small organisms nibbled from corals, rocks, and reefs. Some bottom-dwelling fish, such as skates, rays, and drum, have molarlike teeth that are well adapted for crunching crustaceans, mollusks, and other organisms.

Many fish, including some of the more common types such as carp, minnows, and suckers, have teeth in their throats. These pharyngeal teeth are sharp in some species, molariform in others, and only remnants in still others. There are fish that have teeth on the roof of the mouth (vomerine and palatine) and on the tongue. Pike, pickerel, and muskies, for example, have vomerine teeth that are profuse and closely packed, whereas other fish, such as certain trout, have comparatively few teeth on these areas. One of the distinguishing features between a true trout and a charr (rainbow trout versus brook trout, for example) is the presence or absence of vomerine teeth. The vomerine bone in the center of the charr's mouth has only a few teeth, located on its forward end, whereas the vomer of a true trout is much longer and has teeth all along it. Some fish have teeth on the very edges of their mouths (premaxillary, maxillary, or both). And many planktonic feeders, such as the menhaden, have no teeth at all; instead, their long gill rakers help in retaining the microscopic organisms they take into their mouths.

Fish are a tremendously diversified group of animals, which feed on an extensive variety of foods. Some, when mature, feed exclusively on other fish; others feed entirely on plants. The sea lamprey, a parasitic, highly unattractive eel-like fish, uses its funnel-shaped mouth, lined with radiating rows of sharp teeth, to attach itself to the body of a live fish; then, using its toothed tongue, it rasps a hole in its prey and sucks out blood and body fluids.

In general, the food plan of a fish's life is to eat and to be eaten. Such a scheme involves a food chain. Nutrients in the water nourish various types of free-flowing aquatic plants (phytoplankton) that are eaten by a variety of microscopic animals (zooplankton). A tiny fish feeds on zooplankton, and the bigger fish feeds on the smaller fish. There are many steps in this food chain, as larger fish eat smaller ones until the chain may end with, for example, a bluefin tuna. The tuna eventually expires and sinks to the bottom, where it is eaten by worms, crabs, and other bottom dwellers. Finally, bacteria return the nutrients to the water in a soluble inorganic form, which the phytoplankton again utilize. The food chain is then complete.

Insects, worms, snails, mussels, squid, and crabs are some of the important larger invertebrates that provide food for fish. Amphibians, reptiles, birds, and mammals, as well as other fish, are also included in the diet of fish. Largemouth bass and muskies, for example, commonly eat frogs and occasionally small turtles or snakes. Gar have been caught that contained bird remains in their stomachs. And goosefish—bottom dwellers with huge mouths—will capture such unusual prey as a diving duck.

Fish also differ in the way they feed. Predators entrap or cut their prey by using their well-developed teeth. Grazers or browsers feed on the bottom. Fish that feed on tiny organisms sifted from the water by using their long gill rakers are known as strainers. Suckers and sturgeon have fleshy, distensible lips, well suited to suck food off the bottom, and thus are suckers. Some lampreys depend on the blood and the fluids of other fish to live; they are categorized as parasites.

Here are a few examples of the structural adaptations of fish that assist them in feeding: catfish and sturgeon have whiskerlike feelers for touching and tasting food before accepting it; sailfish, marlin, and swordfish may stun their prey with their clublike bills before devouring it. The paddlefish employs its long, sensitive, paddlelike snout to stir up the bottom organisms on which it feeds. Gar have elongated snouts filled with needlelike teeth that make formidable traps for capturing prey. The goosefish, also known as the angler, has a long, slim appendage with a piece of skin at its tip, located on the forward part of its upper snout; this appendage can be wiggled like a worm and acts as a lure to entice prey.

Generally, fish that live in a temperate zone, where seasons are well defined, will eat much more during the warm months than they will during the cold months. In this zone a fish's metabolism slows down greatly during winter. The body temperature of most fish changes with the surrounding environment; it is not constant, as it is in mammals and birds.

The digestive system of fish, as in all other vertebrates, dissolves food, thereby facilitating absorption or assimilation. This system, or metabolic process, is capable of removing some of the toxic properties that may be present in foods on which fish feed.

The basic plan of the digestive tract in a typical fish differs in some respects from that of other vertebrate animals. The tongue cannot move as it does in higher vertebrates, and it does not possess striated muscles. The esophagus, or gullet (between the throat and stomach), is highly distensible and usually can accept any type or size food that the fish can fit into its mouth. Although choking does happen and has been particularly noticed in pickerel and pike, a fish rarely chokes to death because of food taken into its mouth.

Fish stomachs differ in shape from group to group. The predators have elongated stomachs. Those that are omnivorous generally have saclike stomachs. Sturgeon, gizzard shad, and mullet, among others, have stomachs with heavily muscled walls used for grinding food, just as the gizzard of a chicken does. Some of the bizarre deep-sea fish possess stomachs capable of huge distention, thereby enabling them to hold relatively huge prey. On the other hand, some fish have no stomachs; instead, they have accessory adaptations, such as grinding teeth, that crush the food finely so that it is easily absorbed.

Intestinal structure also differs in fish. The predators have shortened intestines; meaty foods are more easily digested than are plant foods. In contrast, herbivores, or plant eaters, have long intestines, sometimes consisting of many folds. Sharks and a few other fish have intestines that incorporate a spiral or coiled valve that aids in digestion. Lampreys and hagfish have no jaws and do not have well-defined stomachs or curvature of the intestines. Lampreys need a simple digestive system because they are parasites that subsist on the blood and juices they suck from other fish. During the long migration from the sea upriver to spawn, the various species of salmon never feed. Their digestive tracts shrink amazingly, allowing the reproductive organs to fill up their abdomens.

Gills and Breathing

Like all other living things, fish need oxygen to survive. In humans, the organs responsible for this function are the lungs. In fish, the gills perform the job. However, in some scaleless fish, the exchange of gases takes place through the skin. In fish embryos, various tissues temporarily take up the job of breathing. Some fish are capable of obtaining oxygen directly from the air through several adaptations, including modifications of the mouth cavity, the gills, the intestine, and the air bladder.

A fish's gills are much-divided thin-walled filaments where capillaries lie close to the surface. In a living fish, the gills are bright-red feathery organs that are prominent when the gill cover of the fish is lifted. The filaments are located on bony arches. Most fish have four gill arches. Between the arches are openings through which the water passes. In the gills, carbon dioxide, a waste gas from the cells, is released; at the same time, the dissolved oxygen is taken into the blood for transport to the body cells. This happens quickly and is remarkably efficient—about 75 percent of the oxygen contained in each gulp of water is removed in the brief exposure.

Different kinds of fish vary in their oxygen demands. Trout and salmon require large amounts of oxygen. The cold water in which they live can hold a greater amount of dissolved oxygen than can warm water. Furthermore, many live in fast-flowing streams, in which new supplies of oxygen are churned into the water constantly. Most types of catfish are near the opposite extreme; their oxygen demands are so low that they thrive in sluggish warmwater streams and also in ponds and lakes where the oxygen supply is low. A catfish can, in fact, remain alive for a long time out of water if kept cool and moist. Like carp and similar kinds of fish, catfish can be shipped for long distances and arrive at the market alive.

A few fish, such as the various walking catfish, the climbing perch, the bowfin, the gar, the gourami, and others, can breathe air. Air-breathers use only about 5 percent of the oxygen available to them with each breath of air. The best-known air breathers are the lungfish that live in tropical Africa. Their "lung" is an air bladder connected to the lungfish's mouth by a duct, its walls richly supplied with blood vessels. A lungfish gets new supplies of oxygen by rising to the surface and gulping air. It will drown if kept underwater. When the stagnant pool in which it lives dries up, which happens seasonally, the lungfish burrows into the soft mud at the bottom and secretes a slimy coating over its body. It continues to breathe air through a small hole that connects to the surface through the mud casing. When the rains come again and the pool fills, the lungfish wriggles out of its cocoon and resumes its usual living habits.

The lamprey has seven paired gill sacs or bronchial pouches. A lamprey does not take in water through its mouth as other fish do, even when its mouth is not in the act of sucking blood and juices out of its prey. Water, from which the lamprey secures its oxygen, is both taken in and expelled through the gill sacs.

The sea lamprey is a parasitic eel-like creature that exists by sucking out the blood of fish. It attaches itself to the side of its host by means of a funnel-shaped mouth lined with radiating rows of sharp teeth. With its toothed tongue, it rasps a hole in its victim and proceeds to draw out the fish's life blood and body fluids. Surprisingly, fish do not fear the lamprey by sight. The lamprey swims along serenely by the side of a lake trout (or other fish) and simply reaches out, clamping its suction mouth onto the unsuspecting prey. After feasting, it departs and the trout usually dies. If by chance the prey survives, it carries a wound that invites infection.

Rays and skates usually have five paired external gill slits (rarely six or seven) located on the bottom sides of their heads. Sharks also have the same number of gill slits, but they are located laterally (on the sides). In sharks, the water used for respiration is taken in through their mouths and expelled through the gill slits. Rays and skates, however, draw in water through the spiracles located on the tops, or close to the tops, of their heads (an excellent adaptation for bottom-dwelling fish). The water flows over the gills and out the gill slits located on the undersides of their heads.

Because a fish has no opening between its nostrils and mouth cavity as humans do, it has to breathe through its mouth. When the fish opens its mouth, a stream of water is drawn in. During this intake of water, the gill cover is held tight, thereby closing the gill opening. Then the fish closes its mouth and drives the water over the gills and out the external openings by using special throat muscles. As the water passes over the gills, the exchange of gases takes place; that is, oxygen (which has been absorbed from the air by water exposed to it) is taken in through the walls of the fine blood vessels in the gill filaments, and carbon dioxide is given off. The blood, well oxygenated, then travels through the fish's body.

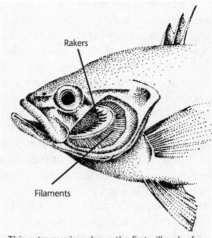

This cutaway view shows the first gill arch of a sunfish. The rakers, which strain the water, are on the left; the filaments, which transfer dissolved oxygen to the blood, are on the right.

The rapidity with which a fish breathes varies with different species. A human in good health under normal circumstances breathes about 20 to 25 times a minute. Some types of fish have a breathing rate as low as 12 times a minute, yet others take as many as 150 breaths per minute. If the fish is exerting itself, or if the oxygen content of the water becomes low, the rate of breathing will be faster, and the fish pants like a runner after finishing the mile.

Although gills play a major role in the respiratory organization of a fish, they also serve another purpose. Gill rakers, located along the anterior margin of the gill arch, aid in several ways. By projecting over the throat opening, they strain water that is passed over the gills. Solid particles are prevented from passing over and injuring the gill filaments. Gill rakers may be short and knobby, as in the pickerel, which is primarily a fish-eater. The shad, on the other hand, feeds on minute organisms. Its gill rakers are numerous, long, and thin, and they serve to sieve out the tiny organisms on which the shad feeds. In between these two extremes in size and shape, gill rakers of various sizes can be found in different types of fish. The number of gill rakers on the first gill arch is sometimes used as an aid in identifying or separating species that closely resemble one another.

Blood Circulation

The circulatory system of a fish, which consists of the heart, the blood, and the blood vessels, carries to every living cell in the body the oxygen and

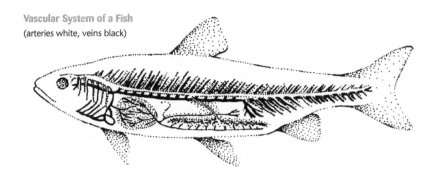

Vascular System of a Fish
(arteries white, veins black)

nourishment required for living; it carries away from the cells the carbon dioxide and other excretory products.

In function, the fish's muscular heart is similar to that of other vertebrates, acting as a pump to force the blood through the system of blood vessels. It differs from the human heart in having only two, rather than four, compartments—one auricle and one ventricle. The fish's heart is located close behind the fish's mouth. Blood vessels are largest close to the heart and become progressively smaller, terminating in a network of extremely fine capillaries that meander through the body tissues. The blood of a fish, like blood in all vertebrates, is composed of plasma (fluid) and blood cells (solid).

A fish's circulatory system is much simpler than that of a human. In humans, the blood is pumped from the heart into the lungs, where it is oxygenated; it then returns to the heart and receives a good thrust to travel throughout the body. In contrast, fish blood passes from the heart to the gills for purification and then travels directly to all other parts of the body.

Fish are often referred to as "cold-blooded" creatures, but this is not entirely true. Some are "warm-blooded," although they cannot sustain a constant body temperature as humans do. Instead, the fish's body temperature approximates that of its surrounding medium: water. Fish blood is thicker than human blood and has low pressure because it is pumped by a heart with only two chambers. Consequently, the flow of blood through a fish's body is slow. Because the blood flows slowly through the gills where it takes on oxygen, and because water contains less oxygen than air, fish blood is not as rich in oxygen as is human blood. Also, because of the slow flow of blood through the gills, the blood cools and approaches the temperature of the water surrounding the fish.

Senses and Nerves

A fish's eyes are adapted or modified for underwater vision, but they are not very different from human eyes. Fish do not have true eyelids. Human eyelids prevent the eyes from becoming dry and also protect against dirt. A fish's eyes are always covered by water; therefore, they require no lids.

The metallic-looking ring, called the iris, encircling the dark center, or lens, of the fish's eye cannot move as it does in the human eye. The human iris can expand or contract, depending upon light conditions. Because light never attains great intensity underwater, a fish needs no such adaptation. The big difference between a human eye and the eye of a fish occurs in the lens. In humans it is fairly flat, or dishlike; in fish it is spherical or globular. Human eyes are capable of changing the curvature of the lens to focus at varying distances—flatter for long-range focusing and more curved for shorter range. Although the eye of a fish has a rigid lens and its curvature is incapable of change, it can be moved toward or away from the retina (like the focusing action of a camera). Scientists note one outstanding similarity between the eye of a human and the fish's eye. In both, six muscles move the eyeball. The six muscles are controlled by the same six nerves and act the same way to provide eye movement.

Although fish have no eyelids, they do sleep. Schooling fish commonly separate periodically to rest. Then they become active again and the schools reassemble. Some fish lie on their sides when they rest; others lean against rocks or slip into crevices. Some kinds wriggle their way into the soft ooze at the bottom to take a nap, and some of the parrotfish secrete a blanket of slime over the bodies at night. The preparation of this "bed" may take as long as an hour.

Important to anglers is the fact that a fish can distinguish colors. Experimenters have found, for example, that largemouth bass and trout quickly learn to tell red from other colors when red is associated with food. They can also distinguish green, blue, and yellow. There are indications that some kinds of fish prefer one color to another and also that water conditions may make one color more easily distinguished than others. Although lure action is most important, anglers can increase their chances of taking a fish by presenting lures of the proper color.

Many kinds of fish have excellent vision at close range. This is made especially clear by the archerfish, which feeds on insects. By squirting drops of water forcefully from its mouth into the air, it may shoot down a hovering fly or one resting on grass or weeds. As an archerfish prepares to make its shot, it approaches carefully to make certain of its aim and range. An archerfish is accurate at distances up to about 3 feet and is sometimes successful with even longer shots.

The four-eyed fish, one of the oddities of the fish world, lives in shallow, muddy streams in Central America. On the top of its head are bulbous eyes that are half in and half out of the water as the fish swims along near the surface. These eyes function as four eyes because of their internal structure—the lens is egg-shaped, rather than spherical. When the fish looks at objects under the water, light passes through the full length of the lens, and the four-eyed fish is as nearsighted as any other fish. When it looks into the air, the light rays pass through the shorter width of the lens, giving the fish good distance vision.

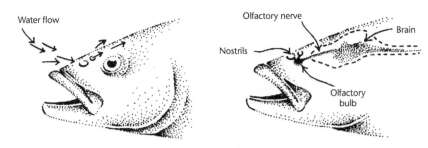

Water flow

Olfactory nerve

Brain

Nostrils

Olfactory bulb

Smell receptors are located in the nostrils, and water (carrying odors) is drawn into sacs that are lined with the organs of smell. Olfactory nerves connect the nostrils and brain.

Fish that live in the dusky or dimly lit regions of the sea commonly have eyes that are comparatively larger than the eyes of any other animal with backbones. Fish that live in the perpetual darkness of caves or other subterranean waters usually have no eyes, but those inhabiting the deep sea, far below the depth to which light rays can penetrate, may or may not have eyes. The reason that most deep-sea fish have well-developed eyes is the prevalence of bioluminescence. Deep-sea squid, shrimp, and other creatures, as well as fish, are equipped with light-producing organs. The light they produce is used to recognize enemies or to capture prey.

Many fish with poor vision have well-developed senses of smell, taste, and touch. Improbable as it may seem, fish do possess nostrils. Four nostrils are located close to the top of the snout, one pair on each side. Each pair opens into a small blind sac immediately below the skin. Water, carrying odors, passes through the sacs, which are lined with the receptors of smell. Some fish, including sharks, possess an extremely acute sense of smell.

Fish have taste organs located in the skin of the snout, the lips, the mouth, and the throat. A fish's tongue, unlike the human tongue, is flat, rigid, and cartilaginous and moves only when the base below it moves; nevertheless, it does possess taste buds that indicate to the fish whether to accept or to reject anything taken into its mouth.

There is a close relationship between the senses of smell and taste in fish, just as in humans. Many types of fish are first drawn to food by its odor. For example, catfish and sturgeon, which are first attracted by food odor, will feel and taste the food with their chin barbels before taking it. These whisker-like appendages contain taste buds. Some catfish have taste buds all over their bodies; certain kinds can actually taste with their tails.

Although fish obviously do not possess outer ears as humans do, they are still capable of hearing. The human ear is composed of an outer, a middle, and an inner ear; each part interacts with the other for both hearing and maintaining equilibrium. A fish possesses only an inner ear, found in the bones of the skull. Outer and middle ears are not necessary in fish, because water is a much better conductor of sound than is air. In many fish, these ear bones are connected to the air bladders. Vibrations are transmitted to the ear from the air bladder, which acts as a sounding board.

The lateral-line system, a series of sensory cells usually running the length of both sides of the fish's body, performs an important function in receiving low-frequency vibrations. Actually, it resembles a "hearing organ" of greater sensitivity than human ears. The typical lateral line is a mucus-filled tube or canal under the skin; it has contact with the outside world through pores in the skin or through scales along the line or in-between them. A nerve situated at intervals alongside the canal sends out branches to it. In some cases the lateral line extends over the fish's tail, and in many fish it continues onto the head and spreads into several branches along the outer bones of the fish's skull, where it is not outwardly visible. The fish utilizes its lateral line to determine the direction of currents of water and the presence of nearby objects, as well as to sense vibrations. The lateral line helps the fish to determine water temperature and to find its way when traveling at night or through murky waters. It also assists schooling fish in keeping together and may help a fish to escape enemies.

Many fish are noisy creatures. They make rasping, squeaking, grunting, and squealing noises. This came as a great surprise to military forces during World War II, when their sound-detecting devices, designed to pick up the noises of submarines, instead were literally jammed by fish noises. Some fish produce sounds by rubbing together special extensions of the bones of their vertebrae. Others make noises by vibrating muscles that are connected to their air bladders, which amplify the sounds. Still other fish grind their teeth, their mouth cavities serving as sound boxes to amplify the noises. Many fish make sounds when they are caught. Grunts and croakers got their names from this habit.

Some fish are capable of generating electricity. To our present knowledge, no other animal possesses organs that can perform such a function. The electric eel can produce an electric current of shocking power. In a properly constructed aquarium, it can be demonstrated that electricity expelled by an electric eel is strong enough to operate light bulbs. The current also stuns enemies and prey and acts as a sort of radar system. Sensory pits located on the fish's head receive the reflections of these electrical currents from objects close by. The electric ray and the electric catfish are also capable of producing electrical currents strong enough to stun prey. South African gymnotids and African mormyrids are among other kinds of fish that produce electric shocks of lesser strength. The electrical field set up around them serves as a warning device to any intruding prey or predator.

Since fish have a nervous system and sense organs, it would appear that they can feel pain. The fish's brain is not highly developed, however. There is no cerebral cortex (the part of the brain in higher animals that stores impressions), and so the fish has little or no memory. It is not uncommon, for example, for an angler to hook the same fish twice within a short time. Many fish are caught with lures or hooks already embedded in their jaws. Fish are essentially creatures of reflex, rather than of action produced or developed by using the brain. In all probability, physical pain in fish is not very acute, and if any impression of pain is made in the brain, it is quickly lost.

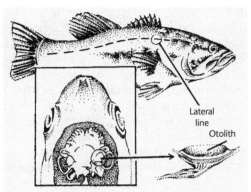

Lateral line

Otolith

Hearing is accomplished primarily through nerves in the lateral line but also through sound waves detected by the otolith.

Reproduction

The fish, like most animals, begins life as an egg, and, as in all other vertebrates, the single-cell egg cannot develop unless it is fertilized by a sperm produced by the male. Fish sperm is most commonly referred to as milt.

Eggs may be fertilized either externally or internally. External fertilization takes place when the egg is penetrated by the sperm after the egg leaves the female's body. Most fish are reproduced by this system. Internal fertilization occurs when the male introduces the sperm into the female's body, where it makes contact with and fertilizes the egg. Some sharks and the live-bearing toothed carp (popular aquarium fish) are ovoviviparous; that is, the egg is fertilized internally and held within the female without attachment to her until it is ready to be extruded alive. In other species, such as some of the sharks and the sculpin, a few catfish, and the skate, the egg is penetrated by the sperm inside the female's body, but it does not hatch until some time after being released from the female.

Reproduction and associated activities in fish are generally referred to as spawning. The spawning season, or breeding period, is that time when the eggs of the female and the milt, or sperm, of the male are ripe. This period may last only a few days, as in some warmwater species like the largemouth bass. Or it may extend into weeks and even months in coldwater species such as the whitefish and the arctic charr. Fish that live in tropical waters of fairly constant temperature may spawn year-round.

Depending on the species, spawning may take place in a variety of environments. But, regardless of where the spawning occurs, all fertilized eggs require special conditions for successful development. Sunlight, oxygen, water agitation, salt and chemicals, water temperature, and other factors have an influence on egg development. In the marine environment, spawning may take place in the open ocean or close to shore. In freshwater, spawning may occur in rapidly moving rivers and streams, where the parents leave the eggs, or in quiet waters, where the fish makes a nest and then protects it. Some fish leave saltwater to travel up rivers and streams to spawn. Eels leave saltwater to enter freshwater but return to the sea to spawn.

Fish such as mackerel, which travel in the open ocean in large schools, take part en masse in external fertilization. They form huge groups and release their reproductive cells indiscriminately into the water. No attempt is made at pairing. The fertilized eggs are at the mercy of temperature, winds, currents, water clarity, salinity, and other factors. In this open-sea type of spawning, the eggs of most species float freely. In other species, the fertilized eggs sink to the bottom, where they are greedily fed upon by bottom-dwelling species. In either system, the parents show no concern for the eggs.

The striped bass, a popular sportfish, is an example of a fish that leaves saltwater to spawn in rivers and streams. Its eggs are fertilized more or less freely, and a single female may be attended by as many as 50 males. The nonadhesive eggs are slightly heavier than water and are rolled along the bottom by the current. The parents protect neither eggs nor young.

Six species of salmon, one on the North American East Coast and five along the Pacific, enter freshwater rivers to spawn. Often they travel hundreds of miles before reaching the spawning site. Unlike the striped bass, they pair off and build a type of nest. These nests, called redds, are built in clear water that is well oxygenated and runs over pebbly areas. The eggs sink in between the pebbles of the nest, where they are safe from predators. The parents, however, do not protect eggs or young. If the nest gets covered by silt, the eggs suffocate.

Trout and bass, among the most popular sportfish, have contrasting spawning habits. Bass usually select quiet, sheltered spawning areas, in water 2 to 6 feet deep. The male excavates a depression in the sand or gravel bottom or among the roots of vegetation. The nest averages 2 to 3 feet in width and 6 inches in depth. It is constructed by the male, who fans the spot with his tail and transports the small pebbles away in his mouth. Depending on her size, a female largemouth bass usually carries from 2,000 to 26,000 eggs, although there are cases on record of a female carrying as many as 40,000 eggs. The pugnacious male guards the nest, the eggs, and the young until the school scatters.

In contrast, the female brook trout usually digs her nest in riffles or at the tail end of pools. She turns on her side and with rapid movements of her tail pushes around the gravel, pebbles, and other bottom materials. When the nest, or egg pit, is of proper size and depth, both male and female assume a parallel position over the area; when ready, the eggs and the milt are extruded at the same time. Young females may carry 200 to 500 eggs, and larger ones may carry over 2,500.

As soon as the spawning procedure is completed, the female brook trout hollows out another nest a short distance upstream from the first nest. The disturbed pebbles from the second excavation travel downstream, covering the eggs of the first nest with a layer of gravel. Several nests may be required before the female has shed all her eggs.

Time requirements for the incubation of eggs depend on the species of fish and the water temperature. For example, largemouth bass eggs hatch in about 5 days in water about 66°F. The incubation period for brook trout is about 44 days at 50°F and about 28 days at 59°F. A sudden 10° drop in temperature during the breeding season is usually enough to kill bass eggs or the newly hatched fry.

Attached to a typical newly hatched young fish, called a larva, is an undigested portion of the yolk. This is usually enough food to last until the little fish can adjust to its aquatic world, before it must begin hunting food for itself. Some kinds of fish start to resemble their parents soon after emerging from the egg and may themselves spawn within the year. Others require years of development before they mature.

Young flounder and other members of the flatfish family start life in an upright position, looking like any other little fish. But during the course of a flatfish's development, the skull twists and one eye migrates to the other side of the head until finally both eyes are on the upper side of the fish. Another startling example of differences in appearance between the young and an adult occurs in the prolific American eel (large specimens deposit 15 to 20 million eggs). The adult eels leave lakes, ponds, and streams to spawn in midwinter in the Sargasso Sea, southwest of Bermuda and off the east coast of Florida. In its larval stage, the American eel is thin, ribbonlike, and transparent. Its head is small and pointed; its mouth contains large teeth, although at this stage it apparently takes no food. The larval form lasts about a year. Then it metamorphoses to the elver, at which time the length and the depth of the body shrink but increase in thickness to a cylindrical form resembling the adult eel. The large, larval teeth disappear, and the head also changes shape. The elver, however, does not take on the adult color, and it does not begin to feed until it reaches North American shores. Averaging 2 to 3½ inches in length, the elvers appear in the spring.

Carp and sturgeon are two of the big egg producers among freshwater fish. When a female sturgeon is full of roe, the eggs may account for as much as 25 percent of her weight. The salted and processed eggs of sturgeon are prized as caviar, as is the roe of salmon, herring, whitefish, codfish, and other fish.

Bullhead and many tropical fish lay their eggs in burrows scooped out of the soft mud at the bottom. Gourami make bubble nests, the males blowing bubbles that rise to the surface, stick together, and form floating rafts. After the nest is built, the female lays her eggs; the male then blows each egg up into the bubbles, where it remains until it hatches. The male stands guard under the raft to chase away intruders.

The male seahorse carries its eggs and also its young in a belly pouch. A female South American catfish carries her eggs attached to a spongy disk on her belly. Sea catfish males use their mouths as brooding pouches for their eggs; once the young are born, the pouches serve as a place of refuge until the young are large enough to fend for themselves.

Many species of fish make nests. Some nests are elaborate, much like those made by birds. The male stickleback, for example, makes a neat nest of twigs and debris and defends it with his life. Other fish simply sweep away the silt and debris where the eggs are to be laid and keep the nest clean and the water aerated until the eggs hatch.

During the spawning season, the sex of most fish is easily discernible. Because of the huge quantity of eggs she carries, the female is usually pot-bellied compared with the male. As the reproductive apparatus becomes ripe, a slight press on the belly will cause the whitish milt of the male or the eggs of the female to be seen in the vent. When the milt and the eggs are in advanced stages of ripeness, they can be forced out by massaging the belly firmly from the head toward the vent. Hatcheries force out the reproductive products in this manner. The eggs are exuded into a pan, and then the milt is forced over them. Milt and eggs are gently mixed, and fertilization takes place. Except in spawning conditions, the sex of many fish cannot be determined unless their bellies are dissected and the immature eggs or the milt sacs are found.

As spawning time approaches, some kinds of fish develop outward signs that make the sexes easily distinguishable. Male trout and salmon acquire hook jaws. Smelt, suckers, and most species of minnows have on their heads and snouts small horny tubercles that disappear shortly after spawning has finished. Males of many species possess larger fins or extensions on the fins. And color is often different in the sexes. The male may sport much brighter and more intense coloration than the female. Some fish have permanent differences in their anatomy; for example, the male bull dolphin has an extended or square forehead, whereas the female's forehead is rounded. Males of many species develop large fins or extensions on some of the fins. Male sharks, skates, and rays have tubelike extensions of the pelvic fins that function in mating.

Age and Growth

Although birds and mammals cease to grow after becoming fully mature, fish continue to grow until they die, provided food is abundant. Growth is fastest during the first few years of life and continues at a decreasing rate. It accelerates during warm-weather months when food is abundant. During the cold months, fish do not feed much; their metabolism slows down, and growth is retarded.

Proper determination of age and growth in fish is important in order to regulate the harvest. In both sport and commercial fish, the age and the growth rate must be known in order to reap the crop wisely. Fisheries are

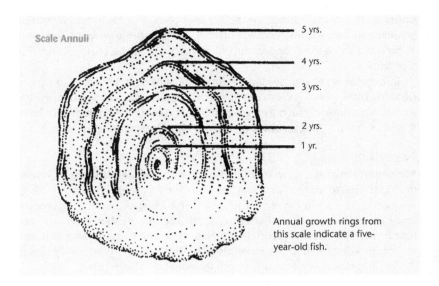

Scale Annuli

5 yrs.
4 yrs.
3 yrs.
2 yrs.
1 yr.

Annual growth rings from this scale indicate a five-year-old fish.

controlled by rules and regulations, based on facts in the life history of fish.

Generally, fish in warm climates reach sexual maturity and grow faster than do their cousins farther north, because the growing seasons are longer and the food supply is not shortened by cold weather. For example, a largemouth bass in Florida may spawn after 1 year; in Wisconsin the same species does not spawn until the third year; and in Canada the largemouth bass may not reach maturity until the fourth or fifth year. Under average conditions, the largemouth bass may attain 3 inches in length in the first 5 months, 5 to 6 inches in 1 year, and 8 to 10 inches in 2 years. By the third year, bass may be 12 or more inches.

A fish's growth rate is also influenced by its environment. A pond or a lake can support only a limited poundage of fish, just as a piece of farmland produces only a limited harvest of vegetables or other crops. In some bodies of water, fish never attain natural size because there are too many of them for the available food supply. Yellow perch are found stunted because only a few, if any, predators, such as bass and pickerel, are present to feed on them. Stunting may also take place because not enough fish are caught, or perhaps because anglers return all the small ones to the water unharmed.

The age of fish that live in temperate climates can be determined fairly accurately from various bony portions of their anatomy, because definite changes in seasons cause annual marks to appear in the bone. These year zones of growth are produced by the slowing down of metabolism in the winter and its rapid increase in the spring. In some species the annual ridges, called annuli, are especially pronounced and easy to read in the scales and cheekbones. In fish with tiny scales, these annuli are difficult to see, even under a microscope. Spines, vertebrae, jawbones, and earbones have to be studied to determine the fish's age. In cross-section, these various bones may show annual rings that appear similar to the rings in the cross-section of a tree trunk.

In tropical areas with seasonal rainfall, the age of freshwater fish can be denoted by seasonal growth marks caused by dry and wet seasons. In uniformly warm waters, such as the equatorial currents, fish demonstrate little, if any, seasonal fluctuation in growth, and age determination is difficult.

Migration

Migration is the mass movement of fish (or any other animals) along a route from one area to another at about the same time annually. This group travel is induced basically by factors of food and spawning. At times, mass movement may take place for other reasons, but such travel should not be confused with migration. Sudden adverse conditions, such as pollution, excessive sedimentation, or water discoloration caused by unusually severe storms, may force large groups of fish to leave the affected area.

Some fish, called "tide-runners," move with the tide to shore and then out again while searching for food. This movement is simply a daily feeding habit and is not considered migration. Some fish remain in deep water during the day and move to shore at night for feeding. In some lakes the entire population of a certain species may move at times from warming shallows to deeper, cooler waters to survive. The lake trout and the walleye are good examples of sportfish that make seasonal movements of this sort.

The bluefin tuna, one of the largest of the oceanic fish, migrates about the same time each year between the coasts of southern Florida and the Bahamas, where it spawns, to waters off Nova Scotia, Prince Edward Island, and Newfoundland. On reaching these far northern waters, the bluefin will find and follow huge schools of herring, sardines, mackerel, or squid in the same localities, year after year. If the temperature rises higher than usual, or other water changes take place, the bait schools will depart from their customary haunts, and the bluefin will follow.

Inshore fish such as the shad and the striped bass may travel varying distances along the coast before arriving in freshwater rivers or brackish stretches that meet the requirements for their spawning activities. Some species do not travel along a coast or migrate north and south; instead, they move offshore into deeper water in cold weather and inshore during warm weather. Others combine a north-south movement with an inshore-offshore migration.

The California grunion, a small, silvery fish, is an example of a unique and precisely timed migration. It spawns at the turn of high tide and as far up the beach as the largest waves travel. This action takes place during that period when the water reaches farthest up shore. The grunion deposits eggs and sperm in pockets in the wet sand. Two weeks or a month later, at the time of the next highest tide, when the water reaches the nests and stirs up the sand, the young are hatched and scramble out to sea before the tide recedes and prevents them from escaping.

Members of the salmon family participate in what may be termed classical migration. All have the same general life pattern. The eggs are hatched in shallow streams; the young spend their early lives in freshwater, grow to maturity in the ocean, and then return to the stream of their birth to spawn. The length of time spent in freshwater and saltwater habitats varies among the species and among populations of the same species. All five species of northwestern Pacific salmon die after their first spawning. The Atlantic salmon drops back to saltwater; those fish that survive the hazards of the sea return to spawn again. Salmon migrate various distances to reach their spawning sites. The chum and the pink salmon usually spawn a few miles from saltwater and often within reach of the tides. The chinook, largest of the salmon family, may cover thousands of miles and surmount many obstacles before reaching its ancestral spawning grounds. And after spending from 1 to about 4 years far out to sea, each individual returns to spawn in the river where it was born.

Alewife
Alosa pseudoharengus

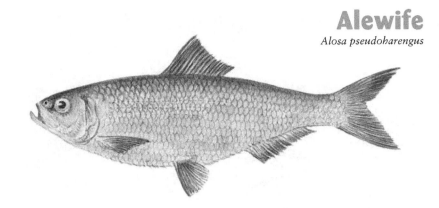

A small herring, the alewife is important as forage for game-fish in many inland waters and along the Atlantic coast. It is used commercially in pet food and as fish meal and fertilizer, and it has been a significant factor in the restoration of trout and salmon fisheries in the Great Lakes.

Identification. Small and silvery gray with a greenish to bluish back tinge, the alewife usually has one small dark shoulder spot and sometimes other small dusky spots. It has large eyes with well-developed adipose eyelids. The alewife can be distinguished from other herring by its lower jaw, which projects noticeably beyond the upper jaw.

Size. Alewives can grow up to a half pound in weight and to 15 inches in length; they usually average 6 to 12 inches in saltwater and 3 to 6 inches in freshwater.

Life history/Behavior. The alewife is a schooling fish and is sometimes found in massive concentrations detectable on sportfishing sonar. In late April through early June, saltwater alewives run up freshwater rivers from the sea to spawn in lakes and sluggish stretches of river. Landlocked alewives move from deeper waters to nearshore shallows in lakes or upstream in rivers, spawning when the water is between 52° and 70°F. Saltwater females deposit 60,000 to 100,000 eggs, whereas freshwater females deposit 10,000 to 12,000 eggs. They deposit the eggs randomly, at night, and both adults leave the eggs unattended. Young alewives hatch in less than a week, and by fall they return to the sea or to deeper waters. Adult landlocked alewives cannot tolerate extreme temperatures, preferring a range of 52° to 70°F—the same temperatures they spawn in.

Food and feeding habits. Young alewives feed on minute free-floating plants and animals, diatoms, copepods, and ostracods; adults feed on plankton, as well as insects, shrimp, small fish, diatoms, copepods, and their own eggs.

OTHER NAMES
herring, sawbelly, gray herring, grayback; French: *gapareau, gaspereau;* Spanish: *alosa, pinchagua.*

Distribution. *Sea-run alewives extend from Newfoundland and the Gulf of St. Lawrence to South Carolina. Alewives were introduced into the upper Great Lakes and into many other inland waters, although some naturally landlocked populations exist.*

Habitat. *Alewives are anadromous, inhabiting coastal waters, estuaries, and some inland waters, although some spend their entire lives in freshwater. They have been caught as far as 70 miles offshore in shelf waters.*

Bass, Florida Largemouth

Micropterus salmoides floridanus

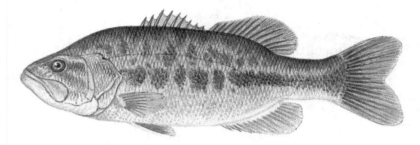

The Florida largemouth bass, also known as the Florida bass, is a subspecies of the largemouth bass *(see: Bass, Largemouth),* which in turn is often called a northern largemouth. This fish occurs naturally in Florida. Mixtures of it and northern largemouth are called intergrades, as they are neither pure Florida nor pure northern strains. These fish occur from northern Florida to Maryland.

Florida bass grow to trophy size more readily than do northern largemouth bass. They have been stocked in many states, including California, which has produced near–world record 22-pounders from transplanted stocks, and in Texas, which has completely transformed its big-bass potential by stocking this fish.

Bass, Guadalupe

Micropterus punctulatus

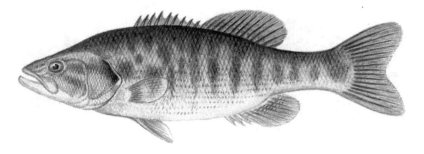

The Guadalupe bass is a member of the Centrarchidae family and is similar to the spotted bass *(see: Bass, Spotted)* in appearance. It has 10 to 12 dark bars along its sides, which are less distinct in older fish; it usually has 16 pectoral rays and 26 to 27 scales around the caudal peduncle. It can grow to almost 16 inches and usually weighs less than a pound. The all-tackle world record is a 3-pound, 11-ounce Texas fish taken in 1983.

In North America, Guadalupe bass are restricted to the Edwards Plateau in the Brazos, Colorado, Guadalupe, San Antonio, and upper Nueces (where introduced) River drainages in southern Texas. They occur in gravel riffles, runs, and flowing pools of creeks, as well as in small to medium rivers.

Bass, Largemouth

Micropterus salmoides

OTHER NAMES

black bass, largemouth, bigmouth, linesides, Oswego bass, green bass, green trout, Florida bass, Florida largemouth, southern largemouth, northern largemouth; French: *achigan à grande bouche;* German: *forellenbarsch;* Italian: *persico trota;* Japanese: *okuchibasu;* Portuguese: *achiga.*

Distribution. *The largemouth bass is endemic only to North America, and its native range was generally the eastern half of the United States and southernmost Ontario and Quebec in Canada. Since the late 1800s, its range has been expanded to include major or minor portions of every state in the United States, except Alaska, and most of the southern fringes of Canada, as well as numerous countries in Europe, Asia, Africa, South America, Central America, and the Caribbean.*

Habitat. *The largemouth bass is typically described as a fish that frequents the*

The largemouth bass is the biggest and most renowned member of the Centrarchidae family of sunfish and its subgroup known as black bass. It is sometimes confused with the smallmouth in places where both species occur, and also with the spotted bass *(see: Bass, Spotted).* One subspecies, the Florida largemouth bass *(see: Bass, Florida Largemouth),* M. salmoides floridanus, is capable of attaining large sizes in appropriate waters but is otherwise similar.

Identification. The largemouth bass has an elongated and robust shape compared to other members of the sunfish family. It has a distinctively large mouth, as the end of its maxillary (jaw) falls below or beyond the rear margin of the eye; the dorsal fin has a deep notch separating the spiny and soft rays; and the tail is broad and slightly forked.

Although coloration varies greatly and is especially dependent on biological factors and host environments, the largemouth bass generally has a light green to light brown hue on the back and upper sides, white lower sides and belly, and a broad stripe of diamond-shaped blotches along the midline of the body. This stripe particularly distinguishes it from its close relative the smallmouth bass, as does the upper jaw, which in the smallmouth does not extend past the eye. The largemouth lacks a tooth patch on the tongue, which helps distinguish it from the spotted bass.

Size/Age. Although the largemouth bass can live up to 15 years, the average life span varies; these fish seldom live more than 10 years. Throughout their range, largemouth bass encountered by anglers average 1 to 1½ pounds (10 to 13 inches) but are commonly caught up to 5 pounds and less commonly from 7 to 10 pounds.

The maximum size attainable may be 25 pounds, but this has not been proven, and only about a dozen bass in the 20-pound class are known to have been caught. The largest specimen is the all-tackle world record of 22 pounds, 4 ounces, caught from Montgomery Lake, Georgia, in 1932.

Life history/Behavior. Largemouth bass spawn from late winter to late spring; the timing depends on latitude and temperature. Southern populations spawn earliest, and most northern populations latest. They begin to spawn about the time the water temperature reaches 60°F. Fish of about 10 to 12 inches are mature enough to reproduce for the first time. The male selects and prepares the nest site, a circular bed usually in 1 to 4 feet of water, often positioned near or including some type of object along the shoreline. The female is nudged to the nest site by the male, deposits her eggs, and leaves; the male guards the eggs, which hatch in a few days, and then guards the young fry for a short period.

Growth rates for largemouth bass are extremely variable, influenced as they are by broad geographical location (north versus south), the specific body of water they inhabit within a particular region, and individual differences even within the same population. Despite these influences, bass are capable of growing quickly under the right circumstances.

Food and feeding habits. Adult bass predominantly eat other fish, including gizzard shad, threadfin shad, golden shiners, bluegills and other sunfish, small catfish, and many other small species, plus crayfish. They are extremely opportunistic, however, and they may consume snakes, frogs, salamanders, mice, and other creatures.

As aggressive predators, bass primarily are ambush feeders, but they may pursue fish in open water, where there are no ambush opportunities. In normally warm waters, digestion occurs fairly quickly; however, at extremely warm or cold temperatures digestion actually slows, causing the bass to feed less frequently and making them less susceptible to anglers.

Bass are well known for their ability to locate prey in turbid water and at night. Although they are primarily sight feeders when water clarity permits, they otherwise use their highly developed lateral line to detect vibrations and locate prey. They can also detect odors, but their senses of smell and taste are poorly understood by scientists and evidently used less for feeding than are their senses of sight or hearing.

weedy sections of ponds and lakes. In reality, the largemouth is highly adaptable to many environments and to many places within various types of water. These bass inhabit creeks, ditches, sloughs, canals, and many little potholes that have the right cover and forage, but they live principally in reservoirs, lakes, ponds, and medium to large rivers, and not always in the weedy sections.

More specifically, however, they orient toward cover and find most of their food in or near some form of cover. Favored haunts include logs, stumps, lily pads, brush, weed and grassbeds, bushes, docks, fencerows, standing timber, bridge pilings, rocky shores, boulders, points, weedline edges, stone walls, creekbeds, roadbeds, ledgelike dropoffs, humps, shoals, and islands. Although much bass cover is nearshore, some bass do spend time away from shore, especially in unvegetated lakes.

Largemouth bass are most active in waters ranging from 65° to 85°F; the lower 70s is likely optimum. Yet they do well in temperatures much higher and lower, including waters that touch the 90°F mark, as well as frozen lakes that dip to the mid-30s.

Bass, Peacock

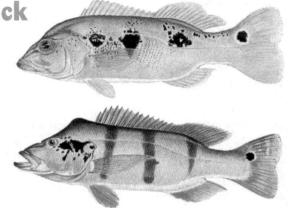

Butterfly Peacock Bass
Cichla ocellaris

Speckled Peacock Bass
Cichla temensis

Distribution. *Though native to South American jungle or rain forest rivers and reservoirs, peacock bass have been introduced in appropriate North American waters through stocking efforts, most notably in small lakes and canal systems in southern Florida and warmwater reservoirs in Texas.*

Peacock bass are among the world's hardest-fighting freshwater fish. They willingly take lures, strike hard, and provide a strong and exciting battle.

The term "peacock bass" is a misnomer, but it is a name that has good marketing value and one that has stuck in the English-speaking world. Species that are called peacock bass in English are formally known as *pavón* in Spanish-speaking countries and as *tucunaré* in Brazil.

Like many other fish that are called bass, peacock bass are not true bass but are members of the Cichlidae family. Their body shape is generally basslike, however. All known species of peacock bass have a prominent black eyespot, surrounded by a gold ring (ocellus), on their tail fin.

Butterfly peacock bass *(Cichla ocellaris).* The butterfly peacock bass is also known as peacock cichlid, tucunare, tuc; in Spanish as *pavón mariposa, pavón amarillo, pavón tres estrellas, marichapa;* in Portuguese as *tucunaré-acu;* and in Hawaiian as *lukanani.* It was introduced in Hawaii (where it is primarily known as *tucunare*) from British Guyana in 1957, and in Florida in 1984 and 1986; it has also been stocked in Puerto Rico, Panama, Guam, and the Dominican Republic.

Butterfly peacock bass possess great variation in color. They are generally yellowish green overall, with three dark, yellow-tinged blotches along the lateral midsection; these blotches intersect with faint bars, which typically fade in fish weighing more than 3 to 4 pounds. The iris of the eye is frequently deep red. A conspicuous hump exists on top of the head in breeding males, and spawning fish have an intensified yellow coloration. They are distinguished by the absence of black markings on the opercula and are believed to attain a maximum size of 11 to 12 pounds; the all-tackle world record is a 12-pound, 9-ounce individual from Venezuela.

Bass, Peacock (continued)

Speckled peacock bass *(Cichla temensis).* The speckled peacock bass is also known as speckled pavon, painted pavon, striped tucunare; in Spanish as *pavón cinchado, pavón pintado, pavón trucha,* and *pavón venado;* in Portuguese as *tucunaré-pacu.* It was introduced to Florida in 1985.

Speckled peacock bass have dark blotches on the opercula and three distinctive vertical black bars on their bodies; these may become more pronounced with age, although this does not appear to be absolute. There are light or faint spots on the dorsal and caudal fins, and a conspicuous hump exists on top of the head in a breeding male. Some individuals (described as another color phase) may have four to six horizontal rows of light-colored dashes or spots along the sides and speckling over the rest of their bodies and fins; these fish are called "spotted peacock bass" by many anglers and were previously thought to be a distinct species.

The speckled peacock bass is the only peacock bass that has broken longitudinal lines and spots on the head, opercula, and caudal and dorsal fin regions, resulting in a speckled appearance. Many speckled peacock bass, however, especially the largest specimens, do not exhibit this speckling along their flanks.

Speckled peacock bass exhibit many color variations, the adults being lighter than the juveniles. Generally, they are dark green to black along the back, golden to yellow or light green along the flanks, and lighter on the belly. The pelvic, the anal, and the lower half of the caudal fins are often reddish in color, sometimes yellowish green. These colors are general conformities, however, and significant variations exist, especially in intensity (some have an orange or a bronze tinge), which may or may not be due to season or habitat.

This species attains the greatest size of all the peacock bass. The current all-tackle world record is a 27-pound speckled peacock bass from Brazil.

Bass, Redeye

Micropterus coosae

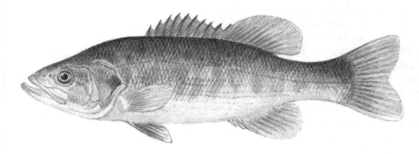

Distribution. *Redeye bass are found in the Alabama, the Savannah, the Coosa, the Chattahoochee, and the Warrior River systems in Georgia and Alabama, and in southeastern Tennessee (Conasauga drainage). They have been introduced to a limited degree in California, Puerto Rico, and Kentucky's upper Cumberland River drainage.*

Shoal bass occur in the Apalachicola River system in Florida and in the Chattahoochee, the Chestatee, and the Flint Rivers in Georgia.

Habitat. *Inhabiting the rocky runs and pools of creeks and small to medium rivers, redeye bass prefer the cold headwaters of small streams. They seldom exist in natural lakes, ponds, or reservoirs, and they prefer water temperatures in the mid-60s. Shoal bass are most likely to thrive in main-channel habitats.*

There are two widely recognized forms of this member of the black bass group of the Centrarchidae family: the Apalachicola, which is called a shoal bass, and the Alabama, which is generally referred to as the redeye bass or the true redeye. The shoal bass has yet to be described fully or given a distinct scientific name, and there is some confusion over the two. A scrappy fighter, the redeye bass often jumps when hooked and is hard to catch. Its white, flaky meat is of good table quality, similar to that of other black bass.

Identification. As its name indicates, the redeye bass is characterized by the considerable amount of red in its eyes. It is bronze olive above, with brownish to greenish sides, and yellow-white to blue below, usually with dark vertical bars on the flanks. The bars on the caudal peduncle are diamond shaped with light centers. It has a prominent dark spot on the gill cover and rows of dark spots on the lower sides, as well as white upper and lower outer edges on the orange-tinged tail. The upper jaw of its large mouth extends to the rear portion of the eye but not beyond, and there is usually a patch of teeth on the tongue. The redeye has redder fins than do other black bass; the first and the second dorsal fins are connected, and the second dorsal and the caudal fins and the front of the anal fin are brick red on young fish. There is a dusky spot on the base of the tail, which is also darkest on a young fish. There are 12 dorsal rays and 10 anal rays.

The shoal bass can normally be distinguished from the redeye bass by a prominent spot immediately before the tail and another on the edge of the gill cover, which is generally indistinct on the redeye. The shoal bass also lacks white outer edges on the tail, has smaller scales, and lacks the patch of teeth on the tongue. It has 12 to 13 dorsal rays and 10 to 11 anal rays.

Size/Age. The redeye bass grows to 18½ inches and

about 3 pounds, although some reach more than 8 pounds and live as long as 10 years. The shoal form grows faster, although it generally reaches about 15 inches in length. The all-tackle world record is an 8-pound, 12-ounce fish taken in Florida in 1995.

Spawning. Spawning occurs in spring, when water temperatures are between 60° and 70°F, usually over coarse gravel at the head of a pool. Males build the nest and guard the eggs and fry.

Food. Redeye feed primarily on terrestrial and larval insects, crayfish, and small fish.

Bass, Roanoke

Ambloplites cavifrons

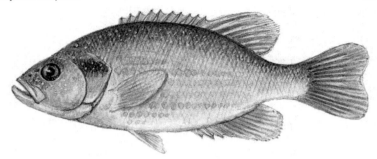

The Roanoke bass is a sunfish and a member of the Centrarchidae family, similar in body shape to a rock bass *(see: Bass, Rock)* or warmouth *(see)*. It can be identified by its unscaled or partly scaled cheek and the several iridescent gold to white spots on its upper side and head. It is olive to tan above, has a dark and light marbling on the sides, and often sports rows of black spots and a white to bronze breast and belly. It is also distinguished by the 39 to 49 lateral scales, 11 anal rays, and 27 to 35 scale rows across its breast between the pectoral fins. The all-tackle world record is a 1-pound, 5-ounce fish taken in Virginia in 1991.

Growing to a maximum of 14½ inches, the Roanoke bass occurs in North America in the Chowan, the Roanoke, the Tar, and the Neuse River drainages in Virginia and North Carolina. It inhabits the rocky and sandy pools of creeks and small to medium clear rivers.

Bass, Rock

Ambloplites rupestris

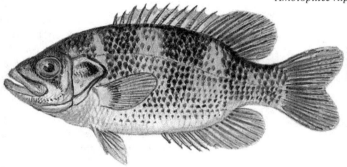

The rock bass is actually a member of the sunfish family and is not a true bass. Rock bass are fun to catch because they can be caught on many types of baits and lures, and they put up a decent fight on ultralight tackle. Rock bass are known to overpopulate small lakes, making population control measures necessary.

Identification. Although it looks like a cross between a bluegill and a black bass, the rock bass is actually a large and robust sunfish with a deep body; it is less compressed than most sunfish and is more similar to a black bass in shape. The back is raised, and the large head is narrow, rounded, and deep. The mouth of the rock bass is large in comparison to other sunfish; the upper jaw reaches beyond the beginning of the eye but not to the back of the eye. It has two connected dorsal fins, five to six anal fin spines, and large eyes.

The rock bass is olive brown or bronze on the back and sides, with faint lines of tiny dark marks; the centers of the scales below the lateral line also have dark markings that form 11 or more rows and give the fish a striped appearance. In some rock bass, the coloring is lighter but consistent underneath, whereas others are silver, gray, or white on the bellies. The ventral fins have pale circular spots, and all fins are usually darker at their margins, although the edges of the anal spines are white, the tips of the pectoral fins are clear, and the pelvic fins sometimes have a white edge. A distinguishing characteristic is the bluish-black blotch found on the tips of the gill covers.

Rock bass are frequently confused with the warmouth (*Lepomis gulosus; see: warmouth*). Warmouth have teeth on their tongue, whereas rock bass do not. There are also six spines in front of the anal fin of a rock bass, as opposed to the three spines in the warmouth. Rock bass may resemble the mud sunfish as well (*see: Sunfish, Mud*); rock bass have

OTHER NAMES

black perch, goggle-eye, red eye, rock sunfish, goggle-eye perch; French: crapet de roche.

Distribution. *Native to the northeastern United States and southeastern Canada, rock bass range from southern Manitoba east to Ontario and Quebec, and southward through the Great Lakes region and the Mississippi Valley to the Gulf of Mexico and as far east as northern Alabama and northern Georgia. They have been introduced into other states, including some in the western United States.*

Habitat. *Rock bass prefer small to moderate streams with cool and clear water, abundant shelter, and considerable current; they are plentiful in shallow, weedy lakes and the outer edges of larger lakes, as well as in thousands of smaller lakes and ponds. Rock bass almost always hold over rocky bottoms (resulting in the name "rock" bass) where there is no silt. Young* *rock bass are frequently found in vegetation. Rock bass tend to frequent the same habitats as do small-mouth bass.*

forked tails and rough scales, whereas mud sunfish have rounded tails and smooth scales.

Size/Age. The most common size for rock bass is about 8 ounces, although they have been known to reach 3 pounds. Often, rock bass in a particular lake will weigh around a pound, with a few fish exceeding 2 pounds. As with most sunfish, however, size is extremely variable, and rock bass living in streams are often stunted. The all-tackle record is a 3-pound Canadian fish.

Rock bass can reach a length of 12 to 14 inches but are usually less than 8 inches long. Although aquarium fish have lived for 18 years, those in the wild live 10 to 12 years on average.

Life history/Behavior. Rock bass are able to reproduce once they are 2 years old or 3 to 5 inches long; spawning occurs from midspring to early summer, when water temperatures range from 60° to 70°F. Males move into the shallows 3 to 4 days prior to the females' arrival, to establish territories. They begin building round nests in gravelly or sandy areas near weedbeds or other protection, such as submerged tree trunks, using their pectoral, anal, and caudal fins to fan the gravel for the nests.

Spawning occurs during the day, usually in the morning. The females spawn at least twice, moving from nest to nest and laying from 3,000 to 11,000 eggs in total. The males guard the nests until the eggs hatch and the young swim away, and many males nest a second or even a third time.

Rock bass are a schooling fish and often cluster with other sunfish and smallmouth bass.

Food and feeding habits. Young rock bass feed on minute aquatic life when young, then on insects and crustaceans as they grow. Adults eat mostly crayfish, as well as minnows, insects, mollusks, and small fish. This diet varies with season and location. They can consume relatively large specimens because of their large mouths. Rock bass generally feed on the bottom but may occasionally feed near the surface.

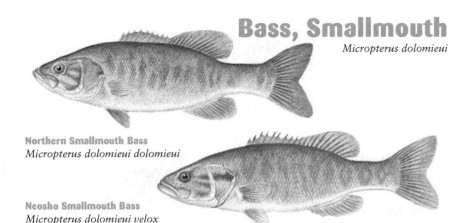

Bass, Smallmouth

Micropterus dolomieui

Northern Smallmouth Bass
Micropterus dolomieui dolomieui

Neosho Smallmouth Bass
Micropterus dolomieui velox

The smallmouth bass is the second largest member of the Centrarchidae family of sunfish and a North American original. To anglers, it is one of the most impressive of all freshwater fish and is coveted for its fighting ability.

The smallmouth is not actually a bass but a sunfish, and its mouth is only small in comparison to that of some relatives. It is naturally a fish of both clear rivers and lakes and has been widely introduced to other waters outside its original range. Smallmouth bass that reside in small to intermediate streams do not grow as large, on average, as those from lakes or reservoirs, although fish from big rivers, and especially those with tailwater fisheries, can attain large sizes. River smallmouth bass are even spunkier than their lake-dwelling brethren, however, and tend to be more streamlined and to lack drooping bellies.

The smallmouth bass is occasionally confused with the largemouth where they both occur, and also with the spotted bass and the redeye bass. They have been known to hybridize with spotted bass. Two subspecies are often recognized: the northern smallmouth, *Micropterus dolomieui dolomieui*, and the Neosho smallmouth, *M. d. velox*.

Identification. The smallmouth bass has a robust, slightly laterally compressed and elongate body; a protruding lower jaw; red eyes; and a broad and slightly forked tail. Its pelvic fins sit forward on the body below the pectoral fins; a single spine is found on each pelvic fin and on the front of the anal fin. The two dorsal fins are joined or notched; the front one is spiny and the second one has one spine followed by soft rays. Its color varies from brown, golden brown, and olive to green on the back, becoming lighter to golden on the sides and white on the belly. Young fish have more distinct vertical bars or rows of spots on their sides, and the caudal, or tail, fins are orange at the base, followed by black and then white outer edges.

OTHER NAMES

black bass, smallmouth, bronzeback, brown bass, brownie, smallie, redeye; French: *achigan à petite bouche;* German: *schwarzbarsch;* Japanese: *kokuchibasu.*

Distribution. *The smallmouth bass is endemic only to North America, and its original range was from the Great Lakes and the St. Lawrence River drainages in Canada south to northern Georgia, west to eastern Oklahoma, and north to Minnesota. It has since been widely spread within and beyond that range, across southern Canada west to British Columbia and east to the Maritimes, west to the Pacific coast states, and into the southwestern United States. It has also been introduced to Hawaii, Asia, Europe, and Africa.*

Habitat. *Smallmouth bass prefer clear, quiet waters with gravel, rubble, or rocky bottoms. They live in mid-size, gentle streams that have deep pools and*

Bass, Smallmouth (continued)

abundant shade or in fairly deep, clear lakes and reservoirs with rocky shoals. Although they are fairly adaptable, they are seldom found in murky water and avoid swift current.

In the typical river, smallmouth bass predominate in the cool middle section where there are large pools between riffles, whereas trout occupy the swifter and colder upper section. In stillwaters, smallmouth bass may occupy lakes, reservoirs, or ponds if these waters are large and deep enough to have thermal stratification, and they are usually located deeper than largemouth bass once the surface layer warms in the spring or early summer.

The smallmouth is easily distinguished from the largemouth by its clearly connected dorsal fins, the scales on the base portion of the soft-rayed second dorsal fin, and the upper jawbone, which extends only to about the middle of the eye. The coloration is also distinctive, being usually more brownish in the smallmouth and more greenish in the largemouth.

Size/Age. The average life span of the smallmouth bass is 5 to 6 years, although it can live for 15 years. Most smallmouth bass encountered by anglers weigh between 1 and 1 1/2 pounds and are from 9 to 13 inches long; fish exceeding 3 pounds are considered fairly large but not uncommon. The largest smallmouth known is the Tennessee state record, a fish that weighed 11 pounds, 15 ounces, when caught from Dale Hollow Lake in 1955.

The Neosho subspecies, which is more slender than the smallmouth, occurs in the Neosho River and tributaries of the Arkansas River in Missouri, Kansas, Arkansas, and Oklahoma.

Life history/Behavior. Smallmouth bass spawn in the spring (or the early summer in most northern waters), when the water temperature is between 60° and 65°F. The male builds a nest in water that ranges from 1 to 12 feet deep, depending on the environment. The nest site is often over a gravel or rock bottom but may be over a sandy bottom in lakes, and it is usually near the protection of a log or a boulder.

Older bass prefer rocky, shallow areas of lakes and rivers and retreat to deeper areas when water temperatures are high. They tend to seek cover and avoid the light and generally do not inhabit the same types of dense, weedy, or wooded cover that largemouth bass prefer. They hide in deep water, behind rocks and boulders, and around underwater debris and crevices, preferring water temperatures between 66° and 72°F.

Food. These highly carnivorous and predatory fish will eat whatever is available, but they have a clear preference for crayfish and small fish. In lakes, this includes small bass, panfish, perch, and assorted fingerling-size minnows in lakes. In rivers, it includes minnows, crayfish, hellgrammites, nymph larvae, and leeches.

Bass, Spotted

Micropterus punctulatus

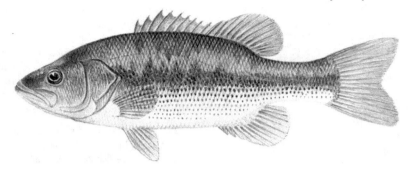

Often mistaken by anglers for the largemouth bass, the spotted bass is a lesser-known member of the black bass group of the Centrarchidae family than either the largemouth or the smallmouth, but this is a spunky and distinguished-looking species that no angler is unhappy about catching, even if most are encountered by accident.

The general term "spotted bass" really incorporates three recognized subspecies: the northern spotted bass *(M. p. punctulatus)*, the Alabama spotted bass *(M. p. henshalli)*, and the Wichita spotted bass *(M. p. wichitae);* the last was previously thought to be extinct and is still rarely encountered.

Spotted bass are scrappy fish whose fight is often compared to that of the smallmouth, although they jump less frequently. Their average and maximum sizes are smaller than those of the largemouth, and they are more likely to utilize and suspend in deep water, even moving about in deep water in loose groups, rather than in schools.

Identification. The spotted bass has a moderately compressed, elongate body, with coloration and markings that are similar to those of the largemouth bass; both have a light green to light brown hue on the backs and the upper sides, white lower sides and bellies, and a broad stripe of diamond-shaped blotches along the midlines of their bodies. Like all black bass except the largemouth, the spotted bass has scales on the base portion of the second dorsal fin, its first and second dorsal fin are clearly connected, and its upper jawbone does not extend back to or beyond the rear edge of the eyes. The spotted bass has a distinct patch of teeth on the tongue, which the largemouth does not, and there is a large spot on the point of the gill cover.

The spotted bass differs from the smallmouth bass in that it lacks the vertical bars that are present on the sides of the body in the smallmouth. It also has small black spots in alternate rows below the lateral line (the rear edges of

OTHER NAMES

Alabama spotted bass, black bass, Kentucky bass, Kentucky spotted bass, lineside, northern spotted bass, redeye, spot, Wichita spotted bass.

Distribution. *Spotted bass were once primarily found in the lower to central Mississippi River drainages of North America, but their range has expanded greatly. They are now found throughout the central and lower Mississippi basin, from southern Ohio and West Virginia to southeastern Kansas and south to the Gulf of Mexico (from Texas to the Florida Panhandle), including the Chattahoochee drainage in Georgia, Alabama, Tennessee, Kentucky, and other nearby states, where they occur naturally or have been introduced. Spotted bass have been introduced as far west as California, where some of the larger specimens are now found, and outside North America, including South Africa, where the species has*

Bass, Spotted (continued)
become established in
several bodies of water.

The infrequently
encountered Wichita
spotted bass appears to be
limited to West Cache
Creek, Oklahoma. The
Alabama spotted bass is
native to Alabama, Missis-
sippi, and Georgia.

Habitat. *The natural habi-*
tats of spotted bass are
clear, gravelly, flowing pools
and runs of creeks and
small to medium rivers, and
they also tolerate the
slower, warmer, and more
turbid sections that are
unlikely to host smallmouth
bass. They are seldom found
in natural lakes but have
adapted well to deep
impoundments, which were
created by damming some
of their natural rivers and
streams. In reservoirs they
prefer water temperatures in
the mid-70s Fahrenheit. The
typical habitat is similar to
that of the largemouth
bass, although the spotted
bass prefers rocky areas and
is much more likely to
inhabit and suspend in open
waters; it may hold in great
depths (between 60 and
more than 100 feet) in
some waters. Rocky bluffs,
deep rockpiles, and sub-
merged humps are among
its haunts.

certain scales are black), unlike either the largemouth or the smallmouth. Reportedly, spotted bass and smallmouth bass have hybridized in nature, which could make identification of some specimens where both species are known to occur even more difficult.

The Alabama spotted bass has a dark spot at the base of the tail and on the rear of the gill cover and 68 to 75 scales along the lateral line. The northern spotted bass also has a spot on the tail, but the spot on the gill cover is not as distinct, and there are only 60 to 68 scales along the lateral line.

Size/Age. Spotted bass seldom exceed 4 to 5 pounds and are rarely encountered up to 8 pounds. The all-tackle world record is a 10-pound, 4-ounce fish taken in California in 2001. Because of the difficulty in recognizing the species, it is probable that larger record-size specimens of spotted bass have gone unnoticed. The life span of about 7 years is much shorter than that of the smallmouth or the largemouth, and the growth rate is intermediate between the two.

Life history/Behavior. Spotted bass spawn in the spring at water temperatures of about 63° to 68°F. Males sweep away silt from a gravel or rock bottom to make the nests, generally near brush, logs, or other heavy cover. The males guard the eggs and then guard the fry after they leave the nests. Fry are extremely active, much more than those of either the largemouth or the smallmouth.

These fish tend to school more than does any other member of the black bass family and are often encountered chasing shad in open water.

Food and feeding habits. Juveniles feed on small crustaceans and midge larvae, whereas adults eat insects, larger crustaceans, minnows, frogs, worms, grubs, and small fish. Crayfish are usually the most important item in the diet, followed by small fish and larval and adult insects.

Bass, Striped

Morone saxatilis

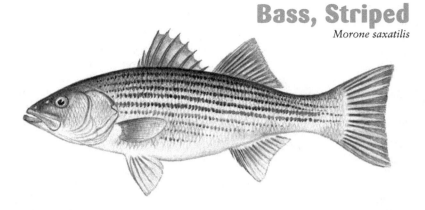

An excellent sportfish that attains large sizes, the striped bass is a member of the temperate bass family (often erroneously placed with the sea bass family). It has been considered one of the most valuable and popular fish in North America since the early 1600s, originally for its commercial importance and culinary quality, and in more recent times for its recreational significance.

Identification. A large fish with a large mouth, the striped bass is more streamlined than its close relative, the white bass. It has a long body and a long head, a somewhat laterally compressed body form, and a protruding lower jaw. Of the two noticeably separate dorsal fins, the first one has 7 to 12 stiff spines, usually 9, which make this fin quite a bit higher than the second; the second dorsal fin has 1 sharp spine and 8 to 14, ordinarily 12, soft rays. The striped bass also has a forked tail and small eyes.

These fish are mostly bluish black or dark green above, fading into silver on the sides and white on their bellies. On each side of a striped bass's body, there are seven or eight prominent black horizontal stripes that run along the scale rows that are the distinctive markings of the striped bass; one of the stripes runs along the lateral line, and the rest are equally divided above and below it. The stripe highest up on the side is usually the most noticeable, although on some fish, one or more of the stripes is interrupted.

In freshwater, the striped bass has been crossed with the white bass to create a hybrid called the whiterock bass or sunshine bass. Striped bass differ from hybrids in the regularity of their stripes, whereas the hybrid usually has interrupted stripes. The narrow body of the striped bass also distinguishes it from the white bass.

Size/Age. Growing rapidly in early life, striped bass average 5 to 10 pounds, although they often reach weights in

OTHER NAMES

striper, rock, rockfish, striped sea bass, striper bass, linesider, squid hound, and greenhead; French: *bar rayé;* Spanish: *lubina estriada.*

Distribution. *On the Atlantic coast of the United States, the striped bass commonly occurs from the St. Lawrence River south to the St. Johns River in northern Florida. It has also ranged along the coasts of Florida, Louisiana, Alabama, and Mississippi in the Gulf of Mexico. Some fish migrate north from North Carolina, Virginia, or Maryland during the summer and return during the fall. Others living in estuarine river systems, such as the St. Lawrence, the Santee Cooper, or the Savannah, are nonmigratory.*

Striped bass were introduced to San Francisco Bay in 1879 and 1882; today, along the Pacific coast, they are abundant in the bay area and extend from Washington to California; some California fish migrate north to Oregon and are occasion-

Bass, Striped (continued)

ally found off the west coast of Vancouver Island.

Habitat. *Striped bass inhabit saltwater, freshwater, and brackish water, although they are most abundant in saltwater. They are anadromous and migrate in saltwater along coastal inshore environs and tidal tributaries. They are often found around piers, jetties, surf troughs, rips, flats, and rocks. A common regional name for stripers is "rockfish," and indeed their scientific name,* saxatilis, *means "rock dweller," although they do not necessarily spend most of their lives in association with rocks. They run far upstream during spawning runs and are also found in channels of medium to large rivers at that time. The striped bass is entirely a coastal species off the coast of the Carolinas and southward, never ranging more than a few miles offshore; along the entire Atlantic coast, they are rarely caught more than a short distance from shore except during migration.*

Striped bass were introduced into freshwater lakes and impoundments with successful results. In some freshwater populations, striped bass were not introduced but were landlocked, due to man-made barriers that blocked their return to the sea. In freshwater, stripers are commonly found in open-water environs or in the tailrace below dams. They are seldom found near shore or docks or piers, except when chasing schools of baitfish.

the 30- to 50-pound range. The maximum size that a freshwater striped bass can achieve is unknown, although the largest sport-caught freshwater striper weighed 67 pounds, 1 ounce. The all-tackle record for the species—78 pounds, 8 ounces—belongs to a saltwater fish, although larger ones have been reportedly taken commercially. Striped bass normally live 10 to 12 years, although most fish more than 11 years old and more than 39 inches long are female.

Life history/Behavior. Striped bass males are sexually mature by their second or third year, whereas females are sexually mature sometime between their eighth and ninth years; males measuring at least 7 inches and females as small as 34 inches are known to spawn. Spawning occurs in fresh or slightly brackish waters from mid-February in Florida to late June or July in Canada, and from mid-March to late July in California, when the water temperature is between 50° and 73°F; peak spawning activity is observed between 59° and 68°F. Striped bass prefer the mouths of freshwater tributary streams, where the current is strong enough to keep the eggs suspended.

When mating, each female is accompanied by several smaller males. The spawning fish swim near the surface of the water, turning on their sides and rolling and splashing; this display is sometimes called a "rock fight." The semi-buoyant eggs are released and drift with the current until they hatch 2 to 3 days later, depending on the water temperature.

Food and feeding habits. A voracious, carnivorous, and opportunistic predator, the striped bass feeds heavily on small fish, including large quantities of herring, menhaden, flounder, alewives, silversides, eels, and smelt, as well as invertebrates such as worms, squid, and crabs. Freshwater striped bass prefer shad, herring, minnows, amphipods, and mayflies. There has been controversy over the effect of freshwater stripers on other gamefish—most notably, on largemouth bass—but bass and other popular sportfish do not appear to be important components in the diet of freshwater stripers.

Bass, Suwannee

Micropterus notius

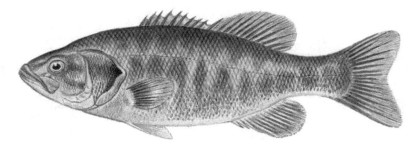

The Suwannee bass is similar in bodily appearance to the smallmouth bass and in markings to the redeye bass, except that it is generally brown overall, and the cheeks, breasts, and bellies of large males are bright turquoise. It, too, has a large mouth, with the upper jaw extending under the eye, and possesses a patch of teeth on the tongue, a spot at the base of the tail, and blotches on the sides. It is further identified by its 59 to 64 lateral scales, 16 pectoral fin rays, 12 to 13 dorsal fin rays, and 10 to 11 anal fin rays.

Growing to just over 14 inches and weighing generally less than a pound, the Suwannee bass is a small species. The all-tackle world record is a 3-pound, 14-ounce fish taken in Florida in 1985. A member of the Centrarchidae family, it has the smallest range of any black bass, occurring in North America, commonly in the Suwannee River drainage in Florida and less commonly in the Ochlockonee River drainage in northern Florida and Georgia. Limited range and small size make this species of minor angling interest, but it is an aggressive species found in rocky riffles, runs, and pools and is typically caught around rocky structures and along steep banks.

Bass, White

Morone chrysops

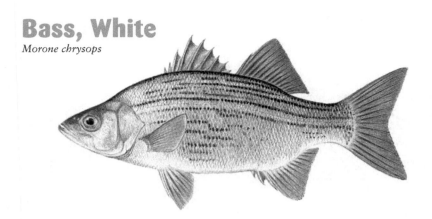

OTHER NAMES

white lightning, barfish, striped bass, silver bass, striper, stripe, sandbass, and sandy; French: *bar blanc.*

Distribution. *White bass have a wide distribution extending throughout river systems in the Mississippi Valley (including Texas, northwest Florida, and Louisiana), the Ohio Valley, and the Great Lakes. Native in the east from the St. Lawrence River, in the north from Lake Winnipeg, and in the west from the Río Grande, white bass are found from Canada to the Gulf of Mexico. They have been stocked within and outside their natural range and transplanted into various states, including California.*

Habitat. *The white bass is most abundant in clear, cool lakes; reservoirs; ponds; and pools of small to large rivers. White bass prefer lakes exceeding 300 acres and with considerable stretches of water at least 10 feet deep.*

A member of the temperate bass family, the white bass is a freshwater fish known for its spunky fighting ability, as well as its merits as an excellent eating fish. Because of its small size, it is often considered a panfish. White bass usually travel in schools and can provide a lot of action, making them highly desirable among light-tackle enthusiasts and for fishing with family and youths.

Identification. The white bass has a moderately deep and compressed body that is raised behind the small head and the large mouth, deepest between the two dorsal fins. It also has 11 to 13 rays on the anal fin and one to two patches of teeth at the back of the tongue. The coloration is mostly silvery with a dark grayish green on the back and anywhere from 4 to 10 dark horizontal stripes running along the sides. It also has yellow eyes, clear to dusky dorsal and caudal fins, and clear to white pectoral and pelvic fins.

The white bass is sometimes confused with other members of the temperate bass family. It resembles the striped bass *(M. saxatilis)* by possessing the same silver sides and black stripes; it is shorter, though, than the striped bass and has a smaller head, a deeper body, a humped back, and dorsal fins that are closer together. The white bass is also similar in appearance to the yellow bass *(M. mississippiensis)* but is more silvery in color and has unbroken stripes, as well as a projecting lower jaw (in yellow bass, the jaws are about even); the white bass has separate spiny and soft portions of the dorsal fins, whereas those of the yellow bass are joined at the base.

The white bass also thrives in some waters inhabited by white perch *(M. americana),* particularly in the Great Lakes and their tributaries. The white bass can be distinguished from the white perch by the lack of distinct stripes on the sides of the body of the white perch, although stripes are occasionally found on the young of that species.

Bass, White (continued)

Size/Age. White bass average between ½ pound and 2 pounds but may weigh as much as 3 to 4 pounds; the all-tackle world record is 6 pounds, 13 ounces. They can grow up to 17¾ inches long, averaging 10 to 12 inches, and can live at least 10 years, but few make it past age 4. Females grow faster and probably live longer than males. Cold water and a lack of shad in the north, and warm water and abundant gizzard and threadfin shad populations in the south, account for regional growth differences.

Life history/Behavior. White bass migrate within freshwater rivers to spawn, specifically 40 miles or less. Two-year-old sexually mature males reach the spawning grounds about a month before the females do, moving into the same spawning grounds every year; they arrive sometime between February and June, depending on when the water temperature rises above 45°F. Several white bass males gather around a female in 6 to 7 feet of water and push her to the surface, where she releases eggs that are quickly fertilized. Settling on rocks and vegetation in shallow water, the tiny, adhesive eggs hatch in 45 hours at 60°F. The adult fish do not protect the eggs or the young, and as a result, very few fish survive their first year. Adults move to deeper water once they have spawned, where they swim in compact schools, often close to the surface.

Food and feeding habits. White bass feed on shad, silversides, crustaceans, yellow perch, sunfish, insects, crayfish, and their own young. Although they stay mostly in deep waters, they usually come to the surface to feed on schools of small shad or other minnows and often make a great commotion; this normally occurs early or late in the day or on overcast days.

Bass, Whiterock

Morone saxatilis x Morone chrysops

Distribution. *Hybrid striped bass distribution is limited to freshwater and to places with a good population of baitfish, principally members of the herring family. Nevertheless, stocking programs have resulted in plantings of these fish in lakes and reservoirs in more than 30 states, from California to New York and from Nebraska to Florida. The greatest concentration is throughout the southern half of the country, and the most fishing opportunities are in the Southeast.*

Habitat. *Whiterock and sunshine bass inhabit the same freshwater habitats as their parents, primarily large lakes and reservoirs, but they also thrive in midsize to large rivers and occasionally in small lakes or ponds. They are largely nomadic in those environments and are found in the same places as their parents, sometimes commingling with them, mostly in open-water environs or in the tailrace below dams. They are seldom found near shore or docks or piers, except when chasing schools of baitfish.*

Hybrid striped bass have become one of the most popular introduced fish in freshwater. Hybrid stripers are the progeny of one pure-strain striped bass parent and one pure-strain white bass parent. When the cross is between the female striper and the male white bass, the result is primarily known as a whiterock bass; in some places it is referred to as a wiper and in some simply as a hybrid striped bass. When the cross is between the male striper and the female white bass, it is called a sunshine bass (primarily in Florida) or simply a hybrid striped bass.

These fish, which usually look like stockier versions of pure-strain stripers, are aggressive and hard-fighting fish that provide great sport. The fact that they are so strong and grow fairly large rather quickly endears them to anglers, not to mention that they can be a more ambitious lure and bait consumer than pure stripers.

Hybrid stripers do not occur in saltwater; they are strictly a freshwater phenomenon. In freshwater, whiterock or sunshine bass may crossbreed naturally in the wild, although this is not the norm. Most hybrid stripers existing in freshwater lakes and rivers are the result of state fish-stocking programs.

Like both of its parents, the whiterock or the sunshine bass is good table fare, and its flesh is virtually indistinguishable from that of the parent fish.

Identification. This fish looks like a stockier version of the striped bass, usually having a shorter length and greater girth but with very similar coloration. The primary means of distinguishing the whiterock or the sunshine bass is by the less distinct and interrupted or broken lines along its sides. The lateral lines of the parent fish are unbroken. Hybrid stripers (and pure-strain stripers) can be distinguished from white bass by the tooth patterns on their tongues. The white bass has a single broad U-pattern, while the striper has two distinctive elongated tooth patches.

The accompanying illustration shows the distinguishing characteristics. It is important to learn the differences between these fish when angling in waters that may contain all three species, as regulations regarding them may differ.

Size/Age. Whiterock and sunshine bass have an extremely fast growth rate in their early stages. Specimens that have been stocked as inch-long fish have grown to 4 inches in just 1 month, and 15 inches by their second summer, so they quickly attain sizes of angling interest. When 18 inches long, a hybrid striper will weigh at least 3 pounds and possibly as much as 5 pounds.

Their maximum attainable size is uncertain, although they grow much larger than a white bass and are much smaller than a pure-strain striped bass. The all-tackle world-record hybrid striped bass is a 25-pound, 15-ounce Alabama fish.

Life history/Behavior. These elements are essentially the same as for the parent species, including spring spawning runs, open-water migrations, schooling, and baitfish-pillaging tendencies. One difference with whiterock and sunshine bass is that when planted in lakes with no other related species with which to interbreed, they can be controlled entirely through stocking programs. Unlike many hybrid fish, which are sterile, these specimens are fertile fish; however, they can reproduce only if they cross with a pure-strain parent. But in lakes where neither pure-strain stripers nor white bass are present (usually in northern states), fisheries managers have stocked hybrid striped bass with the comfort of knowing that the fish wouldn't expand beyond the numbers stocked. Thus, if the fish proved detrimental to baitfish or other game species, they could be eradicated by discontinuing stocking.

Food and feeding habits. The food preferences and the feeding habits of these fish are similar to those of freshwater striped bass and white bass.

Bass, Yellow

Morone mississippiensis

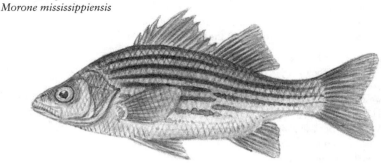

Distribution. *Yellow bass inhabit the Lake Michigan and Mississippi River basins from Minnesota, Wisconsin, and Michigan south to the Pearl River drainage in Louisiana, the Galveston Bay drainage in Texas, the lower Coosa and Mobile Bay drainages, east to western Indiana and eastern Tennessee, and west to western Iowa and eastern Oklahoma. Found mostly in the central Mississippi Valley area, they have been stocked only within their native range and transplanted to nearby states and have been generally unsuccessful elsewhere. They are scattered within this range and vary in abundance from lake to lake.*

Habitat. *Yellow bass thrive in quiet pools, ponds, backwaters of large streams,*

A popular light-tackle quarry and usually lumped into the category of panfish, the yellow bass is a scrappy fighter and provides good sport on light tackle. With white, flaky flesh, it is also a good food fish, on a par with or exceeding white bass and compared by some to the yellow perch.

Many anglers are unfamiliar with this member of the temperate bass family because it is largely restricted to the middle portion of the United States and is smaller than its relatives; a true bass, the yellow is related to the striped bass, the white bass, and the white perch. Those fishing with larger lures and bait for largemouth bass or stripers are likely to encounter only the occasional, and larger, yellow bass specimen, although they can be caught with great frequency where they are abundant and by anglers using light tackle.

Identification. The body shape of the yellow bass is very similar to that of the white bass: moderately long and stocky, with the deepest part between the dorsal fins, as opposed to round and compressed. It has a small head, a large mouth, and connected dorsal fins. Its coloration is a brassy, silvery, or bright yellow, sometimes with a grayish olive on the back, and it has clear to blue-gray fins that are particularly blue when the fish is in water. Five to eight distinctively dark horizontal stripes line the sides, and the lower stripes may be irregularly interrupted and offset above the anal fin; these markings are different on either side of the fish.

The yellow bass can be distinguished from the white bass by its golden coloring and broken stripes. Also, the second spine of the anal fin is longer and thicker than the third on the yellow bass; in the white bass it is noticeably shorter. The yellow bass has even jaws, whereas the white bass has a projecting lower jaw.

Bass, Yellow (continued)

Size/Age. Yellow bass are smaller than the largest bluegills, and the usual size caught by anglers ranges from 4 to 12 ounces. They can grow to 2 pounds and 18 inches, although few are seen over a pound; the all-tackle world record is a 2-pound, 4-ounce Indiana fish caught in 1977. These fish grow slowly after becoming juveniles and rarely achieve the size of white bass, perhaps because they are extremely prolific and often become stunted. In some places, their small size and bait-stealing tendency brand them a nuisance. They have a short life expectancy of about 4 years on average and may live to age 7.

Spawning. Yellow bass spawn in the spring and move into tributary streams when the water temperature reaches the upper 50s. They spawn on shoals and abandon their nesting sites without protecting the young.

Food and feeding habits. Yellow bass feed on insects, minnows, small shad, and small sunfish. Insects and insect larvae constitute a good portion of their diet, especially in smaller sizes. Similar to white bass, they will maraud baitfish in schools, although with less of a tendency to do so on or near the surface. Yellow bass are more active in shallow and nearshore environs early and late in the day and roam deeper open-water expanses during the day.

small to large rivers, large lakes, clear to turbid waters below lakes, and reservoirs; they are somewhat tolerant of weedbeds, more so than are white bass, and are fond of warm water.

Bluegill

Lepomis macrochirus

OTHER NAMES

bream, brim, sun perch, blue perch, blue sunfish, copperbelly, blue bream, copperhead bream, red-breasted bream, bluegill sunfish, roach.

Distribution. *Native to approximately the eastern half of the United States, the bluegill's range extends southward from the St. Lawrence River through the Great Lakes and the Mississippi River basin, eastward from New York to Minnesota and draining south from the Cape Fear River in Virginia to the Río Grande in Texas, including states as far east as Florida and as far west as New Mexico. Also found in a small portion of northeastern Mexico, the bluegill has been widely introduced elsewhere in North America, as well as in Europe, South Africa, Asia, South America, and Oceania.*

Habitat. *Although mainly lake fish, bluegills inhabit sluggish streams and rivers, vegetated lakes and ponds, swamps, and pools of creeks. They prefer quiet*

At times easily caught by novice and experienced anglers alike, bluegills are among the most popular panfish species in North America. This notoriety is the result of their vast distribution, spunky fight, and excellent taste. Commonly referred to as "bream," bluegills are the most widely distributed panfish and are found with, or in similar places as, such companion and related species as redbreast sunfish, green sunfish, pumpkinseeds, shellcrackers, and longear sunfish, all of which are similar in configuration but different in appearance.

Despite their abundance and popularity, bluegills are not heavily targeted in some waters and are thus underutilized. Bluegills are so prolific that their populations can grow beyond the carrying capacity of the water, and as a result many become stunted; these stunted fish are regarded as pests, and waters containing them must often be drained and restocked. There are three subspecies of bluegills in existence, although stocking has intermingled populations and subspecies.

Identification. The bluegill has a significantly compressed oval or roundish body, a small mouth, and a small head, qualities typical of members of the sunfish family. The pectoral fins are pointed.

Its coloring varies greatly from lake to lake, ranging from olive, dark blue, or bluish purple to dappled yellow and green on the sides with an overall blue cast; some fish, particularly those found in quarry holes, may actually be clear and colorless. Ordinarily, there are six to eight vertical bars on the sides, and these may or may not be prominent. The gill cover extends to create a wide black flap, faint in color on the young, which is not surrounded by a lighter border as in other sunfish. Dark blue streaks are found on the lower cheeks between the chin and the gill cover, and often there is a dark mark at the bottom of the anal fin. The

Bluegill (continued)

breeding male is more vividly colored, possessing a blue head and back, a bright orange breast and belly, and black pelvic fins.

Size/Age. These fish range from 4 to 12 inches in length, averaging 8 inches and reaching a maximum length of 16¼ inches. The largest bluegill ever caught was a 4-pound, 12-ounce specimen taken in 1950. The growth of the bluegill varies so much that estimates of age as it relates to size are at best inexact. Bluegills are estimated to live for 10 years.

Life history/Behavior. The age of sexual maturity varies with environment and locale, although most bluegills reach spawning age when 2 or 3 years old. Spawning occurs between April and September, starting when water temperatures are around 70°F.

The males build shallow, round nests in water up to 6 feet deep over sandy or muddy bottoms. These nests occur in colonies of up to 500 along the shoreline, densely concentrated and easily spotted by anglers. Females may lay between 2,000 and 63,000 eggs, which hatch 30 to 35 hours after fertilization. It is common for fish to spawn many times, with a particular fish laying eggs in several nests and a single nest containing eggs from more than one female. Males guard the eggs throughout the incubation period and stay to protect the hatched young. Having reached lengths of ¼ to ⅓ inch, the young leave their nests for deeper waters. Bluegills travel in small schools, typically made up of similar-size individuals.

Food and feeding habits. A variety of small organisms serves as food for bluegills, including insects, crayfish, fish eggs, small minnows, snails, worms, and sometimes even plant material. The young feed mostly on crustaceans, insects, and worms. Adults will feed at different depths, depending on temperature, so they obtain food on the bottom, as well as on the surface. Active mostly at dusk and dawn, the larger bluegills move inshore in the morning and the evening to feed, staying in deeper water during the day.

waters and may hold in extremely shallow areas, especially early in the season and during spawning time, although when the surface and shallow water temperature is warm in the summer, they may go as deep as 30 or more feet. They occupy the same habitat as their larger relative the largemouth bass.

Bowfin

Amia calva

OTHER NAMES

dogfish, freshwater dog-
fish, blackfish, mudfish,
western mudfish, mud
pike, cabbage pike,
shoepike, griddle, grindle,
spottail grindle, grinnel,
lawyer, scaled ling, speckled cat, cypress trout,
cypress bass, cottonfish,
John A. Grindle; French:
*choupiquel, poisson de
marais.*

Distribution. *Bowfin occur
only in North America, from
the St. Lawrence River and
Lake Champlain drainage of
Quebec and Vermont west
across southern Ontario to
the Mississippi drainage,
from Minnesota south to
Texas and Florida.*

Habitat. *Bowfin are generally a big-water fish and
inhabit warm and swampy
lakes with vegetation, as
well as weedy rivers and
streams. With a significant
tolerance for high temperatures and a modified air
bladder, the bowfin is able
to live in stagnant areas by
taking in surface air.*

Described as a living fossil, the bowfin is the only existing
member of the Amiidae family, a group of fish that origi-
nated in the Cretaceous period more than 100 million years
ago. Of little commercial value because of their poor-tasting
flesh, bowfin are excellent fighters and are caught by
anglers wherever they are abundant, although mostly unintentionally. When not abundant, they are a rare catch, and
many anglers are unfamiliar with them. Although they are
sometimes considered pests or nuisances by anglers seeking
other quarry, bowfin are helpful in constraining otherwise
large, stunted populations of smaller fish.

Identification. An ancient fish in design and described by
some as looking more like a serpent than a fish, the bowfin
has a rounded tail and a considerable amount of cartilage in
its skeletal system. Underneath its head is a large, bony
gular plate, with several other bony plates protecting the
skull. Distinctive qualities include a large flattened head with
tubelike nostrils and long, sharp teeth, as well as a long,
spineless dorsal fin that extends almost the entire length of
the body. Another interesting feature of the bowfin's
anatomy is a modified, lunglike air bladder, in addition to
gills; as in the gar, which possesses a similar organ, the
bowfin is able to breathe surface air and, consequently, live
in water too polluted or stagnant for most fish.

Its long, thick, cylindrical body is covered with large
olive-colored scales, although it occasionally has a brownish
or gray cast that fades to white or cream underneath. The
male has a dark spot on the upper tail with a yellowish
orange rim around it, and the female has a less conspicuous
spot without a rim.

Size/Age. The bowfin can grow to up to 43 inches in
length but averages 2 feet. The world-record bowfin
weighed 21 pounds, 8 ounces, although the average

weight is in the 2- to 5-pound range. The male is smaller than the female, and they survive up to 12 years in the wild and 30 years in captivity.

Life history/Behavior. When bowfin are 3 to 5 years old, they reach sexual maturity. They spawn between early April and June, when water temperatures are between 60° and 66°F. Males move into the weedy shallows after dark, before the females, and build bowl-shaped nests of plant material among tree roots or under fallen logs. A single male may try to mate with more than one female, and sometimes several pairs of bowfin will use the same nest.

The male is left to protect the eggs, which hatch in 8 to 10 days. The newly hatched bowfin use adhesive organs on their snouts to attach themselves to the bottom of the nest as they grow to about ½ inch long. Once they reach this length, the fry school and follow the male, which guards them for several weeks against potential predators. Adult coloration appears when they are about 1½ inches long, and the young begin to protect themselves at this stage. They stop schooling entirely when they reach 4 inches in length.

Bowfin swim slowly along the bottom, although they can move very quickly if disturbed or when in pursuit of prey.

Food and feeding habits. Bowfin can be extremely ravenous and eat a large variety of food, including crayfish, shrimp, adult insects and larvae, small fish, frogs, and large amounts of vegetation. Scent is as important as sight in obtaining food, and bowfin have the habit of gulping water to capture their prey. Although bowfin are always ready to feed, they are most active in the evening.

Buffalo, Bigmouth

Ictiobus cyprinellus

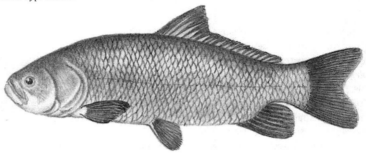

Distribution. *Found only in North America, bigmouth buffalo occur in the Nelson River drainage of Hudson Bay, the lower Great Lakes, and the drainages of Lake Erie and the Ohio and Mississippi Rivers, from Ontario to Saskatchewan and Montana south to Louisiana and the Gulf of Mexico. They have also been introduced in Arizona, California, and Cuba with success.*

Habitat. *Bigmouth buffalo have a preference for pools and backwaters of small to large rivers and are found in lakes and impoundments.*

A member of the Catostomidae family of suckers, the bigmouth buffalo is so called because of its humped back.

Identification. The robust and deep-bodied bigmouth buffalo has a large head with a big, distinctively oblique, and toothless mouth. This terminal, thin-lipped cavity angles downward when closed, although the edge of the upper lip is practically on a level with the eyes. The sickle-shaped dorsal fin is characterized by a taller lobe at the middle of the back that tapers off into a shorter lobe; the whole fin extends to the caudal peduncle. It is the only member of the sucker family with its mouth directly in the front of the head.

The color of the bigmouth buffalo may be gray, coppery olive brown, or slate blue on the back, and the sides are yellowish olive, fading to a white belly; all the fins are blackish in tint.

Size/Age. The largest of all the suckers, the bigmouth buffalo is said to grow to 80 pounds, although the all-tackle rod-and-reel record is a 70-pound, 5-ounce fish. It typically weighs between 3 and 12 pounds, and it has been known to grow as long as 40 inches. Most fish will live only 6 to 8 years and grow to 20 pounds.

Life history/Behavior. Adults spawn at about 3 years of age, in April or May, when water temperatures reach the 60° to 65°F range. Adults seek weedy areas in 2 to 3 feet of water to lay their eggs, which hatch in 10 to 14 days. They travel in schools throughout their lives and are capable of tolerating temperatures of up to 90°F in waters with little dissolved oxygen.

Food and feeding habits. Roughly 90 percent of the food a bigmouth buffalo eats consists of small crustaceans.

Buffalo, Smallmouth

Ictiobus bubalus

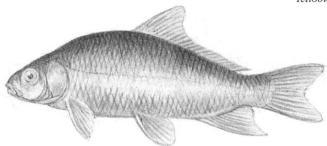

The smallmouth buffalo is second only to the bigmouth in the sucker family in terms of size and commercial importance, although it has a better reputation as a food fish than does its larger relative. The smallmouth buffalo, however, is less abundant and subsequently less commercially important.

Identification. A deep-bodied and compressed fish, the smallmouth buffalo has a small conical head, a high-arched back, and a long dorsal fin. It also has a small, thick-lipped mouth with distinct grooves on the upper lip; the upper jaw is considerably shorter than the snout. Usually lighter in coloration than other buffalo, it is gray, olive, or bronze on the back; black to olive yellow on the sides; white to yellow on the belly; and it has an olive bronze sheen. The pelvic fins are olive or grayish black, and the other fins are indistinctly dark.

It bears a noticeable resemblance to the bigmouth buffalo, but it can be distinguished by a more compressed body and a more steeply arched back. It also possesses a smaller, subterminal mouth that lies laterally; the bigmouth buffalo's mouth lies at a slant. Characteristic of all suckers, the mouth extends downward, a noticeable feature when the smallmouth buffalo is feeding.

Size. Growing slower than the bigmouth, a smallmouth buffalo can reach 36 inches in length. The average commercially taken fish are in the 2- to 10-pound range, although some specimens weigh 15 to 20 pounds. The all-tackle world record for a smallmouth buffalo is 82 pounds, 3 ounces.

Life history/Behavior. Spawning and schooling habits are similar or identical to those of the bigmouth buffalo.

Food and feeding habits. Smallmouth buffalo feed on shellfish and algae, grinding them with the bony plates in their throats designed for that purpose; they eat more insects and bottom organisms than bigmouth buffalo do.

OTHER NAMES
razorback buffalo, roach-back, thick-lipped buffalo, channel buffalo, hump-backed buffalo, high-back buffalo, river buffalo.

Distribution. Found only in North America, the smallmouth buffalo has a range similar to that of the bigmouth buffalo. It occurs in the Lake Michigan drainage and the Mississippi River basin, from Pennsylvania and Michigan to Montana and south to the Gulf of Mexico, and from Mobile Bay, Alabama, west to the Rio Grande in Texas and New Mexico. It is also found in Mexico and was introduced in Arizona. It is most abundant in the central states.

Habitat. Smallmouth buffalo inhabit pools, backwaters, large streams, and main channels of small to large rivers, as well as warm lakes and reservoirs. They prefer slightly cleaner and deeper waters than do bigmouth buffalo, an explanation for their relatively smaller numbers.

Bullhead, Black

Ameiurus melas

OTHER NAMES

catfish, black catfish, yellow belly bullhead, horned pout; French: *barbotte noire.*

Distribution. *The black bullhead is found from southern Ontario west to Saskatchewan and throughout the Great Lakes, the Hudson Bay, the St. Lawrence, and the Mississippi River basins, extending to New York in the east, the Gulf of Mexico in the south, and Montana in the west. Introduced populations exist in Arizona, California, and other states.*

Habitat. *Black bullhead inhabit pools, backwaters, and slow-moving sections of creeks and small to large rivers; they also inhabit impoundments, oxbows, and ponds. They have a preference for muddy water and soft mud bottoms and are able to tolerate polluted water better than other catfish do. They prefer water in the 75° to 85°F range and tend to avoid cooler, clearer water.*

A smaller member of the catfish family, the black bullhead is very popular due primarily to its fine culinary appeal. It is often stocked in farm ponds and raised commercially.

Identification. Although the name would imply something else, the "black" bullhead may actually be yellowish green, dark green, olive, brown, or black on the back; bronze or green on the sides; and bright yellow or white on the belly. The entire body possesses a lustrous sheen. Only the young and spawning males are truly black.

Distinguishing the black bullhead from the brown or the yellow bullhead can be done by noting the rear edge of the pectoral fin in the latter two, which have a spine that is serrated with numerous sharp, thorny protrusions; those found on the spine of the black bullhead's pectoral fin are much less prominent and may be absent altogether. The black bullhead has dark chin barbels that may be black-spotted, a chubby body, and a squarish tail.

Size/Age. Black bullhead reportedly grow to 24½ inches in length, but they are most common at 6 to 7 inches and are seldom larger than 2 pounds. The maximum life span for black bullhead is approximately 10 years, although most live only 5 years. The world record is 7 pounds, 7 ounces.

Spawning behavior. Spawning takes place in May, June, and July, usually at water temperatures between 66° and 70°F. In weedy sections, the female clears away debris and silt to prepare the nest. Spawning up to five times an hour, the female releases roughly 200 eggs each time, fanning the eggs in-between spawning. Both parents fan the eggs until these hatch, and they guard the fry, which leave the nest in compact schools.

Food and feeding habits. Adults forage primarily at night, feeding on clams, snails, plant material, and fish.

Bullhead, Brown

Ameiurus nebulosus

With its firm, pink flesh of excellent quality, the brown bullhead is an exceedingly popular species, sometimes included in the panfish category.

Identification. The head of the brown bullhead is large for its round and slender body, and the skin is smooth and entirely scaleless. The coloring of the brown bullhead is not always brown, but it may actually range from yellowish brown or chocolate brown to gray or olive with brown or black scattered spots; the belly is yellow or white.

The brown bullhead is distinguished from the yellow bullhead by having a mottled coloring and dark brown to nearly black chin barbels. There are sharp, toothlike serrations on the pectoral spine of the pectoral fin, and the tail is squarish or somewhat notched.

Size/Age. The average weight of the brown bullhead is less than a pound, and although fish in the 2- to 4-pound range are occasionally caught, this species seldom exceeds 3 pounds in weight. A 6-pound, 5-ounce fish is the largest ever caught on rod and reel. Brown bullhead can grow to 21 inches in length, although they are most commonly 8 to 14 inches long. Their life span is 6 or 7 years.

Spawning behavior. Spawning takes place in April and May. Nests are made by one or both sexes by fanning out dish-shaped hollows in mud or sand. The eggs are guarded by one or both parents, although some fish have been said to eat them. Young brown bullhead are jet-black and resemble tadpoles, forming large schools that swim in surface waters. The male continues to guard the young until they reach 2 inches in length and are able to protect themselves.

Food and feeding habits. Brown bullhead feed mainly at night on immature insects, worms, minnows, mollusks, crayfish, plankton, and offal.

OTHER NAMES
bullpout, horned pout, brown catfish, mudcat, common bullhead, marbled bullhead, squaretail, minister; French: *barbotte brune*.

Distribution. *Brown bullhead range from Nova Scotia and New Brunswick to Saskatchewan, from North Dakota to Louisiana in the west, and from Maine to Florida in the east. Native to the eastern United States and southern Canada, they have been widely introduced elsewhere.*

Habitat. *Brown bullhead inhabit warm and even stagnant waters, as well as sluggish runs over muddy bottoms. They occur in farm ponds, pools, creeks, small to large rivers, lakes, and reservoirs. Unlike other bullhead, they are found in large and deep waters, although they are able to withstand low oxygen concentrations and are known to bury themselves in mud to survive such conditions.*

Bullhead, Yellow

Ameiurus natalis

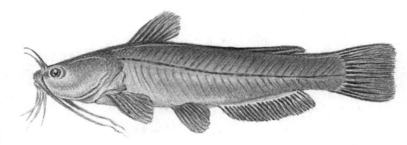

yellow cat, creek cat, white-whiskered bullhead, greaser.

Distribution. *Yellow bullhead inhabit most of central and eastern North America, ranging in the east from New York to Florida and in the west from southern Quebec to central North Dakota and south to the Gulf of Mexico. As with other bullhead, this fish has also been introduced outside its original range.*

Habitat. *With a preference for clear waters, gravel or rock bottoms, sluggish currents, and heavy vegetation, yellow bullhead are found in pools, ponds, streams, small to large rivers, and small, shallow lakes. They are common in small, weedy, and shallow bodies of water and are more tolerant of polluted water and low oxygen levels than are most other types of bullhead. They are most abundant at water temperatures between 75° and 80°F.*

Although the least commercially important of the catfish, the yellow bullhead can provide decent angling and is a good food fish.

Identification. A moderately slim fish, the yellow bullhead has leathery skin without scales. The coloring ranges from yellowish olive to brown or almost black on the back with yellowish olive or brown sides, yellow or white on the belly, and dusky fins. Juveniles are dark brown or jet-black.

The rounded tail helps to distinguish the yellow bullhead from other bullheads, which have squarish or truncated tails. The yellow bullhead has sharp, toothlike serrations on the back edge of the spine at the top of the pectoral fins. The chin barbels are white, yellow, or pale pink.

Size/Age. Yellow bullhead usually weigh less than a pound, although they sometimes reach a weight of 3 pounds. The most common length is between 7 and 11 inches, and they can be as much as 18.3 inches long. The world-record fish is a 4-pound, 4-ounce specimen. Yellow bullhead can live up to 7 years.

Spawning behavior. In May and June, sexually mature fish of 3 years and older move into shallow water at temperatures in the upper 60s or low 70s. After finding a suitable site, one or both of the parents constructs the nest, which consists of either a shallow depression in an open area or a 2-foot-deep burrow in the bank in a protected area. The male guards the eggs and the fry hatch in 5 to 10 days, after which the young continue to be protected by the male in a tight group until they are able to protect themselves.

Food and feeding habits. Yellow bullhead are nocturnal scavengers that feed by smell and taste. They eat crustaceans, immature aquatic insects, snails, small fish, dragonfly nymphs, crayfish, mollusks, and bits of aquatic vegetation.

Burbot
Lota lota

The only freshwater member of the Gadidae family of cod-fish found in North America, Europe, and Asia, the burbot is often caught accidentally by anglers fishing for other species. Although it is a popular food fish in Europe, its ugly appearance makes it unappetizing to a fussy majority of Americans. It is mainly sold in salted form for ethnic consumption in North America but is also a source of oil and is processed into fishmeal; the liver is high in vitamins A and D and is sold smoked or canned in Europe.

Identification. The elongate shape of the burbot resembles an eel or a cross between an eel and a catfish. It has been mistaken for a catfish, and in some places it is called an eel, although it is neither. It also looks like a smaller and slimmer version of the saltwater cod. Other distinctive features include tubular nostrils, a single chin barbel, and a rounded tail. The soft-rayed fins are also noteworthy in appearance: The pectoral fins are large and rounded, the first dorsal fin is small and short, and the second dorsal and anal fins start near the middle of the body and continue to the tail. It has a wide head, small eyes, and small, embedded scales that produce a slick skin.

The burbot has a mottled appearance, due to a dark brown or black pattern scattered over a yellow, light brown, or tan background; there may be regional color variations, including light brown, dark brown, dark olive, or even yellow. The anal fins have a dark edge to them.

Size/Age. Full-grown fish average 15 inches in length and less than a pound in weight. Burbot that are caught by anglers usually weigh several pounds and are occasionally in the 8-pound class, although they can grow much larger. An 18-pound, 11-ounce fish holds the all-tackle world record, but Alaska has produced larger fish, at least one of which was reportedly almost 60 pounds. Some are able to live for 20 years.

OTHER NAMES
eelpout, pout, ling, cusk, lawyer, lingcod, gudgeon, freshwater ling, mud blower, lush (Alaska), maria (Canada); French: *lotte, lotte de riviére;* Spanish: *lota.*

Distribution. *The burbot is common throughout the circumpolar region above 40° north, especially in Alaska, Canada, the northern United States (including the Missouri and Ohio River drainages), and parts of Europe. It is absent from Scotland, Ireland, the Kamchatka Peninsula, the west coast of Norway, extreme western British Columbia, Nova Scotia, and the Atlantic Islands.*

Habitat. *Occurring in large, deep, cold rivers and lakes, burbot are found in depths of up to almost 700 feet. They inhabit deep water in summer and move shallower during summer nights.*

Spawning behavior. By the time it is 3 years of age, the burbot is sexually mature. It is one of the few species that spawns in mid- or late winter under ice, doing so at night in shallow bays in 1 to 4 feet of water over sand or gravel; occasionally, it will spawn in rivers in 1 to 10 feet of water. A burbot may produce more than a million spherical, amber eggs at one time, although the average amount is half that number. Without a nest or parental protection, the eggs hatch in 4 to 5 weeks.

Food and feeding habits. Young burbot feed on plankton and insects, graduating to a diet made up almost entirely of fish, especially perch, cisco, and whitefish. They will also eat mollusks, fish eggs, plankton, and crustaceans. Rocks and other indigestible items have been found in their stomachs.

Carp, Common
Cyprinus carpio

One of the largest members of the minnow family and a close relative of the goldfish, the common carp was also one of the first fish whose populations were regulated to increase production. Propagated for centuries and distributed widely, common carp are both beloved and despised. In North America, they are abundant but among the least-favored targets of freshwater anglers.

Three varieties of common carp exist—the scaleless leather carp, the partially scaled mirror carp, and the fully scaled common carp, which is the most abundant of the three.

Identification. The common carp has a deep body form and a heavy appearance. Distinctive features include a short head, a rounded snout, a single long dorsal fin, a forked tail, and relatively large scales. The mouth is toothless and suckerlike, adapted to bottom feeding, and the upper jaw projects slightly past the lower one. It has a single serrated spine at the front of the dorsal and the anal fins and two pairs of fleshy barbels on either side of its mouth.

The pigmentation of the common carp ranges from gold to olive to brown, with a yellowish coloring on the lower sides and belly and a reddish tint to the lower fins. Each scale on the upper sides of the fish has a concentrated dark spot at its base and a conspicuous dark rim. Juveniles and breeding males are usually a darker green or gray, with a dark belly instead of a yellowish one, and females are lighter. Males develop tiny tubercles, which are found in a random pattern on the head and the pectoral fins. The common carp superficially resembles the bigmouth buffalo.

Size/Age. Growing quickly and to moderately large sizes, the common carp is said to reach weights in the 80-pound range, although the average fish is considerably smaller.

OTHER NAMES

European carp, French carp, Italian carp, German carp, Israeli carp, leather carp, mirror carp, king carp, koi, sewer bass, buglemouth; French: *carpe, carpe commune;* German: *karpfen;* Japanese: *koi;* Spanish: *carpa.*

Distribution. *The common carp was one of the first species to be introduced into other countries. Its native range was restricted to temperate Asia and the rivers of the Black Sea and the Aegean basins in Europe, specifically the Danube. At some point, the carp found its way to England, and in the nineteenth century it was brought from Germany to the United States.*

Habitat. *Common carp are incredibly hardy and flexible in their preferences for living conditions. Primarily bottom-dwelling fish, carp like quiet, shallow waters with a soft bottom and dense aquatic vegetation. Although they favor*

Carp, Common (continued)
*large turbid waters, they
also thrive in small rivers
and lakes. They can live in
low-oxygen environments
and can tolerate tempera-
ture fluctuations and
extremes, with the ability
to survive in 96°F water for
24 hours. They tend to
monopolize some of the
bodies of water they
inhabit.*

*Most of the time carp
prefer to hold in quiet, shallow places with a muddy or
sandy bottom, which they
browse over. In some northern waters where the fish
are abundant and such
terrain is lacking or offers no
food, carp will cruise over
shallow, rocky flats and
shoals, browsing along the
rubble bottom. They are
often observed during the
day in protected areas,
sometimes adjacent to deep
water, although they are
seldom caught in deep
water.*

The all-tackle rod-and-reel record is 75 pounds, 11 ounces. The maximum life span is disputed but may be a half century; the average carp seldom exceeds 15 years of age.

Life history/Behavior. By their second year, males are able to reproduce, whereas females are able to do so once they are 3 years old. Carp spawn in the spring and the summer, depending on latitude, becoming active once temperatures rise to the 60°F range. During the day or the night, several males will accompany one or two females to shallow, vegetated waters and splash and thrash as the eggs are released and fertilized. A large female can carry millions of adhesive eggs, but the average amount is 100,000 eggs per pound of body weight.

The eggs go unattended, hatching in 3 to 10 days. Each fry is born with an adhesive organ that it immediately uses to adhere to bottom vegetation; after the first day, fry must go to the surface and gulp air to survive. Common carp fry are quick to grow and may reach about 9 inches in length during the first year of their lives, if they escape the hungry jaws of their primary predators. Juvenile carp make good baitfish, but their use is forbidden in some areas where trout are the main species.

Food and feeding habits. Omnivorous feeders, carp favor predominantly vegetarian diets but will feed on aquatic insects, snails, crustaceans, annelids, and mollusks. Aquatic plants and filamentous algae are the most popular food groups of common carp. Their feeding habits are noteworthy, because they grub sediment from the bottom with their suckerlike mouths, uprooting and destroying vegetation and muddying the water. They have done severe damage to habitats by causing the loss of large quantities of plant life. This has proved detrimental to native fish populations and other animals.

Carp primarily spend their lives in small groups and are inclined to roam for food. They can gain several pounds a year in rich fertile environments but may remain smaller in those that are less fertile and where there is overcrowding.

Carp, Grass

Ctenopharyngodon idella

A large member of the minnow family and an aquaculture species of worldwide importance, the grass carp is used for weed control because of its aggressive and herbivorous feeding habits. In the United States, where it was introduced in the early 1960s, it has become an extremely controversial species because of the biological damage it inflicts in the process of eliminating vegetation. This species is called the grass carp by critics, whereas supporters often refer to it as the white amur to avoid the negative connotations associated in North America with the name "carp."

Identification. The grass carp has an elongate and fairly compressed body, a wide and blunt head, a very short snout without the barbels found on common carp, a short dorsal fin, and a moderately forked tail. The terminal and nonprotractile mouth has thin lips and sharp pharyngeal (throat) teeth especially suited to its feeding habits. The grass carp is covered with large scales; the ones on the upper sides of the body have a dark border and a black spot at the base and give the fish a cross-hatched appearance. It is colored gray or green on the back, shading to white or yellow on the belly, and has clear to dark fins.

Size/Age. The grass carp grows quickly and to large sizes; some have been reported at 100 pounds in native waters. It can add 3 to 5 pounds a year to its weight under favorable conditions. The largest fish taken by rod and reel was a 68-pound, 12-ounce Arkansas specimen.

Life history/Behavior. Spawning takes place once a year over gravel bottoms in rivers, between April and September, according to temperature; adults will migrate upstream to find acceptable spawning sites. The round eggs of the grass carp are semibuoyant and amber colored, hatching in 24 to 30 hours without the protection of the parents. After they absorb the nutrients in their yolk sacs in the first 2 to 4 days

OTHER NAMES

white amur, amur, carp;
French: *carpe amour, carpe herbivore, amour blanc;*
German: *graskarpfen;*
Japanese: *sogyo.*

Distribution. *Found originally in China and eastern Siberia, specifically in the Amur River basin from which it gets its name, the grass carp has been widely introduced to more than 20 countries. Only those in certain areas have been able or allowed to reproduce naturally; these places include the Danube River in central Europe, the Mississippi River in North America, and Russia and southern Africa. In the United States, the grass carp was first stocked in Arkansas waters in 1963 and intentionally released in 35 states, although it has subsequently spread to other bodies of water where it was unwanted. In fact, many states have made it illegal to stock grass carp within their borders, unless a permit issued by the appropriate fisheries management agency has been obtained.*

Habitat. *Occurring in freshwater, grass carp inhabit lakes, ponds, pools, and backwaters of large rivers, with a preference for slow-flowing or standing bodies of water with vegetation. They are able to withstand temperature variation, extreme salinity, and low oxygen concentrations.*

of their lives, the larvae feed on microplankton in quiet waters. The young hide in deep holes in riverbeds during the winter.

Food and feeding habits. Primarily vegetarians, grass carp have earned their name by eating aquatic plants and submerged grasses, adding the occasional insect or invertebrate. With the help of teeth on the pharynx, they tear off vegetation with jerking motions. Unlike common carp *(see: Carp, Common)*, grass carp do not muddy the water with their browsing, but their aggressive feeding habits cause other problems. Grass carp tend to break off the upper portions of grasses, leaving the roots to grow, so they are not as useful in eradicating vegetation as they are supposed to be. Also, grass carp cannot digest all the plant matter they take in, so instead of eliminating a vegetation problem, they make it worse by excreting plant material and distributing it to new areas. In addition, they contribute to increased water turbidity and to eutrophication. Finally, heavy browsing may stimulate faster than normal growth in certain kinds of plants.

Triploid grass carp. A technique that consists of exposing fertilized eggs to heat shock was invented by researchers in 1981 to produce sterile grass carp. This method creates nonreproducing fish of both genders. They are called triploid grass carp because they have three sets of chromosomes, instead of the usual two sets (those fish are called diploid). They are as hardy as the ordinary variety of grass carp, but they have the benefit of not being able to overpopulate their habitats. They look like large creek chub, flourish in warm water, and may reach weights of 25 pounds or more. Triploid grass carp are useful in controlling unwanted aquatic plants, but the water clarity may deteriorate due to the substantial passing of plant material as fecal matter.

Catfish

Channel Catfish
Ictalurus punctatus

Catfish comprise a large group of predominately freshwater fish that is distributed around the world. Some accounts peg the total number of catfish species worldwide at more than 2,200. Many of the world's significant river systems are home to at least one species of catfish, and in most cases these fish rank among the largest fish of the river system. The same applies to large lakes, especially in reservoirs that are impoundments of large rivers. Many catfish are important for commercial and recreational purposes.

Species. Most catfish are scaleless, but some are armored with heavy scales. They vary in size from tiny versions that are popular for aquarium use, the smallest of which grow no larger than ½ inch, to huge specimens, the largest of which has been recorded at more than 600 pounds. Most catfish prefer the sluggish localities of lakes and rivers; some do best in fairly swift waters. Tenacious fish, they can stay alive out of water for a considerable time, especially if kept moist. They are characterized by having a single dorsal fin and an adipose fin; strong, sharply pointed spines in the dorsal and pectoral fins; and whiskerlike sensory barbels on the upper and lower jaws. The head and the mouth are generally broad, and the eyes small.

North American freshwater catfish. Members of the family Ictaluridae, North American freshwater catfish are distributed from Canada to Guatemala and contain about 50 species. These bottom-loving fish are important commercially, and many millions are harvested annually, some from natural environments and some from aquaculture or fish-farming operations.

Thousands of anglers pursue these fish, employing a wide variety of methods to catch them. All species obtained from fairly clear waters are delicious on the table. Many fish farms specialize in raising and marketing catfish. All members of this group have scaleless skins and a stiff, sharp spine at the leading edge of the dorsal fin and pectoral fins. Just in front of the tail, on the dorsal surface, is a fleshy adipose fin. Its eight barbels are sensory structures that help the catfish to locate food.

Nearly all North American catfish live in sluggish streams or in the quiet waters of lakes and ponds. They are bottom feeders, taking both live and dead foods. They are typically active at night—although some are more active than others during the day—and on dark, overcast days or in roiled, murky water. Catfish spawn in the spring and the early summer, fanning nest areas in the sand or the mud. One or both parents stand guard until the eggs hatch and then shepherd the young until they are large enough to fend for themselves.

Perhaps the most abundant and best-known members of the clan of about a dozen species of the genus *Ictalurus* are the three principal species of bullhead: brown bullhead, black bullhead, and yellow bullhead.

Also of commercial and recreational importance in some areas are channel catfish, blue catfish, white catfish, and flathead catfish. The largest is the blue catfish, which may tip the scales at more than 150 pounds.

The foregoing North American catfish are not finicky about what they eat. They will accept almost anything offered for bait, although some are more finicky than others, and this is not to imply that they will strike anything at any time, only that they have eclectic tastes. Biologists have found strange collections of debris in the stomachs of catfish. Most catfish, in fact, have taste glands located over much of their body, although these glands are concentrated in their long sensory whiskers.

The North American freshwater catfish family includes the various madtoms, about two dozen of which are in the genus *Noturus*. All are small, most of them less than 5 inches long. Madtoms are recognized by their unique adipose fin. A non-madtom catfish has a fleshy fin protruding from its back just ahead of the caudal fin. The adipose fin of a madtom is continuous with its caudal fin.

Catfish, Blue

Ictalurus furcatus

This is a popular species within its range and prized for its flesh, as well as for its sporting value. The blue catfish is a strong, stubborn fighter. It can grow quite large, which enhances its appeal. It is considered good table fare and is widely pursued by commercial fishermen for the market. Its flesh is white, delicate, and tender, especially in smaller specimens.

Identification. Blue catfish are generally blue gray or slate blue and possess no spots or other markings, although they may be almost pale blue or silvery; their flanks taper in color to their bellies, which are light gray or white. They have deeply forked tails, and their anal fins have straight margins. They resemble channel catfish and when small are most easily confused with that relative. A larger blue cat has a distinct humped-backed appearance, with the hump occurring at and in front of the dorsal fin; its head is generally larger than that of a channel cat, and its body is less sleek. It can be distinguished from a channel cat by its longer and straight-edged anal fin, which has 30 to 35 rays. In smaller specimens, a distinguishing characteristic is their lack of black body spots. Internally, the blue catfish has three chambers in the swim bladder, whereas the channel cat has two.

Like the channel catfish and the little-known Yaqui catfish of Mexico, the blue cat has a deeply forked tail, a characteristic that distinguishes these three from the flathead catfish and the bullhead, and to some degree also from the white catfish, which has a moderately forked tail. As with other catfish, channel cats have heavy, sharp pectoral and dorsal spines, as well as long mouth barbels.

Size/Age. Blue cats are capable of growing to gargantuan sizes but are rarely found at the upper limits of their capabilities. Most anglers catch blues in the 5- to 20-pound

OTHER NAMES
catfish, chucklehead cat, white catfish, forktail cat, Mississippi cat, Fulton cat, blue Fulton cat, great blue cat, silver cat, blue channel cat, highfin blue cat.

Distribution. *Blue cats are native to the Mississippi, Missouri, and Ohio River basins in the central and eastern United States, extending north into South Dakota and south into Mexico and northern Guatemala. Dams and commercial harvest are among the factors that have affected their population and perhaps their size in some parts of their native range. They have been introduced with good success into some large river systems outside of that range, most notably in the Santee Cooper waters of South Carolina. They are now most abundant in the deep, warm waters of the South.*

Habitat. *Blue catfish inhabit rivers, streams,*

Catfish, Blue (continued)

lakes, reservoirs, and ponds but are primarily a fish of big rivers and big lakes/reservoirs. They have been introduced into smaller lakes and ponds but seldom attain large sizes in such places. This species prefers the deep areas of large rivers, swift chutes, and pools with swift currents. Like the channel catfish, it prefers locations with good current over bottoms of rock, gravel, or sand.

range. Fish in the 20- to 50-pound class are not uncommon in waters with a good population of fish, but blue catfish in that range are infrequently caught and specimens exceeding that size are rare. The all-tackle world record for the species is a 116-pound, 12-ounce fish caught in the Mississippi River in Arkansas in 2001. A 116-pounder caught on a trotline was reportedly taken at Lake Texoma, Texas, in 1985, and in 1879 a 150-pounder from the Mississippi River near St. Louis was found at a local market and shipped to the U.S. National Museum. Historical accounts describe 100-pounders at the turn of the twentieth century, and individuals between 200 and 400 pounds have been reported but undocumented, perhaps being more lore than likelihood.

There is similar haziness concerning the blue cat's growth and longevity. Several scientific reports indicate that these fish grow up to 14 years of age, and they have been reported to live to 21 years, but greater longevity for the biggest specimens is evidently possible.

Spawning behavior. Blue catfish spawn in the spring or early summer, when the water temperature is between 70° and 75°F. Nests are constructed by one or both parents, usually among crevices and holes under logs and trees and in undercut banks. Secluded and dark places are often preferred.

Food and feeding habits. Blue catfish evidently eat most anything they can catch; their diet includes assorted fish, crayfish, aquatic insects, and clams. Herring and gizzard shad are part of their diet, especially when the catfish are larger and in places where these are abundant. Blue cats primarily feed on or near the bottom, and they are principally nocturnal foragers.

Catfish, Channel
Ictalurus punctatus

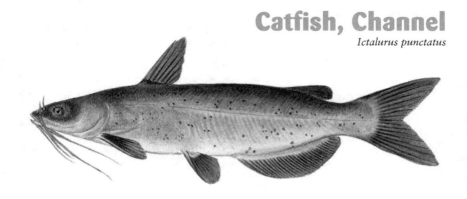

The most widely distributed of all freshwater catfish, the channel cat is a significant component of recreational angling efforts, as well as a mainstay of commercial fishing; its tender, white, and nutritious flesh is highly valued as table fare. It has been stocked widely in lakes and ponds, and provides the backbone of catfish farming activities. In some states, the sporty channel cat is ranked at or near the top among all species in angling popularity. Channel catfish have the potential to attain large sizes, although less gargantuan than other species, but their general willingness to strike baits, their wide distribution, and their high food esteem primarily account for their popularity.

Identification. Channel catfish are often recognized at a glance, owing to their deeply forked tails and small irregular spots on the sides. The spots may not be present in all specimens but generally are obvious in smaller individuals. These pigmented spots are most noticeable on younger fish and obscure on older ones. The blue catfish also has a forked tail but no spots, and the same is true for the Yaqui catfish (*Ictalurus pricei*; a species in the Yaqui River drainage of Mexico). The channel cat is more slender than other catfish, perhaps owing to its native riverine existence, and it has a relatively small head. It is distinguished from the white and the blue catfish by its 24 to 29 anal fin rays.

The body of a channel catfish is pale blue to pale olive with a bit of silvery tint, but the color variation is subject to location and water conditions. Male channel cats during the spawning season may be entirely black dorsally, and other channel cats may be dark blue, with little or no spotting, or uniformly light blue or silvery, like the blue catfish or the white catfish. Another feature distinguishing a channel catfish from a blue catfish is the anal fin; this is shorter and more rounded on a channel catfish than on a blue catfish.

OTHER NAMES

catfish, river catfish, fiddler, blue channel catfish, Great Lakes catfish, willow catfish, spotted catfish, forked-tail catfish, lady catfish.

Distribution. Channel cats exist in freshwater throughout most of the United States and parts of southern Canada and northeastern Mexico. In the United States, they are most abundant in the central region east to the Appalachian Mountains, and sparser on the West and East Coasts, where they are present mostly through introduction.

Habitat. The channel catfish inhabits rivers, streams, lakes, reservoirs, and ponds. Of all the catfish, the channel cat shows the greatest preference for clear, flowing waters, although it does equally well in lakes and ponds. It prefers clean bottoms of sand, rubble, or gravel in large lakes and rivers. Although it tolerates some amount of current, it is more likely to inhabit warm, quiet, slow-moving areas.

Like other catfish, channel cats have heavy, sharp pectoral and dorsal spines, as well as long mouth barbels.

Size/Age. The maximum age for these fish varies by latitude; some fisheries sources report a maximum longevity of 15 to 20 years, although it is believed their age can exceed 20 years. Those commonly caught weigh from 1 to 7 pounds; fish exceeding 15 pounds are infrequent, and a 20-pounder would be considered extremely large. The all-tackle world-record specimen, a fish caught in 1964, weighed 58 pounds.

Spawning behavior. Channel catfish spawn in the spring or the early summer, when the water temperature is between 70° and 85°F. Nests are constructed by one or both parents, sometimes over the open bottom but more likely among crevices and holes under logs and trees and in undercut banks. Secluded and dark places are often preferred. The male guards the eggs and aerates them and has been reported to eat some of the eggs during incubation, although it guards the young until they disperse. Ten-inch females may lay only 2,000 eggs, whereas fish over 30 inches long may lay 20,000 eggs.

Food and feeding habits. Channel catfish are primarily but not exclusively bottom feeders. They are omnivorous and consume insects, crayfish, clams, snails, crabs, fish eggs, and assorted small fish, including sunfish, darters, shiners, and gizzard shad, plus a variety of plants.

Catfish, Flathead

Pylodictus olivaris

A common and large-growing species, the flathead is one of the ugliest members of the freshwater catfish clan. Nevertheless, large specimens are commonly caught, and the fish provides a good struggle on hook and line. It is important for both commercial and recreational use and produces good table fare when taken from clean environments.

Identification. The flathead catfish is distinctive in appearance and not easily confused with any other species. It has a squared, rather than a forked, tail, with a long body and a large flattened head. Medium to large specimens are rather pot-bellied and have wide heads and beady eyes. With their distinctly flat-looking oval shape, the eyes accentuate the flatness of the head, and the lower jaw further accentuates this trait by protruding beyond the upper jaw. Compared to that of other catfish species, the anal fin of the flathead is short along its base, possessing 14 to 17 fin rays.

Flathead color varies greatly with environment, and sometimes within the same environment, but is generally mottled with varying shades of brown and yellow on the sides, tapering to a lighter or whitish mottling on the belly. As with other catfish, flatheads have heavy, sharp pectoral and dorsal spines, as well as long mouth barbels.

Size/Age. Flathead catfish are a large and fairly quick-growing species, especially in the southern and warmer parts of their range. Most anglers encounter flatheads weighing from several pounds to 10 or 15 pounds; fish up to 20 pounds are not uncommon, and fish to 50 pounds are a possibility in better waters. Many of the state records for flatheads are in the 60- to 80-pound range, and the all-tackle world record, established in Kansas in 1998, is a 123-pounder. Flatheads do grow larger, however; Texas produced a 122-pounder caught on a trotline, and Arkansas has reported flatheads up to 139 pounds. The upper limits

OTHER NAMES

mud cat, muddy, shovel-head, shovelnose, yellow cat, appaloosa, goujon, johnnie cat, pied cat, Morgan cat.

Distribution. *Flatheads are native to the lower Great Lakes and the Mississippi, Missouri, and Ohio River basins from southern North Dakota to western Pennsylvania and south to northern Mexico, reaching as far east as the western tip of the Florida Panhandle. They are widely dispersed within that range and have been transplanted successfully well beyond this.*

Habitat. *This species is primarily found in large bodies of water, especially reservoirs and their tributaries and big rivers and their tributaries. In rivers, they prefer deep pools where the water is slow, as well as depressions or holes, such as those that exist in eddies and adjacent to bridge pilings. They are also commonly found in tailraces below dams. Their chosen*

Catfish, Flathead (continued)

habitat often has a hard bottom, sometimes mixed with driftwood or timber. In large reservoirs, they are usually found deep, often in old river beds, at the junction of submerged channels, and near the headwater tributary.

are generally unknown, although this species reportedly does not reach the maximum size of the blue catfish. The chances of catching a really big flathead are better than those of catching a big blue catfish, though, because the former species has a wider range and because more large flatheads seem to be available.

Flatheads have been reported to attain 30 pounds at less than 10 years of age, and presumably the largest specimens are 20 to perhaps 30 years old, although there is scant information on their absolute longevity. A Texas flathead that was tagged at 1.76 pounds was recaptured many years later when it weighed 31 pounds; analysis showed it to be 12 years old.

Spawning behavior. Flathead catfish spawn in the spring or the early summer, when the water temperature is between 70° and 80°F. Nests are constructed by one or both parents, usually among crevices and in holes under logs and trees and in undercut banks. As with other catfish, secluded and dark places are often preferred, and there is often a log, a tree, or another object at the nest site. The male guards the eggs and aerates them and then guards the young until they disperse.

Food and feeding habits. Like its brethren, the flathead is omnivorous and opportunistic and consumes diverse and available foods. Flathead catfish are primarily but not exclusively bottom feeders and consume insects, crayfish, clams, and assorted small fish, including sunfish, shiners, and shad. Adults consume larger prey, including bullhead, gizzard shad, and carp, and, reportedly, some terrestrial animals that have the misfortune of finding themselves in the water. Live fish are a popular bait for flatheads, more so than for other catfish species, as these fish are more reluctant to consume old and smelly bait. Although not exclusively nocturnal, flatheads are more active at night and may spend the day inactive in deep water or under cover. At night they may move shallower and feed at different levels.

Catfish, White

Ameiurus catus

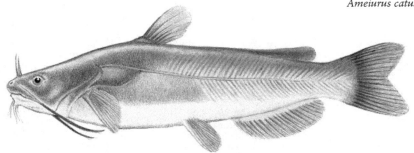

White catfish are a common and popular fish with more limited range than other catfish species, and with commercial as well as recreational value. They have been successfully stocked in pay-to-fish ponds and are also cultivated for commercial bulk harvest. Their flesh is white and fine, and they make excellent eating, especially when caught from clean environments.

Identification. The white catfish looks somewhat like a cross between a channel cat *(see: Catfish, Channel)* and a bullhead *(see)*, owing to its slightly forked tail, broad head, and squat body. Midsize specimens are often thought to be huge bullhead. The white catfish has a moderately forked tail, which distinguishes it from the flathead catfish *(see: Catfish, Flathead)* and the bullhead, whose tails are not forked. Its anal fin is rounded along the edge and has 19 to 23 fin rays, fewer than in either the blue catfish *(see: Catfish, Blue)* or the channel cat. Without close inspection, it could be confused with other catfish, although it doesn't possess the spots seen on young channel catfish. This fish is olive gray or slate gray on the head and bluish gray or slate gray on its back and sides, tapering to a white belly. As with other catfish, the white cat has heavy, sharp pectoral and dorsal spines, as well as long mouth barbels; its chin barbels are white.

Size/Age. White catfish are smaller than their blue, channel, and flathead brethren but may grow larger than bullhead. The all-tackle world record for this species is a Connecticut fish that weighed 21 pounds, 8 ounces, but a 22-pounder has been reported from California. These are the known upper limits for this species, but it may grow larger. Most white catfish are small, averaging 10 to 14 inches, and are often confused with bullhead. They are a relatively slow-growing fish, reaching sexual maturity at 3

OTHER NAMES

catfish.

Distribution. *The native range of the white catfish is freshwater and the slightly brackish water of rivers along the Atlantic coast from southern New York to Florida. It exists along the Gulf Coast from Florida to Texas and has been introduced to some inland waters in the eastern and western parts of the United States, including several New England states, plus Oregon and Nevada; it is well established in California.*

Habitat. *White catfish inhabit the silty bottom areas of slow-moving streams and rivers, as well as ponds, lakes, and the low-salinity portions of tidal estuaries. They generally avoid the swift water of large rivers and do not thrive in weedy or muddy shallow ponds.*

to 4 years. They have been reported to live 14 years but may get older.

Spawning behavior. This species spawns in the spring and the early summer, depending on latitude, and its spawning behavior is generally similar to that of the bullhead. The parents build a nest on sand or gravel substrate, usually near shore and often in places associated with some form of sheltering cover; spawning occurs when the water reaches approximately 70°F, and both parents guard the eggs and the young.

Food and feeding habits. White catfish have a broad appetite and consume aquatic insects, crayfish, clams, snails, mussels, fish eggs, assorted small fish, and some aquatic plants. Adults primarily feed on fish and are active at night, although they are less nocturnal than are other catfish.

Charr

Brook Trout
Salvelinus fontinalis

The term "charr" (or "char") is used to describe five members of the genus *Salvelinus*. They are members of the Salmonidae family, which also includes trout, salmon, whitefish, and grayling, all of which are endemic to the temperate and cool regions of the Northern Hemisphere but have been introduced widely outside their native range.

The charr group includes only one species that is actually called a "charr" in the English language, the arctic charr (*Salvelinus alpinus*), which is also referred to in some scientific texts as the *S. alpinus complex,* because in modern times it has come to represent many fish that were previously thought to be separate species or subspecies. The arctic charr's four cousins include two of the most prominent species that are referred to as "trout," the lake trout (*S. namaycush*) and the brook trout (*S. fontinalis),* and two less widely known species, the Dolly Varden (*S. malma*) and the bull trout (*S. confluentus).*

Charr and other members of the Salmonidae family are primitive fish; their fossil remains date to more than 100 million years ago. Evidence indicates that many of the more advanced or specialized families of modern-day bony fish have ancestral stocks closely resembling these primitive fish.

The most clearly evident primitive feature of the group is the lack of spines in the fins. Most of the soft rays in the fins are branched. The pelvic fins are situated far back on the body—in the "hip" region, where the legs of amphibians articulate with the body. This position differs from the location of the pelvic fins in many other species, including largemouth bass, for example, whose pelvic fins are so far forward, they are almost directly beneath the pectoral fins. Other indications of its primitive nature are an adipose fin and a crude type of air bladder.

Charr, as a group, are among the most distinguished-looking and prettiest fish that appear in freshwater. Some are especially colorful, particularly in spawning mode. All have distinctive body markings, although there are great variations, depending on their environments. The lake trout found deep in one of the Great Lakes, for example, is rather bland compared to the lake trout caught in more sterile waters of the far north.

Most members of the Salmonidae family are in some way associated with cold, often rushing waters and high oxygen demands. Some, including two of the charr, are also tied to the sea, spending a portion of their lives there. All members of the family spawn in freshwater, and most require cold running water. Members of some of the sea-running species, including at least arctic charr, have become accidentally or deliberately landlocked, living and reproducing successfully entirely in freshwater, without ever taking a journey to saltwater.

Some charr species, especially arctic charr and lake trout, are of great historical, cultural, and food significance to native peoples of the Arctic or the near-Arctic and to settlers, and they have had—and, to some degree, still have—both subsistence and commercial value. All native charr have rich red flesh and are excellent eating, primarily when fresh or smoked.

Some populations of the various charr have declined dramatically, and most are not what they were decades ago, in terms of overall size, as well as in the number of large individuals. In addition, some landlocked forms with limited distribution (blueback trout, Quebec red, and Sunapee trout) have become extinct, their loss in some cases hastened by stocking of nonnative salmonids.

The subject of the proper spelling of this group—charr or char—has generated spirited debate in the scientific community. The original and historical spelling is reportedly Celtic (from *ceara,* meaning "blood red"), and became "charre" in seventeenth-century England, then "charr." The general public, especially the popular media, today predominantly uses "char." Many Canadian ichthyologists, who arguably have a greater claim to the group because of the abundance of these species and studies of them, use "charr."

Charr, Arctic

Salvelinus alpinus

Arctic Charr
(sea-run phase)

Arctic Charr
(spawning phase)

The arctic charr is one of five species that are actually classified as charr. It varies so greatly in coloration that many specimens are thought to be species or subspecies, resulting in a great deal of confusion and a tremendous problem for taxonomists. This confusion extended to anadromous and nonanadromous forms, the latter including three New England charr—the blueback trout, the Sunapee trout, and the Quebec red trout, which were once separately recognized species but which were all reclassified and folded under the highly inclusive umbrella *S. alpinus* in 1974.

The arctic charr exists in anadromous (migrating annually to the sea) and nonanadromous (landlocked or living entirely in freshwater) forms. Because of plentiful food resources in the ocean, the anadromous version tends to be larger than the landlocked one and of more importance. The landlocked charr is blocked from the sea by some physical barrier. It is found everywhere that the sea-run charr exists but also occurs in smaller numbers much farther to the south.

Identification. Like all members of the *Salvelinus* genus, the arctic charr has light-colored spots on its body, including below the lateral line, and the leading edges of all fins on the lower part of the body are milk white. It is a long and slender fish with a small, pointed head; an adipose fin; an axillary process at the base of each pelvic fin; and a slightly forked tail that almost appears squared. It also has very fine scales, so deeply embedded that the skin has a smooth, slippery feel. Unlike the trout, it has teeth only in the central forward part of its mouth.

Coloration is highly variable among seagoing and landlocked forms and can change even within individual stocks. In a general sense, the arctic charr is silvery in nonspawning individuals, with deep green or blue shading on the back and upper sides and a white belly. Spawning males exhibit

OTHER NAMES

Seagoing fish
char, red charr; Cree: *awanans*; Danish: *fjeldørred*; French: *omble chevalier*; German: *saibling*; Greenlandic: *eqaluk*; Icelandic: *bleikja*; Inuit: *iqalugaq, iqaluk, ilkalupik, ivisaaruq, kisuajuq, majuq-tuq, nutiliarjuk, situajuq, situliqtuq, tisuajuq*; Japanese: *iwana*; Norwegian: *arktisk roye, royr*; Russian: *goletz*; Swedish: *röding*.

Landlocked fish
blueback charr, blueback trout, Sunapee trout, golden trout (Sunapee), Quebec red.

Distribution. *The most northerly ranging fish, the arctic charr is circumpolar in distribution, occurring in pure and cold rivers and lakes around the globe, from the northeastern United States north and west across northern Canada, Alaska, and the Aleutian Islands, and from northern Russia south to Lake Baikal and Kamchatka, as well as in Iceland, Great Britain, Scandinavia, the*

Charr, Arctic *(continued)*
Alps, and Spitsbergen,
among other places.

In North America, they
occur from Alaska around
the Bering Sea and along
the Arctic coast to Baffin
Island, along the coastline
of Hudson Bay, and from
the northern Quebec coast
easterly and southerly to
Maine and New Hampshire.
Except in larger rivers, they
seldom range far inland
here, although there are a
few pockets of landlocked
charr. In the Northwest
Territories and Nunavut
Territory, where they are
especially known, charr
distribution includes most
coastal rivers, some coastal
lakes, the streams of the
high-arctic islands, and sev-
eral islands in Hudson Bay.

Habitat. *In their ocean*
life, arctic charr remain in
inshore waters; most do not
migrate far. In rivers, they
locate in pools and runs.
The lakes inhabited by
anadromous and landlocked
charr are cold year-round,
so the fish remain near the
surface or in the upper levels
and may gather at the
mouths of tributaries when
food is plentiful.

brilliant red or reddish-orange coloration on the sides, the underparts, and the lower fins; their backs are muted, sometimes without the blue or green coloration or possibly with orange to olive hues. A spawning male of some populations will develop a kype, and some have humped backs. Spawning females are also colorful, although the red is less intense and present only on their flanks and bellies; their backs remain bluish or greenish.

Size. Arctic charr may live up to 30 years and grow to 3 feet in length. Sea-run charr grow much larger, and the all-tackle world record is a 32-pound, 9-ounce sea-run fish that was caught in 1981 in the Tree River of Canada's Northwest Territories. In most places, sea-run arctic charr range up to 10 pounds and average 7 pounds; landlocked fish normally weigh a few pounds. A sea-run arctic charr weighing more than 15 pounds is a trophy in most waters.

Life history/Behavior. The charr spawns in September or October in colder regions and later if it lives farther south; a water temperature of around 39°F is preferred. The spawning female seeks out a suitable bed of gravel or broken rock. The anadromous charr lives in its birth river for at least 4 years before migrating to the sea for the first time. It will return anywhere between mid-August and late September, before the ice begins to form again. The larger fish return first. Unlike other salmonids, all arctic charr leave the sea and overwinter in rivers and lakes, although not all are spawners; some go back and forth several times before they first spawn. Nonanadromous or landlocked charr tend to reach maturity when they are smaller and younger. They have the same lifestyle as their anadromous brethren.

Food. Insects, mollusks, and small fish constitute the diet of arctic charr. Ninespine sticklebacks are important forage in some places. The charr often does not eat in the winter, when its metabolic rate slows in tune with a cooling environment. Rather, it lives on the fat it has accumulated during the summer, and growth is accordingly limited during the cold months and greatest when at sea.

Chub

Creek Chub
Semotilus atromaculatus

In North America, the term "chub" is used to describe many unrelated fish, all of which are members of the largest fish family in the world, minnows. Although the word *minnow* is commonly applied to many small fish, to scientists the minnow family is a large and old group of bony fish, Cyprinidae, which includes river chub, as well as countless species of shiners, dace, and carp.

Confusion about the chub branch of this family exists, nevertheless; this is particularly evident when one sees "smoked chub" on a menu or in a fish market. This is actually a fish-market description for species of whitefish *(see)* or cisco *(see)* from the Great Lakes, which are not cyprinids. True chub are rather bony and do not make admirable table fare.

Species and habitat. Twenty-six minnows merit the name "chub" and inhabit waters from the Appalachians to the Pacific Coast. The larger, primitive chub of the genus *Gila* inhabit western North America. The most familiar chub may be the creek chub, an inhabitant of creeks and lakes throughout eastern and central North America. Also well known are the various river chub, which are members of the genus *Nocomis* and famed architects of the fish world.

River chub are olive-colored minnows with stout bodies, large scales, and light yellow to red-orange caudal fins. The seven *Nocomis* species are identified by unique patterns and the size of the tubercle spots on the heads and snouts of males. Female and young chub lack tubercles.

The largest river chub are bull chub and bigmouth chub, and the largest males range from 12 to 15 inches. Bull chub and bigmouth chub are rivaled in size only by the fallfish, the largest native eastern minnows. The closely related creek chub rarely reaches 12 inches in length.

River chub are widely distributed in streams of eastern and central North America, although some have restricted distribution: redspot chub in eastern Oklahoma and parts of Kansas, Missouri, and Arkansas; redtail chub in the highland rim of the Cumberland River drainage of southern Kentucky and north-central Tennessee; bigmouth chub in the New River drainage of North Carolina, Virginia, and West Virginia; and bull chub from parts of Virginia and North Carolina.

Other species (hornyhead, river, and bluehead) are more widely distributed. The hornyhead is a common baitfish, often called redtail chub. The wide distribution of chub stems from past geological events, such as glaciation and changing river courses.

Chub often occur in schools with other minnows, particularly stonerollers, in runs and pools of clear, moderately sloping gravel and rock-bottomed streams and rivers. It is not unusual to see young smallmouth bass swimming and actively feeding near chub. Chub and young bass may be eating the same prey, but older smallmouth bass readily consume chub. Bluehead chub, redspot chub, and redtail chub more commonly inhabit smaller streams, whereas river chub, bull chub, and bigmouth chub are more common in main stems and large tributaries.

Chub are primarily sight feeders, taking small invertebrates from the bottom or from the drift. Although they have small barbels, these may not be useful for feeding, more likely being a trait retained from a primitive ancestor. Chub primarily eat immature insects, although they also eat aquatic worms, crustaceans, mollusks, water mites, small fish, and aquatic plants. Chub prefer to feed in the swifter-flowing sections because more food is available there, but to avoid sapping their energy, they usually stay within 4 inches of the streambed, often behind larger stones.

Spawning. Chub spawn in the spring when water temperatures are between 60° and 75°F. During the breeding season, males develop large hornlike tubercles and spectacular coloration—pink, rose, yellow, orange, and blue, depending on the species. The "bluehead" name comes from the intense slate blue head of the spawning male. Colors and tubercles signal spawning readiness to nearby ripe females.

Chub, Creek
Semotilus atromaculatus

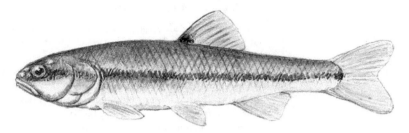

The creek chub is one of the largest chub and a member of the minnow, or Cyprinidae, family, making it a distant relative to carp. Occurring in great abundance in North America, it is important forage for sportfish, often competes with those larger predators for food, and, because it is hardy and lively, is also a prominent bait used by anglers.

Identification. The snout of the creek chub is pointed and its mouth large, with a single small barbel in the corner of each jaw, sometimes hidden between the maxillary and the premaxillary. The body is stout, colored olive brown on the back, silvery on the sides with shades of iridescent purple, and whitish on the underside. A juvenile will have a blackish stripe along its back and a black caudal spot; an adult will also have the stripe on its back, but the black caudal spot will be faint or absent. There is a large black spot at the front of the dorsal fin. A breeding male takes on an orange hue, also gaining 4 to 8 large, thornlike tubercles (thus the name "horned dace") on its opercles, body scales, and fins. The creek chub may occasionally appear to be speckled with black sand, but this is the result of being heavily covered with the parasite that causes black spot disease (which is harmless to the fish and is not transmittable to humans) and not as a result of natural coloring.

Other characteristics include a complete lateral line with 47 to 65 scales, 8 anal fin rays, 8 dorsal fin rays, and a pharyngeal tooth count formula of 2-5-4-2 (2 teeth in minor rows and 4 or 5 teeth in major rows).

The creek chub can be distinguished from the pearl dace (*Semotilus margarita*, a.k.a. *Margariscus margarita*) by its larger mouth. The fallfish (*Semotilus corporalis*) is a strikingly similar fish to the creek chub, but with larger scales and larger eyes and without a black spot on the dorsal fin.

Size/Age. The creek chub can attain a maximum length of between 6 and 12 inches, depending on its environment;

Distribution. Creek chub are found from the Maritime Provinces of Canada west to Montana and south to Texas and northern Georgia. Their distribution extends throughout the eastern half of southern Canada and the central and eastern United States. They occur in the Atlantic, Canadian, Great Lakes, Gulf Coast, Hudson Bay, and Mississippi drainages.

Habitat. These fish prefer cool, clear water in the gravel-bottomed pools and runs of creeks and streams. In dry weather and during low water, they can survive in isolated pools. They are seldom found in lakes. Some ichthyologists refer to the creek chub as the "king of the headwaters" because it is often the largest fish found in very small streams. Deeper pools usually contain the largest individuals. Creek chub are tolerant of some pollution and can be the average is 4 to 6 inches long. Adult males grow faster than females do, and the largest creek chub are usually male. They can live up to 7 years.

Spawning behavior. Creek chub are pit-ridge spawners that build their gravel nests in runs and the downstream sections of pools. Nest building and spawning occur between March and June, in water temperatures ranging from 54° to 68°F. Creek chub have an interesting spawning ritual, which begins in the spring when the male digs a pit in the stream bottom by removing bits of gravel with his mouth. He carefully guards the pit where the spawning occurs and attracts a female. Adult males are territorial during the breeding season and can be observed swimming in parallel, chasing each other, and ramming their tuberculate heads against each other. Some males attempt to spawn over the nests built by other males. Spawning occurs when the male wraps his body around the female and eggs are released over the nest. A single female can produce more than 7,000 eggs, but only a portion of these are released during a single spawning event. Females are often observed floating belly up for a few seconds after spawning. They quickly recover and can spawn again.

Food. Creek chub are omnivores that feed on a variety of foods, including zooplankton, aquatic and terrestrial insects, crayfish, mollusks, frogs, and fish. Adult creek chub have been shown to primarily consume fish, including the young of their own species.

Chub, Hornyhead

Nocomis biguttatus

The hornyhead chub is a member of the large Cyprinidae family and a fairly common stream and river resident; smaller specimens are used as bait by anglers.

Identification. The body of a hornyhead chub is slender with a rounded snout. The mouth is large, almost terminal, with a small barbel above the jaws, and it has pharyngeal (throat) teeth. The hornyhead chub has dark-edged scales, a complete lateral line, and seven anal rays. Its coloring is bluish olive on the back, yellowish with iridescent green on the sides, and whitish on the underside. On the adult male, there is a bright red dot behind each eye; on the female, the dot is brassy colored. Yellow iridescent stripes run along the back and the sides. There is a dark caudal spot, which is darkest on juveniles, around the snout. Breeding males are colored pink with pinkish-orange fins and have many tubercles on their heads.

The hornyhead chub can be distinguished from a bull chub *(Nocomis raneyi)* by its shorter snout, larger eyes, and a red dot behind each eye. The bluehead chub *(Nocomis leptocephalus)*, although strikingly similar, has no red dot behind each eye, and it has a large loop on the right side of its intestine, distinguishing it from the hornyhead.

Size. The average size for a hornyhead chub is 8 inches, although some can grow to up to 10 inches.

Spawning behavior. The spawning season for hornyhead chub is from late May through June, when the male develops tubercles on the head. The male builds a nest from pebbles. Other kinds of fish use this nest for spawning, but the male hornyhead will ward off other fish of the same species.

Food. The hornyhead chub is omnivorous, feeding primarily on insect larvae but also consuming small crustaceans, earthworms, and algae.

OTHER NAMES
redtail chub.

Distribution. *The hornyhead chub is found from New York west to Wyoming and Colorado and south to northern Arkansas; in its easternmost range in New York, it can be found in the Niagara River and several streams in the Mohawk River system, but it does inhabit the Susquehanna, Delaware, and Hudson Rivers.*

Habitat. *This species lives in small to medium-size rivers and streams. It prefers warm, clear waters with a moderate to sluggish current, especially with a sandy, gravelly bottom and aquatic vegetation.*

Chubsucker

Lake Chubsucker
Erimyzon oblongus

Distribution. *Creek chub-suckers inhabit waters from the Great Lakes and the Mississippi River drainages south to Georgia and Gulf slope waters. Lake and sharpfin chubsuckers inhabit waters similar to those favored by creek chubsuckers, including waters as far west as Oregon and as far south as Florida.*

Habitat. *Lukewarm, clear waters of creeks, small rivers, lakes, ponds, and swamps or other waters without turbidity are favored environments. Chubsuckers are seldom found in streams, favoring the depths of still, calm waters. As bottom dwellers, chubsuckers prefer sand, gravel, or silt bottoms with abundant vegetation.*

Chubsuckers are members of the sucker family, Catostomidae. They are divided into three separate species: the creek chubsucker *(Erimyzon sucetta)*, the lake chubsucker *(Erimyzon oblongus)*, and the sharpfin chubsucker *(Erimyzon tenuis)*. All species are extremely similar and are interchangeably referred to as "suckers" or "mullet" in different locales.

Chubsuckers are of little importance commercially and are predominant ignored for sportfishing. When taken from cold water, however, chubsuckers have good-flavored, firm flesh. Because of their abundance and their large size, chubsuckers often account for the greatest biomass in streams and lakes, making them important forage for predator species.

Identification. Chubsuckers are characteristically defined by their small, protruding, suckerlike mouths and thick fleshy lips. Creek, lake, and sharpfin chubsuckers are similarly colored a greenish bronze, without a lateral line. There are usually 10 to 12 dorsal rays and 7 anal rays. The scales are dark-edged and, on the creek chubsucker, accompanied by dark blotches. A young chubsucker has a concentrated black band from the tip of the snout to the tail, on top of which is a yellow band. A breeding male is dark with a pink-orange tint and several tubercles on each side of the snout. The creek chubsucker has a chubby body, whereas the lake and sharpfin chubsuckers are slightly more elongated.

All suckers excepting the chubsucker have a fully developed lateral line.

Size/Age. Chubsuckers can grow to 13 to 15 inches, but they rarely exceed 10 inches in length. The average age for a chubsucker is 5, although one can live up to 8 years.

Life history/Behavior. Spawning occurs in the early spring in small tributary waters. Sometimes the male builds a nest, but the eggs are usually scattered randomly over sand, gravel, or vegetation bottoms and left to hatch unattended.

Food and feeding habits. Chubsuckers are bottom feeders, consuming insect larvae, aquatic plants, and small crustaceans.

Cisco

Coregonus spp

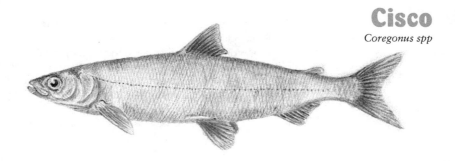

There are a number of similar species under the *Coregonus* genus, which is classified as a member of the Salmonidae family and generally acknowledged as a subfamily of whitefish. Whitefish and cisco inhabit many of the same waters and may be confused, although cisco are generally smaller. One of the most common of these is *Coregonus artedii*, simply referred to as cisco. This species is often portrayed as the only cisco because the differences between species are only minor variations in body or snout shape, depth preference, or number of eggs. However, there are, or were, perhaps as many as 11 species of cisco, some of which were primarily very deep-dwelling fish.

In the Great Lakes, cisco have evidently suffered from competition with more aggressive plankton feeders (like alewives and smelt) and from predation by salmon and sea lampreys, all of which were nonnative species. The bloater (*C. hoyi*) has suffered the least of the Great Lakes species. Bloaters do not support any sportfishing effort, as they dwell far from shore and have mouths too small for ordinary lures. They are efficient feeders, however, and grow more on less food than do alewives.

Bloaters, as well as other Great Lakes cisco, are commonly called "chub." The bloater, in fact, is also known as a bloater chub. These small, soft-fleshed, and oily fish are tasty table fare and are popular for commercial smoking, usually bearing the name "smoked chub."

Cisco provide some sportfishing opportunity, especially for ice fishing, and are important forage fish for other species, particularly northern pike, walleye, perch, and rainbow trout. They are especially significant to lake trout.

Identification. Characterized by an adipose dorsal fin and a forked tail, the cisco has a terminal mouth (a lower jaw projecting slightly beyond the upper jaw). The body is elongate and slender, with less than 100 scales in the lateral line. The pelvic axillary process, or daggerlike progression, is well developed. Its coloring is dusky gray to bluish on the back, silvery on the sides, and white on the underside. All fins are

OTHER NAMES
gray back, tullibee, lake herring, whitefish.

Distribution. *Cisco are primarily inhabitants of Canada, where they range from roughly east of the Mackenzie River through Ontario and north throughout the Northwest Territories, as well as throughout much of Quebec. They inhabit the Great Lakes and its tributaries (including the St. Lawrence River). They are found in some lakes of states bordering the Great Lakes, including the Finger Lakes in New York, and in upper Mississippi River drainages.*

Habitat. *Coldwater lakes are the favored dwelling places of cisco. They may be near the surface when the water is cold or at depths of several hundred feet, but they generally remain below the thermocline in lakes where this stratification occurs. They tend to school in midwater and move into shallower areas when the water cools in the fall. Water temperatures ranging above 60°F are lethal to cisco, and as the surface waters warm, these fish* *move deeper. Many swim close to the surface during the winter, providing opportunities for ice fishing.*

relatively clear, although the anal and the pelvic fins may be milky on adults.

As a group, cisco (and whitefish) are quickly differentiated from other species by the presence of an adipose fin. Cisco can be differentiated from lake whitefish *(Coregonus clupeaformis)*, which inhabit the same deeper waters, by their pointed snouts, terminal mouths, and lack of teeth; the cisco's mouth is at the end of the head, whereas the whitefish's mouth is behind and under the snout. Cisco are differentiated from lake trout *(Salvelinus namaycush)*, by having larger scales, bigger mouths, and lack of teeth.

Size. Cisco can vary in length from 6 to 25 inches, the average size being between 10 and 14 inches and ½ pound; the all-tackle world record is a Manitoba fish *(C. artedii)* that weighed 7 pounds, 6 ounces. The average life span is 8 years. In some lakes, the cisco population may be stunted, and most fish are small.

Life history/Behavior. Cisco are schooling fish that spawn in large congregations in the late fall after moving into shallow water roughly 3 to 10 feet deep, often on reefs, and when the water temperature is about 39° to 41°F. Females can lay up to 30,000 eggs on the lake bottom, usually over gravel or stones. The eggs are given no parental care and hatch within 4 months. Nearly all cisco reach maturity by their fourth season. Some, such as the least cisco *(C. sardinella)*, are anadromous but do not stray far from river mouths during migration.

Food and feeding habits. Plankton is the main food source of cisco. During the early spring, which is their most active (and shallow) feeding season, they may also consume minnows, crustaceans, and mayflies.

Crappie, Black
Pomoxis nigromaculatus

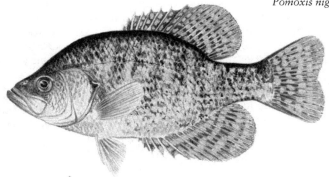

Crappie are like that Chinese dog called a Shih Tzu. Most people don't say the name of that dog in a way that sounds flattering. Ditto for the poor crappie. If its name were pronounced by more folks as if it contained the letter *o* instead of *a*, as in *crop*, we would all be better off. No matter how you pronounce the name, both the black crappie and the white crappie are the most distinctive and largest members of the Centrarchidae family, which includes sunfish and black bass. Both species are considered excellent food fish and sportfish and have white, flaky meat that makes for sweet fillets. In many places crappie are plentiful, and creel limits are liberal, so it does no harm to keep a batch of these fish for the table.

Identification. The black crappie and the white crappie are similar in color—a silvery olive to bronze with dark spots, although on the black crappie the spots are irregularly arranged instead of appearing in seven or eight vertical bands, as they do on the white crappie. Both species are laterally compressed and deep-bodied, although the black crappie is somewhat deeper in body, and it has a large mouth that resembles the mouth of a largemouth bass. It also has distinct depressions in its forehead and large dorsal and anal fins of almost identical size. The gill cover comes to a sharp point, instead of ending in an earlike flap. The best way to differentiate the two species of crappie is by counting the dorsal fin spines, as the black crappie usually has seven or eight, the white crappie six. The breeding male does not change color noticeably, as happens in the white crappie species.

Size/Age. With lengths of up to 13 inches, the black crappie can weigh up to 5 pounds but usually weighs less than 2 pounds and is commonly caught at a pound or less. It is thought to live to 10 years of age. The all-tackle world record is a 4-pound, 8-ounce fish taken in Virginia in 1981.

OTHER NAMES

speckled perch, calico bass, grass bass, speckled bass, strawberry bass, oswego bass, sacalait, barfish, crawpie, bachelor perch, papermouth, shiner, moonfish; French: *marigane noire*.

Distribution. *Black crappie have been so widely introduced in North America that the native range is uncertain, although it appears to start at the Atlantic slope from Virginia to Florida, the Gulf slope west to Texas, and the St. Lawrence-Great Lakes and Mississippi River basins from Quebec to Manitoba, Canada, south to the Gulf of Mexico.*

Habitat. *Black crappie prefer cooler, deeper, clearer waters with more abundant aquatic vegetation than do white crappie. This includes still backwater lakes, sloughs, creeks, streams, lakes, and ponds. Because crappie form schools, an angler who comes across one fish is likely to find others nearby. They are*

Crappie, Black (continued)

especially active in the evening and the early morning and remain active throughout the winter. An abundant species, black crappie occur in smaller concentrations than do white crappie.

Life history/Behavior. Spawning occurs in the early spring and the summer in water temperatures between 62° and 68°F. These fish spawn over gravel areas or other soft material and nest in colonies. The males excavate the nests, and the females lay the eggs, sometimes in several of these. The eggs incubate for 3 to 5 days, and the young mature sometime between their second and fourth years.

Food and feeding habits. Black crappie tend to feed early in the morning on zooplankton, crustaceans, insects, fish, insect larvae, young shad, minnows, and small sunfish. Small minnows form a large part of the diet of adults; in southern reservoirs, gizzard or threadfin shad are the major forage, and in northern states, insects are dominant. Crappie also consume the fry of many species of gamefish. They continue to feed during the winter and are very active under the ice.

Crappie, White
Pomoxis annularus

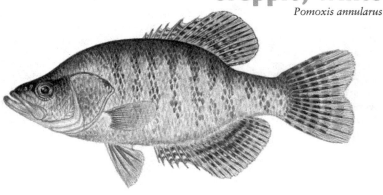

Members of the Centrarchidae family, which includes sunfish and black bass, white crappie are usually thought of in the same breath as black crappie. Both species are considered excellent food fish and sportfish and have white, flaky meat that makes for sweet fillets. In many places, crappie are plentiful, and creel limits are liberal, so it does no harm to keep a batch of these fish for the table.

Identification. The white crappie and the black crappie are essentially the same color, a silvery olive to bronze with dark spots, although the white crappie is somewhat paler; in the white crappie the spots are arranged in seven or eight vertical bands on its sides, whereas in the black crappie the spots are scattered. Deep-bodied and laterally compressed, the white crappie has a large mouth, an upper jaw that extends under the eye, and a lower jaw that seems to protrude. It also has distinct depressions in its forehead and large dorsal and anal fins of almost identical size. The best way to differentiate these fish is by counting dorsal fin spines, as the white crappie has six, and the black crappie usually has seven or eight. The white crappie is also the only sunfish with the same number of spines in both the dorsal and the anal fins. The breeding male grows darker in color and is often mistaken for the black crappie.

Size/Age. The white crappie can reach a weight of 5 pounds but usually weighs less than 2 pounds and is commonly caught at a pound or less. The all-tackle world record is a 5-pound, 3-ounce fish taken in Mississippi in 1957. White crappie live for a maximum of 10 years.

Spawning behavior. Spawning occurs in the early spring and the summer in water temperatures between 62° and 68°F, and during that time the male grows dark on the sides of its head, lower jaw, and breast. Spawning takes place in sandy, muddy, and weedy areas, and the fish nest

OTHER NAMES
crappie, speckled perch, speckled bass, calico bass, sacalait, papermouth, bachelor perch; French: *crapet calicot.*

Distribution. *Widespread in North America, white crappie are found in the Great Lakes, Hudson Bay, the Mississippi River basins from New York and Ontario west to Minnesota and South Dakota and south to the Gulf of Mexico; they also inhabit the Gulf of Mexico drainages from Mobile Bay in Georgia and Alabama to the Nueces River in Texas. They have been introduced widely elsewhere.*

Habitat. *White crappie occur in creek backwaters, slow-flowing streams, sand- and mud-bottomed pools, small to large rivers, and lakes and ponds. They prefer shallower water than do the black crappie and can tolerate warmer, more turbid, and slightly alkaline waters. They are usually found near dropoffs, standing timber, brushy cover, or*

Crappie, White *(continued)*

other artificial cover. Because white crappie school in loose groups, when an angler catches one, others are likely to be around. They are especially active in the evening and the early morning and remain active throughout the winter.

in colonies. In moderately deep water, the male brushes away sediment to form a shallow nest and guards the 27,000 to more than 68,000 eggs. The eggs incubate for 2 to 4 days, and the young white crappie mature in 2 to 4 years.

Food and feeding habits. White crappie feed on small crustaceans, zooplankton, insects and insect larvae, minnows, young shad, small sunfish, and other small fish. Small minnows of many species are probably the most common food item for adults.

Dace

Longnose Dace
Rhinichthys cataractae

Dace belong to the largest family of freshwater fish, Cyprinidae, which includes assorted minnows and carp. These are small and extremely hardy fish.

In North America, dace are distributed widely in small streams, lakes, and ponds, providing an important food source for many species sought by anglers. They inhabit colder, moving, clear water that runs over gravel or pebbles. Adults generally inhabit deep water, and juveniles hold in shallow water closer to shore.

Commonly referred to in North America by the all-encompassing generic term "minnows," dace are small (2 to 3 inches in length) and have slender bodies. Most dace species have terminal barbels. On the pearl dace *(Semotilus margarita margarita),* the barbel is sometimes hidden or even absent. The *Clinostomus* species has no barbels.

Dace are greatly valued as bait for larger gamefish. They can survive in very crowded or stagnant waters, due to low oxygen demand, so anglers who want lively and sturdy bait value this kind of resilience.

Identifying and distinguishing between the different species of dace are difficult. Although not all dace are identical, the variations are minor, such as a slightly longer snout. The coloring is extremely similar on all dace: olive green fading to white on the belly, with silvery overtones. The small scales are pronounced and have dark patterns that can change not only from species to species but also among individual fish.

All dace, especially males, have well-developed tubercles on their bodies, primarily around their heads and snouts. These tubercles, also called pearl organs, are used for nest building, in fighting and courtship rituals, and for maintaining contact with the opposite sex during spawning.

Eggs are given little or no parental care after spawning, and the young feed on zooplankton and phytoplankton for the first several months of life. Adults feed on insect larvae, worms, and algae.

Dace, Blacknose

Rhinichthys atratulus

OTHER NAMES

eastern blacknose dace, brook minnow, potbelly, redfin dace, chub.

Distribution. The range of the blacknose dace spans from North Dakota to the St. Lawrence drainage and south to Nebraska and North Carolina.

Habitat. These fish are commonly found in rapid, clear streams and the rocky runs and pools of small rivers; they can survive in stagnant summer waters and tolerate crowded conditions.

A member of the Cyprinidae family of minnows and carp, the blacknose dace makes excellent bait due to its small size and hardiness and, like many small minnows, provides excellent forage for predator fish, especially bass and trout. It is not sought by anglers but may be netted for use as bait.

Identification. The blacknose dace has a long slim body with a slightly protruding snout. The barbels, which are characteristic of most minnows, corner both sides of the mouth. The coloring is silvery, with dark olive gray fading to white on the belly. A dark lateral line runs along either side onto the head. It can be distinguished from the longnose dace (*Rhinichthys cataractae*) by its shorter snout.

Size/Age. Blacknose dace generally live 2 to 3 years and have an average size of 2 to 3 inches.

Spawning behavior. Blacknose dace spawn in the spring, starting in late May or early June. They build no nests; the fertilized eggs are dropped over the gravel bottom. The male, however, is known to defend spawning territories. The female releases approximately 750 eggs, and little or no parental care is given to them.

Food and feeding habits. Blacknose dace feed on insect larvae, small crustaceans, small worms, and plant material.

Dace, Longnose

Rhinichthys cataractae

A member of the Cyprinidae family of minnows and carp, the longnose dace has many valuable functions. Easily obtainable, small, and extremely hardy, it is prized as exceptional bait and is especially significant for bass fishing. Primarily feeding on blackfly larvae, it is also valued for its control of the blackfly population. And, like many small minnows, it provides excellent forage for predator fish, especially bass and trout. It is not sought by anglers but may be netted for use as bait.

Identification. The longnose dace is a distinctive minnow with a long fleshy snout, a subterminal mouth, and a deep caudal peduncle. The head and the nape slope downward from its cylindrical body, giving this minnow a streamlined appearance. Pigmentation is widely variable; the dorsum can be greenish, brown, or reddish purple, and the lower sides and the venter may be silvery, white, or yellow. The sides are sometimes marked by darkened scales, a lateral stripe, and a blotch near the tail. The longnose dace can quickly be distinguished from most other minnows by the presence of a frenum, a small fleshy bridge between the snout and the upper jaw. It can be distinguished from other species of *Rhinichthys* by its long snout. Other characteristics of the longnose dace are small barbels in the corner of the mouth, small scales, a complete lateral line with 48 to 76 scales, and eyes that are situated near the top of the head. A breeding male has red coloration on the head and the fins and develops small tubercles on the head, the body, and the ventral fins.

Size/Age. Adults can reach lengths exceeding 6 inches, but most are less than 4 inches long. They have been known to live up to 5 years.

Spawning behavior. Longnose dace mature within 2 years but may live up to 5 years. Females often grow larger

OTHER NAMES

dace; French: *naseux de rapide.*

Distribution. *The longnose dace has the widest distribution of any minnow in North America and is an important forage species where it is abundant. Several subspecies are recognized, but further study may reveal the occurrence of unique populations or additional subspecies. The distribution of the longnose dace spans the entire continent, ranging throughout the southern half of Canada and the northern United States. It extends southward to Georgia within the southern Appalachian Mountains and into northern Mexico through the Rocky Mountains. Its northern limit is the Mackenzie River drainage, Canada, which lies within the Arctic Circle.*

Habitat. *Longnose dace occur in a wide variety of habitats. They are found in the riffles, runs, and pools of creeks, streams, and rivers. Within lakes, they usually prefer areas around rocky*

shorelines. These stream-
lined fish are well adapted
to fast-moving waters.

and live longer than do males. Reproduction occurs between the late spring and the early summer. Interestingly, an eastern subspecies spawns during the day, whereas a western subspecies spawns at night. Longnose dace are categorized as broadcast spawners, scattering their eggs in shallow, fast-flowing areas and over chub nests. Males aggressively defend spawning areas, but more than one male may line up next to the female during spawning. Spawning occurs on the stream bottom and may result in the burial of eggs within the substrate. The female deposits between 200 and 1,200 eggs during spawning.

Food and feeding habits. Longnose dace feed on aquatic insects (especially midges and blackfly larvae), worms, small crustaceans, mites, algae, and plants. They have taste buds on their ventral fins, lower heads, lips, and snouts, which may enable them to find food along the stream bottom.

Darters

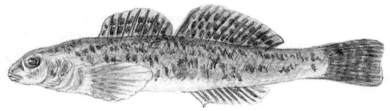

Johnny Darter
Etheostoma nigrum

Darters are an incredibly diverse and colorful group of fresh-water fish, which rival saltwater fish in brilliance. They are actually small representatives of the perch family (Percidae) and are closely related to yellow perch and walleye. The darter group consists of approximately 160 species, all of which are restricted to North America. As such, they represent 20 percent of all fish in the United States.

Identification. Three genera of darters are recognized: *Percina,* which includes roughly 40 species; *Etheostoma,* which includes roughly 112 species; and *Ammocrypta,* with 7 species. The genus *Percina* contains the largest darters. Most are rather drab and cryptic in coloration, although the males of some species exhibit impressive spawning coloration. The genus *Etheostoma* is diverse in the shape and the coloration of its representatives. The bodies and fins of many of these darters are painted with shades of red, blue, yellow, green, and orange interspersed with black blotches. Members of the genus *Ammocrypta* are dull and sand-colored. This camouflages them from predators in the large, sand-bottomed rivers they inhabit.

Darters can reach a length of 12 inches (*Percina lenticula,* the freckled darter), although most are only a few inches long, even as adults. The smallest is the fountain darter (*Etheostoma fonticola),* which reaches an adult size of only 1½ inches. The darter has two dorsal fins, the front with hard spines and the rear with soft rays. The caudal fin is usually rounded or emarginate. Many darters are sexually dimorphic, and the males are usually larger and brightly colored. Males also develop thickened body tissues, fleshy knobs on the dorsal fin rays and spines, and breeding tubercles during spawning. The showy appearance of courting males is thought to attract females during spawning and accounts for the large amount of angling interest in this group.

Distribution. *Darters range from northern Mexico into Canada and from the eastern coastal plains west to the Continental Divide. Only one species, the Mexican darter* (Etheostoma pottsi), *occurs west of the Continental Divide, in northern Mexico. Darters are most diverse in the southern Appalachian Mountains of Tennessee and Virginia and in the Ozark plateau of northern Arkansas. The johnny darter* (Etheostoma nigrum) *is the most widely distributed, followed by the orange-throat darter* (Etheostoma spectabile) *and perhaps the logperch darter* (Percina caprodes).

Habitat. *Darters are found in all types of freshwater habitats. They may inhabit small streams, large rivers, spring seeps, ponds, lakes, or reservoirs. They are most frequently found in fast-moving water, however.*

Life history/Behavior. As a group, darters are well adapted to life in fast water and on the stream bottom. Their rounded bodies and slightly flattened head regions are especially hydrodynamic. In addition, most members of the group have completely absent, or poorly developed, swim bladders. They use their enlarged pectoral fins to perch on rocks, allowing them to remain on the stream bottom, out of the current. Their body style is suited to the unique swimming manner for which this group as a whole is named. Darters do not swim in the same way that most fish do; instead, they leap from one spot to another with short jumps or "darts."

Darters display much variability in reproductive strategies. Most produce few, relatively large eggs and provide some degree of parental care. Most members of the genus *Etheostoma* are cavity spawners and lay adhesive eggs on the undersides of medium-size rocks, usually in fast water. Males of this genus are often brightly colored to attract females to nest sites that they have prepared for egg laying. Members of the genera *Percina* and *Ammocrypta* spawn in a simpler manner. Two or more individuals group together in fast-water areas over sand between larger rocks. Males and females align their bodies next to each other, then simultaneously release sperm and eggs into the substrate and bury them. This protects the eggs from predation and floods.

Most darters spawn in the spring to early summer. Several species are believed to spawn multiple times per year. Darters are not a long-lived group. Most species live less than 5 years. Sexual maturity is usually attained at between 1 and 3 years.

Food and feeding habits. Darters primarily feed on bottom-dwelling organisms, mostly small insects, worms, and snails. However, as a group they exhibit a diversity of feeding strategies that corresponds to morphological differences. Large darters feed on insects on top of rocks or pick them out of sand and gravel. Shorter, more flexible darters often feed on clinging insects between and underneath rocks. As a result of these different feeding strategies, several darter species can coexist in the same area of a stream.

Dolly Varden
Salvelinus malma

Bull Trout
Salvelinus confluentus

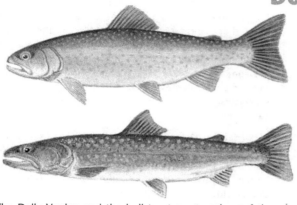

The Dolly Varden and the bull trout are members of the charr group of the Salmonidae family and close relatives of arctic charr. Early studies described these two fish as a variant of the arctic charr and as one distinct species, and for a long time the bull trout was considered just a localized version of the Dolly Varden. Today many fisheries scientists believe that the Dolly Varden and the bull trout are two distinct species that look amazingly similar.

Found in lakes, rivers, and small headwater streams, sometimes migrating back and forth between freshwater and saltwater, and sometimes not, these fish have puzzled fisheries biologists and ichthyologists since they were first discovered. About the only thing everyone agreed on was that they were charr, although somehow the incorrect name "trout" stayed with the bull trout, when the species should have been called bull charr.

Why it is called bull, in fact, is unclear. The Dolly Varden, according to legend, received its moniker because its unique coloration was associated with the colorful clothing of a character in the Charles Dickens novel *Barnaby Rudge*.

Identification. These two charr, as well as the arctic charr, are difficult to distinguish from external characteristics alone, even for specialists. In general, the Dolly Varden and the bull trout can be distinguished by their size and habitat. The Dolly Varden is usually a coastal species, whereas the larger bull trout inhabits inland waters—namely, large, cold rivers and lakes draining high, mountainous areas. Although both can grow large, they seldom do. Dollies are typically smaller and tend to have a more rounded body shape. Bull trout have larger, flattened heads and more pronounced hooks in the lower jaws.

The color of both varies with habitat and locality, but their bodies are generally olive green, the backs being

OTHER NAMES

Dolly Varden
Dolly
Bull Trout
bull charr, western brook trout, Rocky Mountain trout, red spotted salmontrout, red spotted charr.

Distribution. *Dolly Varden occur from the Sea of Japan, throughout the Kuril Islands to Russia's Kamchatka Peninsula, throughout the Aleutian Islands, and around Alaska and the Yukon Territory to the Northwest Territory, as well as in the northwestern United States. In North America, they are especially abundant in Alaska and parts of British Columbia.*

The bull trout is endemic to the Pacific Northwest and inhabits most of the significant drainages on both sides of the Continental Divide. It seems to prefer large, cold rivers and lakes draining high mountainous areas and tends to frequent the bottoms of deep pools. It has been recorded in

northern California, Oregon, Washington, northern Nevada, Idaho, western Montana, Alberta, and British Columbia.

Habitat/Life history. Bull trout and Dolly Varden prefer deep pools of cold rivers, lakes, and reservoirs. Streams with abundant cover (cut banks, root wads, and other woody debris) and clean gravel and cobble beds provide the best habitat. Their favored summer water temperature is generally less than 55°F, but they nevertheless tolerate temperatures less than 40°F. Spawning during the fall usually starts when water temperatures drop to the mid- to low 40s. Cold, clear water is required for successful reproduction.

darker than the pale sides; cream to pale yellow spots (slightly smaller than the pupil of the eye) cover the backs, and red or orange spots cover the sides; and the pectoral, pelvic, and anal fins have white or cream-colored margins. The male in full fall spawning dress sports a dark olive back, sometimes bordering on black; an orange-red belly; bright-red spots; and fluorescent white fin edges, rivaling fall's spectacular colors. Sea-run Dollies are silvery, and the spots can be very faint.

Size. Sea-run Dolly Vardens generally range from 1 to 3 pounds, and freshwater specimens seldom weigh more than 8 pounds. The all-tackle world record is a 20-pound, 14-ounce Alaskan fish. Bull trout are larger growing than Dollies, although the typical fish weighs between 2 and 5 pounds. The all-tackle world record is a 32-pounder that was 40½ inches long and was caught in Lake Pend Oreille, Idaho, in 1949.

Life history. Bull trout and Dolly Varden have complex but similar life histories. Anadromous (seagoing) and migratory resident populations (for example, lake-dwelling stocks and main-stem rearing stocks) often journey long distances in the summer and the fall to spawn, migrating to the small headwater streams where they hatched. Mature adults with these characteristics are generally 4 to 7 years old and 18 to 22 inches in length when they make their first spawning run, although they may be older in some populations.

Spawning begins in late August, peaks in September and October, and ends in November. Fish in a given stream spawn over a short period of time, 2 weeks or less, making redds in clean gravel. Almost immediately after spawning, adults begin to work their way back to the main-stem rivers, lakes, or reservoirs to overwinter. Some of these fish stay put; others move on to saltwater in the spring, evidently not wandering far.

Food. Bull trout and Dolly Varden are opportunistic feeders, eating aquatic insects, shrimp, snails, leeches, fish eggs, and fish.

Drum, Freshwater

Aplodinotus grunniens

The freshwater drum is the only North American freshwater representative of the Sciaenidae family, which includes the croaker, the drum, the corbina, and the seatrout, among others. It also has the greatest range of any North American freshwater fish, is highly adaptable, and is an excellent battler on light tackle, although it is extremely underrated and underutilized as a sportfish.

A unique feature of the freshwater drum is its oversize otolith—a flat, egg-shaped "ear bone" used for hearing and balance. It is surrounded by fluid and has a white, enameled surface with alternating light and dark bands that can be used to determine the age of the fish. These are often kept as good luck charms or made into jewelry. Excavated from Indian village sites, huge otoliths from freshwater drum indicate that at one time the fish grew as large as 200 pounds.

Although a strong fighter with some commercial value, the freshwater drum is not generally highly sought as either a sport or a food fish. It is deliberately sought by some anglers in the southern and midwestern regions of the United States, although it is mostly caught accidentally by anglers. The freshwater drum is often confused with a carp in both appearance and taste, although on close examination it does not look like a carp. The drum's flesh is white with large, coarse flakes. It has been described by some as being of low quality, but this determination is inaccurate. Often found in clear waters, it is a relative of the saltwater drum and the croaker, which are highly valued as food. The freshwater drum, too, is fine table fare. Perhaps 5 to 10 million pounds are taken annually for commercial purposes, mostly from Lake Erie, and mostly for animal feed.

Identification. The body is deep with a humped back, a blunt snout, and a subterminal mouth adapted for bottom feeding. A set of powerful teeth is in the pharynx. It has two dorsal fins, the first having eight to nine spines. The anal fin

OTHER NAMES

sheepshead, croaker, grunt, drum, silver bass, thunder pumper; French: *malachigan.*

Distribution. *The freshwater drum occurs over much of the United States, between the Rockies and the Appalachians southward throughout eastern Mexico to Guatemala's Río Usumacinta system and northward through Manitoba, Canada, all the way to Hudson Bay. It also occurs in some areas of Ontario, Quebec, and Saskatchewan.*

Habitat. *Although it prefers clear waters, the freshwater drum is adaptable and can withstand turbid water better than can many other species. It is commonly found in large lakes and in the deep pools of rivers. It favors deep water, staying at the bottom but moving shoreward at dusk. The drum is rarely found in small streams or small lakes.*

has two spines, the second of which is long and extremely stout. The caudal fin is bluntly pointed. Its coloring is green to gray on its back, with silvery overtones and a white belly. The large, silvery scales are rough to the touch.

The freshwater drum's two dorsal fins and rounded tail distinguish it from the carp and the buffalo. Also, the first dorsal fin of the freshwater drum is composed of eight to nine spines, whereas the carp has only one spine at the beginning of its single soft-rayed dorsal fin, and the buffalo has no spines at all. The freshwater drum can be distinguished from all other freshwater fish by the lateral line, which extends to the tip of the tail and is characteristic of sciaenids.

Size/Age. The average size of a freshwater drum is 15 inches and 3 pounds, although they can grow to 50 pounds. The average commercial catch usually weighs 1 to 5 pounds. The all-tackle record is 54 pounds, 8 ounces. Freshwater drum can live up to 20 years.

Spawning. The freshwater drum spawns in the spring when the water temperature reaches 65° to 70°F. The eggs are released over shallow gravel and sandy stretches near shore. They stick to pebbles or stones on the bottom and hatch within 2 weeks. Neither the eggs nor the young receive parental care.

Food and feeding habits. Young drum feed on minute crustaceans. Adults consume mollusks, insects, and fish. Using their snouts, they slowly move small rocks and other bottom materials to find food. Their pharyngeal teeth crush snail or clam shells, and they spit out the shells and swallow the soft bodies.

Drum, Red

Sciaenops ocellatus

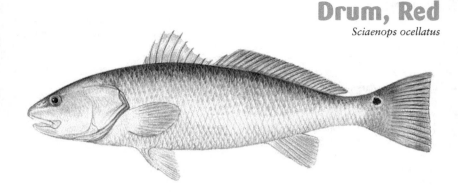

An excellent food fish commonly known as a channel bass and a redfish, the red drum is second only to the black drum in size among members of the drum family, Sciaenidae, but probably first in the hearts of anglers. The common term "drum" refers to the loud and distinctive "drumming" noise that occurs when the fish raps a muscle against the swim bladder. The noise is voluntary and is assumed to be associated with locating and attracting mates, and it can sometimes be heard from a good distance, sometimes even by people above the water.

The red drum is also a popular surf fish, often caught under classic surf conditions. Although it isn't a flashy fighter, it is stubborn and determined, persistent on heading for the bottom. Large red drum, which are primarily found in the mid-Atlantic states, are powerful, premier coastal sportfish.

Identification. The red drum is similar in appearance to the black drum, although its maximum size is smaller and it is more streamlined. The body is elongate, with a subterminal mouth and a blunt nose. On adults the tail is squared, and on juveniles it is rounded. There are no chin barbels, which also distinguishes the red from the black drum. Its coloring is coppery red to bronze on the back, and silver and white on the sides and the belly. One black dot (also called an eyespot) or many are found at the base of the tail.

Size/Age. The average adult red drum is 28 inches long and weighs roughly 15 pounds. Although red drum can attain enormous sizes, they seldom do so. A 30-pounder is generally rare south of the Carolinas or in the Gulf of Mexico, although fish weighing up to 60 pounds are caught in offshore locations. Only smaller fish are found in freshwater.

Red drum can live 50 or more years. They are reported to

OTHER NAMES

channel bass, redfish, rat red (schooling juveniles less than 2 pounds), bull red (more than 10 pounds), puppy drum (under 18 inches), drum, spottail bass, red bass, red horse, school drum; French: *tambour rouge;* Spanish: *corvinón ocelado, pez rojo, corvina roja, pescado colorado.*

Distribution. *Red drum are found in the western Atlantic Ocean from the Gulf of Maine to the Florida Keys (although they are rare north of Maryland), and all along the Gulf coast to northern Mexico.*

Habitat. *An estuarine-dependent fish that becomes oceanic later in life, the red drum is found in brackish water and saltwater on sand, mud, and grass bottoms of inlets, shallow bays, tidal passes, bayous, and estuaries. The red drum also tolerates freshwater, in which some have been known to dwell permanently. Larger red drum*

Drum, Red *(continued)*

prefer deeper waters of lower estuaries and tidal passes, whereas smaller drum remain in shallow waters near piers and jetties and on grassy flats.

Red drum can survive wide ranges of salinity and temperature. Smaller drum prefer lower salinity levels than do larger ones. Optimum salinity levels range from 5 to 30 parts per thousand, optimum temperatures from 40° to 90°F.

More big reds and fewer small ones exist in a fairly short stretch of the mid-Atlantic because of the rich feeding opportunities. This is said to keep the fish from migrating southward each fall, as they prefer to move offshore to warmer continental shelf waters until spring.

live to at least 40 years in the Gulf of Mexico, and the all-tackle record, a North Carolina fish of 94 pounds, 2 ounces, was reportedly 53 years old.

Life history/Behavior. Males are mature by 4 years of age at 30 inches and 15 pounds, females by 5 years at 35 inches and 18 pounds. The spawning season is during the fall, although it may begin as early as August and end as late as November. Spawning takes place at dusk in the coastal waters near passes, inlets, and bays. Currents and winds carry the larvae into estuarine nursery areas.

Food and feeding habits. As a bottom fish, this species uses its senses of sight and touch, and its downturned mouth, to locate forage on the bottom through vacuuming or biting the bottom. In the summer and the fall, adults feed on crabs, shrimp, and sand dollars. Fish such as menhaden, mullet, pinfish, sea robin, lizardfish, spot, Atlantic croaker, and flounder are the primary foods consumed during the winter and the spring. In shallow water, red drum are often seen browsing head-down, with their tails slightly out of the water, a behavior called "tailing."

Eel, American

Anguilla rostrata

American eels are members of the Anguillidae family of freshwater eels and are preyed upon by many species at different stages of their existence. They are important forage for such large offshore predators as sharks, haddock, and swordfish; for inshore species like striped bass; and for many species of birds, including bald eagles and various gulls. Larger individuals (10 to 16 inches or so) are used as bait by anglers, especially those seeking big striped bass, and they may be sold as bait in coastal shops.

Identification. The body is elongate and snakelike, with a pointed head and many teeth. It is covered with thick mucus, hence the phrase "slippery as an eel." The large mouth extends as far back as the midpoint of the eye or past it. There is a single gill opening just in front of the pectoral fins. There are no pelvic fins, and the soft-rayed dorsal, anal, and caudal fins form one continuous fin. There are no visible scales. Coloring changes with maturity, as described later in this text.

Size/Age. American eels grow to 50 inches and 16 pounds. The average size for adult females is about 3 feet, whereas adult males are considerably smaller, rarely growing more than a foot long. They can live longer than 9 years in rivers, streams, and lakes.

Life history/Behavior. When it comes time to spawn, the males and the females stop feeding, change in color from olive to black, and move out to sea. Eels spawn in the same area of the Atlantic Ocean, in deep water at the north edge of the Sargasso Sea. There each female lays as many as 10 to 20 million eggs, and both sexes die after spawning.

The eggs float to the surface and soon hatch into slim, transparent larvae (glass eels). The sex an eel becomes is thought to be partly determined by environmental conditions, such as crowding and food abundance, but it is not

OTHER NAMES
silver eel, Atlantic eel, common eel, yellow-bellied eel, freshwater eel, bronze eel, water snake, whip; Dutch: *amerikaanse aal;* Finnish: *amerikanan kerias;* French: *anguille d'Amerique;* Italian: *anguilla americana;* Japanese: *unagi;* Portuguese: *enguia-americana;* Spanish: *anguila, anguila americana;* Swedish: *amerikansk ål.*

Distribution. *The American eel occurs from southwest Greenland to Labrador, south along the North American coast to Bermuda, the Gulf of Mexico, Panama, and the Caribbean islands. Within this region, inland it occurs from the Mississippi River drainage east, and northeast to the Great Lakes and to the Atlantic Ocean.*

Habitat. *American eels are catadromous, spending most of their lives in freshwater and returning to saltwater to spawn. They prefer to dwell in heavy vegetation or to burrow in the sandy bottom. Their physical*

Eel, American (continued)

structure is such that they can easily swim backward and dig tail first into soft bottom sediments.

determined until they are about 8 to 10 inches long and living in their freshwater habitat.

The larvae drift and swim for 1 year with ocean currents toward river mouths. Males stay near the mouths of rivers, whereas females travel upstream, mostly at night. Eels can absorb oxygen through their skin, as well as through their gills, and are known to travel overland, particularly in damp, rainy weather. Balls of intertwined eels have been seen rolling up beaches in search of freshwater for overwintering.

Food. The diet of the nocturnal feeding American eels includes insect larvae, small fish, crabs, worms, clams, and frogs. They also feed on dead animals or on the eggs of fish and are able to tear smaller pieces of food that are too large to be swallowed whole.

Their feeding habits are rather unusual with respect to large quarry. These eels have relatively weak jaws that are mainly suited to grasping, yet they possess many small, round, and rather blunt teeth. Because they are palindromic—that is, they can move equally well forward or backward forcefully—they are able to pull, twist, and spin when tearing apart prey that is too large to be consumed whole.

Fallfish

Semotilus corporalis

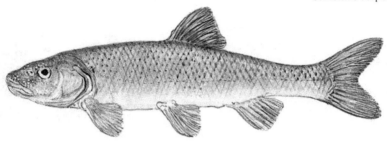

The fallfish is a member of the Cyprinidae family, the largest family of freshwater fish, which also includes minnows and carp. Often confused with the creek chub, the fallfish is the largest in its minnow clan.

Identification. The body of the fallfish is slender, with a bluntly pointed head. There is a single, long dorsal fin. On an adult, the scales are arranged in a pattern of dark, triangular black bars. The mouth is terminal and has barbels—which are characteristic of cyprinids—that are sometimes hidden. Its coloring is olive on the back, silvery on the sides, and white on the belly. A breeding male has tubercles on the snout and a pinkish coloring. A juvenile has a dark black line along the sides. The fallfish can be distinguished from the creek chub by the absence of a black spot at the base of the dorsal fin.

Size/Age. Fallfish may grow to 16 inches or more in length. In smaller streams, they are more likely to be smaller, averaging 10 to 15 inches. A common weight is 1 to 2 pounds. Fallfish have been known to live as long as 10 years.

Spawning behavior. The spawning season is from spring through summer, beginning in early May when the water warms. The male builds a pit-ridge nest out of small stones and pebbles in shallow areas or quiet pools over a clean gravel bottom. The nest can reach 6 feet in length and 3 feet in height. It can weigh up to 200 pounds, due to the volume of pebbles, and is the largest stone mound nest built by any fish. The male repeatedly spawns over one nest with several different females.

Food. Adult fallfish consume aquatic and terrestrial insects (such as mayflies, beetles, wasps, and ants), small crustaceans, small fish, and algae. Juveniles feed on zooplankton and phytoplankton.

OTHER NAMES
windfish, silver chub.

Distribution. *These fish are commonly found from eastern Canada into the James Bay drainage, and south on the east side of the Appalachian Mountains to Virginia.*

Habitat. *Fallfish inhabit the gravel- and rocky-bottomed areas of cold, clear streams, as well as the edges of lakes and ponds. In rivers and streams, adults prefer deeper, quieter waters, whereas juveniles often frequent swifter, shallower water.*

Gar, Alligator

Lepisosteus spatula

OTHER NAMES

garpike; French: *garpique alligator*; Spanish: *gaspar baba.*

Distribution. *The range of the alligator gar extends from the Mississippi River basin of southwestern Ohio and southern Illinois south to the Gulf of Mexico, and from the Enconfina River of the western Florida Panhandle west to Veracruz, Mexico. It has reportedly been taken from Lake Nicaragua, but this catch could have been confused with a large relative, L. tristoechius, taken from Cuban, Central American, and Mexican waters—a fish that rivals the alligator gar in size.*

Habitat. *Large lakes, bays, backwaters, bayous, and coastal delta waters along large southern rivers are the preferred habitat of the alligator gar, although this fish is seldom found in brackish or marine waters. It favors shallow, weedy environs and the sluggish pools and backwaters of large rivers and can survive in hot and stagnant waters. Alligator gar*

The alligator gar is the largest member of the gar family, Lepisosteidae, and one of North America's largest inland fish. It is a primitive species, dating from the Mesozoic era, 65 to 230 million years ago. Fossil remains of gar are often found in limestone quarries throughout the southern United States. The tough, armorlike scales of this species were once used by Indians as arrowheads, and pioneer farmers covered their wooden plowshares with gar hides.

The gar is a resilient fish with an adaptable specialized air bladder that enables it to take in air at the surface, allowing it to survive in the poorest water conditions. Holding a strong resemblance to its namesake, the alligator gar is strong and voracious, and a tough fighter when hooked. It is capable of jumping spectacularly.

The alligator gar has been under siege for most of the twentieth century, eagerly sought and killed. Efforts to eradicate them existed in many of their natural habitats under the ill-advised notion of ridding the waters of gamefish-killing monsters. Many huge fish, including specimens from 100 pounds to more than 300 pounds, were removed by commercial netters, anglers using big-game tackle, and others using steel-tipped arrows while bowfishing. Although their numbers are drastically reduced today, alligator gar are not classified as gamefish by most state fisheries agencies and are not regulated as to size or manner of fishing. There is virtually no concerted sportfishing for this species today.

Identification. The alligator gar's body is long and cylindrical, covered with heavy, ganoid (diamond-shaped) scales. The snout is short and broad like an alligator's, and there are two rows of teeth on either side of the upper jaw (other gar have only one). It has a single dorsal fin that is far back on the body above the anal fin and just before the tail. The tail is rounded, and the pectoral, ventral, and anal fins

Gar, Alligator (continued)

are evenly spaced on the lower half of the body. Its coloring is olive or greenish brown above and lighter below. The sides are mottled with large black spots.

These and other gar are often mistaken for floating logs. The alligator gar can be distinguished from all other gar by the two rows of teeth in the upper jaw, its broader snout, and its large size when fully grown. The alligator gar most closely resembles members of the pike family in body shape and fin placement, although the tail of this fish is forked, not rounded.

are often seen floating at the surface. They occasionally come to the surface layer to expel gases and to take air into their swim bladders.

Size. The alligator gar is the giant of the gar family. It still attains weights in excess of 100 pounds, although such fish are not common; larger fish are occasionally captured in commercial fishing nets. The maximum size of alligator gar is not certain, although the figure evidently exceeds 300 pounds, and they can reach more than 10 feet in length. The all-tackle rod-and-reel record is a 279-pound fish captured in the Rio Grande River in Texas in 1951. There are reports, however, of larger fish. A 190-pounder caught in a net in Arkansas in 1997 was 7 feet, 11 inches long.

Spawning behavior. Spawning occurs in the spring and the early summer in shallow bays and sloughs. The female lays dark green eggs that stick to vegetation and rocks until they hatch in 6 to 8 days. The female is capable of producing as many as 77,000 eggs at once. The young are solitary and float at the surface like sticks.

Food. Although the alligator gar is infamous for eating almost anything, from dead animals to ducks and popular gamefish, studies have revealed that most of its diet consists of gizzard shad, threadfin shad, golden shiners, and rough or coarse fish species.

Gar, Florida

Lepisosteus platyrhincus

Distribution. *The Florida gar ranges throughout peninsular Florida and into the Panhandle as far as the Apalachicola River drainage, where there is evidence that it hybridizes with the spotted gar. The Florida gar also occurs throughout part of southern Georgia to the Savannah River drainage.*

Habitat. *The Florida gar is common in medium to large lowland streams and lakes with mud or sand bottoms and an abundance of underwater vegetation. It is also abundant in canals. Gar can be found resting both on the bottom or at the surface. They live in freshwater but can survive in stagnant water that is intolerable to most other fish.*

The Florida gar is a member of the Lepisosteidae family, an ancient group of predaceous fish once in abundance and widely distributed. Its specialized air bladder enables the gar to take in air at the surface, allowing it to survive in the poorest waters. Although edible, Florida gar are unpopular as food. They are caught by anglers, although not extensively pursued. The roe is highly toxic to humans, animals, and birds.

Identification. The body of the Florida gar is cigar-shaped, and it has a broad, tooth-filled snout. The single dorsal fin is located directly above the anal fin. Its tough scales form a bricklike pattern. Like the spotted gar, it has spots on top of the head, as well as over the entire body and on all the fins. These spots sometimes run together to form stripes.

The Florida and the spotted gar can be distinguished from each other mainly by the distance from the front of the eye to the back of the gill cover. In the Florida gar, it is less than two-thirds the length of the snout; in the spotted gar, it is more than two-thirds the length of the snout. The Florida gar can be distinguished from the longnose gar—the only other gar occurring in the Florida's range—by the absence of spots on its head and by the elongated beak of the longnose.

Size. The average size rarely exceeds 2 feet. The all-tackle record is 10 pounds.

Spawning behavior. The spawning season is from May through July in backwaters and sloughs. A female can lay up to 6,000 eggs at once. Florida gar often travel in groups of 2 to 10 or more.

Food. Forage and coarse fish make up much of the adult gar's diet, although it also consumes shrimp, insects, crayfish, and scuds.

Gar, Longnose

Lepisosteus osseus

The longnose gar is the most common and widely distributed member of the gar family, Lepisosteidae, one of the few remaining ancient groups of predaceous fish once in abundance. Its long endurance is due to a specialized air bladder that enables the gar to take in air at the surface, allowing it to survive in the poorest waters.

Identification. The body of the longnose gar is long and slender. It has an extended narrow beak (18 to 20 times as long as it is wide at its narrowest point). The skeleton is part cartilage and part bone. Both upper and lower jaws are lined with strong, sharp teeth. The nostrils are located in a small, bulbous, fleshy growth at the very tip of the beak.

The body is covered with bony, ganoid (diamond-shaped) scales. The dorsal and the anal fins are set far back. Its coloring is olive brown or deep green along the back and the upper sides, with a silver white belly. There are numerous black spots on the body, although not on the head or the jaws. The longnose gar can be distinguished from other gar by its elongated snout.

Size. The average fish is 2 to 3 feet in length but occasionally reaches 5 feet. The all-tackle record is 50 pounds, 5 ounces.

Life history/Behavior. Groups of adult gar often lie motionless at the surface, strongly resembling floating sticks. In the summer, they will roll over and break the surface to gulp air (usually in extremely murky water) and release gases from their air bladders. Males mature when they are 3 or 4 years old, females at 6 years old. The spawning season is in the spring in shallow water.

Food and feeding habits. Longnose gar feed on shiners, sunfish, gizzard shad, catfish, and bullhead. They sometimes slowly stalk their prey but are generally known to lie in wait for it to come close.

OTHER NAMES

French: *garpique longnez;* Spanish: *gaspar picudo.*

Distribution. *The longnose gar is the most common and widely distributed of all gar. It is primarily found throughout the eastern half of North America, within the Mississippi River system and other drainages. Its range generally encompasses an area from Minnesota and the Great Lakes to Quebec, southward to southern Florida and the Gulf states, and westward to the Rio Grande bordering Texas and Mexico. It may reach as far as Montana in the north and the Pecos River in New Mexico to the south. Large concentrations exist along the Atlantic coast.*

Habitat. *Longnose gar inhabit warm, quiet water, frequenting shallow weedy areas and the sluggish pools, backwaters, and oxbows of large and medium rivers and lakes. They occasionally enter brackish water and can tolerate murky and stagnant environments.*

Gar, Shortnose

Lepisosteus platostomus

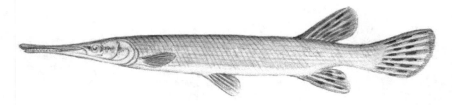

Distribution. *The short-nose gar occurs from the Great Lakes south to the Gulf of Mexico but is essentially limited to the low-gradient portions of the Mississippi River basin. In the United States, it is found from northern Alabama to Oklahoma and down through Louisiana to the Gulf of Mexico. In the north, it has a broad range in the river systems that feed the Mississippi, from southern Ohio to Montana.*

Habitat. *This species is common in quiet water, including the pools and backwater areas of creeks and small to large rivers, and in swamps, lakes, and oxbows, often near vegetation. The shortnose gar is even more tolerant of muddy water than are other gar, and it prefers warm water.*

The shortnose gar is the smallest member of an ancient family, Lepisosteidae, of predaceous fish. It is the most tolerant of all the gar, as it is capable of withstanding murky and brackish water with the help of its specialized air bladder. The bladder allows the gar to gulp in supplementary air and to release gases.

Because large numbers of coarse fish and panfish exist in many waters inhabited by gar, the shortnose gar (as well as other gar) can be useful in controlling these populations. In some areas, however, it is considered a nuisance by anglers and sometimes even a problem because of its abundance.

The shortnose gar has good sporting virtues but is not widely pursued. It is often caught incidentally by anglers pursuing other fish. It is not considered a good food fish, and its roe is toxic.

Identification. The body is long and cylindrical, covered with ganoid (diamond-shaped) scales. There is a single row of teeth in the upper jaw, compared with the alligator gar's two rows. It has a short, broad snout. Unlike its relatives the Florida gar and the spotted gar, it has no spots on its head, but it does have spots on its dorsal, anal, and caudal fins.

Size. The shortnose gar rarely exceeds 2½ feet in length. The all-tackle world record is a 5-pound, 12-ounce fish caught in 1995 in Illinois.

Spawning behavior. Spawning occurs in the spring in shallow bays and sloughs. The eggs attach to weeds or other objects.

Food. The diet of the shortnose gar is similar to that of other gar; forage and rough fish comprise the bulk of its food.

Gar, Spotted

Lepisosteus oculatus

The spotted gar is a member of an ancient family, Lepisosteidae, of predaceous fish. It is often confused with its close relative, the Florida gar. The spotted gar has good sporting virtues but is not widely pursued, and it is often caught incidental to other fishing activities. It is not considered a good food fish, and its roe is toxic to humans but not to other fish.

Identification. The body of the spotted gar is long and cylindrical, covered with hard, ganoid (diamond-shaped) scales. It has a single row of teeth in each jaw. The spotted and the Florida gar are the only two gar that have spots on the top of the head, as well as over the entire body and on the fins. The spots on other gar are limited to the fins and the posterior portions of the body, usually after the pelvic (ventral) fins. The two are generally distinguished by the distance between the front of the eye and the rear edge of the gill cover. If the distance is less than two-thirds the length of the snout, it is a Florida gar; if it is more than two-thirds the length of the snout, it is a spotted gar.

Size. The spotted gar rarely exceeds 3 feet and averages 2½ feet. The all-tackle world record is a 9-pound, 12-ounce fish caught in Texas in 1994.

Life history/Behavior. Like other gar, this species is often observed basking on the surface on warm days, resembling a floating log. It occasionally breaks the surface and gulps air from its specialized bladder. Spawning occurs in the spring in grassy sloughs.

OTHER NAMES
French: *garpique tachetée;* Spanish: *gaspar pintado.*

Distribution. *The spotted gar ranges from the Great Lakes to the Gulf of Mexico and down through the Mississippi River drainage system. It occurs all along the Gulf Coast from central Texas to the western portion of the Florida Panhandle. In the north of its range, it occurs eastward to the north and south shores of Lake Erie in northern Ohio, Michigan, and Ontario, but it seldom occurs much west of Illinois.*

Habitat. *The spotted gar is common in the pools and backwaters of creeks and small to large rivers and in swamps, lakes, and oxbows, often near vegetation. It occasionally enters brackish water and is highly tolerant of warm, stagnant water.*

Goldeye

Hiodon alosoides

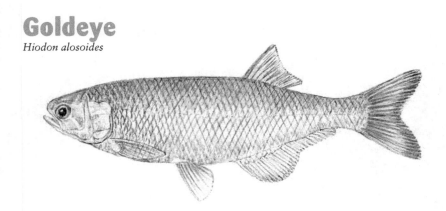

OTHER NAMES

Winnipeg goldeye, western goldeye, shad mooneye, toothed herring, yellow herring; French: *la queche, laquaiche aux yeux d'or.*

Distribution. *Endemic to North America, goldeye are found in both Canadian and American waters. They occur from western Ontario to the Mackenzie River at Aklavik in the north, from below the Great Lakes south throughout the Ohio and Mississippi River drainages on the east, and from western Alberta throughout eastern Montana and Wyoming to Oklahoma on the west. Lake Winnipeg in Manitoba has historically been the largest commercial producer of these fish.*

Habitat. *Throughout their geographical range, goldeye are most often found in warm, silty sections of large rivers and in the backwaters of shallow lakes connected to them.*

A member of the Hiodontidae family of mooneye, the gold-eye is one of Canada's most celebrated freshwater fish, from an epicurean viewpoint. Although often called a herring or a shad, it is neither. The goldeye provides good sport for light-tackle anglers, but it is not pursued in many parts of its range.

Identification. The goldeye is a small fish whose compressed body is deep in proportion to its length and is covered with large, loose scales. Dark blue to blue green over the back, it is silvery on the sides, tapering to white on the belly. It has a small head and a short, bluntly rounded snout with a small terminal mouth containing many sharp teeth on the jaws and the tongue.

The color of its eyes and the position of its anal fin distinguish it from the mooneye. The irises of the large eyes are gold and reflect light. The goldeye's dorsal fin begins opposite or behind its anal fin (the mooneye's begins before the anal fin). The goldeye can be distinguished from the gizzard shad by the absence of a dorsal fin ray projection.

Size/Age. Adults average from 10 ounces to slightly more than a pound in weight and seldom exceed 2 pounds in most waters. They can grow to 5 pounds. The Manitoba record is a 5.06-pound fish from the Nelson River. They reportedly can live for 14 years.

Spawning behavior. In the spring, mature goldeye move into pools in rivers or backwater lakes of rivers, to spawn when the water temperature is between 50° and 56°F.

Food and feeding habits. Goldeye feed on a variety of organisms, from microscopic plankton to insects and fish. They do most of their foraging on or near the surface and predominantly on insects, although they will eat minnows and small frogs.

Grayling, Arctic

Thymallus arcticus

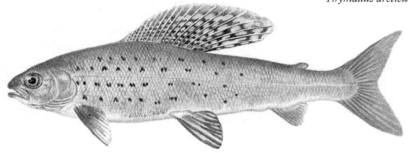

Grayling belong to the Salmonidae family and are related to trout and whitefish. They are distinctive-looking fish, with a sail-like dorsal fin, and are a superb sportfish known primarily in the cool- and coldwater northern regions of North America. Their firm, white flesh is good table fare, although it is not on a par with that of the wild trout and the charr that inhabit similar ranges. Grayling are excellent when smoked, however.

Identification. With its graceful lines, large fin, and dramatic coloration, the grayling is a striking fish. Most striking is its large purple to black dorsal fin, which extends backward and fans out into a trailing lobe, speckled with rows of spots. This fin may look bluish when the fish is in the water. Grayish silver overall, grayling usually have shades or highlights of gold, lavender, or both, as well as many dark spots that may be shaped like an X or a V on some fish.

Young arctic grayling can be distinguished from similar-looking young whitefish by narrow vertical parr marks (whitefish have round parr marks, if any). When the arctic grayling is taken from the water, a resemblance to the whitefish is especially apparent, as the beautiful colors fade to a dull gray. It has a small, narrow mouth with numerous small teeth in both jaws. The arctic grayling also has a forked caudal fin and relatively large, stiff scales.

Size. A small fish, with maximum lengths to 30 inches, the grayling can reach a maximum weight of about 6 pounds. The all-tackle world record for arctic grayling is a 5-pound, 15-ounce fish from the Northwest Territories in Canada, but any arctic grayling exceeding 3 pounds is considered large, and a 4-pounder is a trophy.

Life history/Behavior. Adult grayling spawn from April through June in rocky creeks; fish from lakes enter tributaries to spawn. Instead of making nests, they scatter their

OTHER NAMES

American grayling, arctic trout, Back's grayling, bluefish, grayling, sailfin arctic grayling; French: *ombre artique, poisson bleu.*

Distribution. *Arctic grayling are widespread in arctic drainages from Hudson Bay to Alaska and throughout central Alberta and British Columbia, as well as in the upper Missouri River drainage in Montana. Previously known to inhabit some of the rivers feeding Lakes Huron, Michigan, and Superior in northern Michigan, arctic grayling have been considered extinct there since 1936. They have been widely introduced elsewhere, especially in the western United States.*

Habitat. *Grayling prefer the clear, cold, well-oxygenated waters of medium to large rivers and lakes. They are most commonly found in rivers, especially in eddies, and the heads of runs and pools; in lakes, they prefer river mouths and rocky*

Grayling, Arctic **125**

shorelines. They commonly seek refuge among small rocks on the streambed or lake bottom.

eggs over gravel and rely on the action of the water to cover the eggs with a protective coating. The eggs hatch in 13 to 18 days. Grayling are gregarious and flourish in schools of moderate numbers of their own kind. Arctic grayling of northern Canada may be especially abundant in selected areas of rivers.

Food and feeding habits. Young grayling initially feed on zooplankton and become mainly insectivorous as adults, although they also eat small fish, fish eggs, and, less often, lemmings and planktonic crustaceans.

Herring

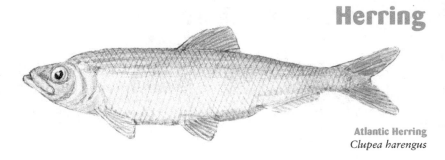

Atlantic Herring
Clupea harengus

Herring and their relatives are among the most important of commercial fish worldwide. They are also extremely important as forage fish for a wide variety of predatory fish, sea birds, seals, and other carnivores. In the past, some countries depended entirely on herring (or related species) fishery for their economic survival. Wars have been waged over the rights to particularly productive herring grounds, which are found in all seas except the very cold waters of the Arctic and the Antarctic.

Most members of the herring family are strictly marine. Some are anadromous and spawn in freshwater, and a few species (those of freshwater origin) never go to sea. Herring typically travel in extensive schools; in the ocean, such schools may extend for miles, which makes harvesting possible in great quantities.

Herring are plankton feeders, screening their food through numerous gill rakers. As such, and because they are generally small, herring are seldom a deliberate quarry of recreational anglers (American and hickory shad are notable exceptions). They are primarily used as bait, either in pieces or whole, by freshwater and saltwater anglers for various game species.

Prominent species with the herring name include Atlantic herring, Pacific herring, blueback herring, and skipjack herring. At least two members of the herring family, alewife and blueback herring, are collectively referred to as river herring.

There is minor angling effort for some species, such as blueback and skipjack herring, when they ascend coastal rivers en masse to spawn; this fishery is generally geared more toward procuring food or bait than to pure angling sport. They may, however, be caught on light spoons and small jigs or flies. When massed, they are taken by snagging (where legal) and in cast nets as well. Coastal herring are sometimes also caught, snagged, or taken by a cast net, mainly for use as bait.

American Shad

Alewife

Atlantic Herring

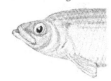

Threadfin Shad

Members of the herring family have a wide lower jaw that curves, a short upper jaw that reaches only to below the middle of the eye, and a cheek that is longer than it is deep.

Hogsucker, Northern

Hypentelium nigricans

OTHER NAMES

sucker, hog sucker.

Range. *The northern hogsucker is widely distributed across central and eastern North America, occurring in the Great Lakes, Mississippi, Ohio, and some Atlantic drainages.*

Habitat. *The northern hogsucker inhabits primarily large streams and small rivers. It is usually found in areas with high water quality and clean substrate, free of heavy siltation. It is well suited to a benthic lifestyle, remaining close to the bottom in areas of various depths and flow velocities. Adults may inhabit deep pools and runs, as they are too large to be preyed upon by bass and other predators. The young and the subadults live in faster water and in the stream margins.*

This is a widespread and distinctive-looking member of the sucker family.

Identification. The northern hogsucker gets its name from its piglike appearance, particularly its head. It has a very steep forehead and long, protruding lips, bearing a strong likeness to a pig's snout. Its head also has a concave depression between the eyes, a trait distinctive among suckers. The body is conical, with the head region much thicker than the caudal peduncle. The body is marked with four lateral bars that come together on the fish's back to form saddles. The northern hogsucker is generally darkly pigmented on the back and lightly pigmented on the belly.

Food. Like most suckers, the northern hogsucker preys upon many varieties of benthic organisms, the most common of which are insect larvae, small crustaceans, detritus, and algae. It feeds by disturbing the stream bottom with its large snout and sucking up organisms that it dislodges. It can often be seen with its body angled upward, tail high, nearly perpendicular to the stream bottom as it forages around larger rocks. Its small air bladder and large pectoral fins help support it in the current while feeding.

Size/Age. The northern hogsucker is a medium-size sucker, reaching up to 12 to 14 inches in length. Sexual maturity is reached between 2 and 3 years old, although most fish do not spawn until age 4. The northern hogsucker may live for 8 years.

Spawning behavior. Northern hogsuckers spawn in mid- to late spring as the water begins to warm. They do not make long upstream migrations, as many suckers do, but spawn in pool tails, riffles, and stream margins near where they reside. Like most suckers, northern hogsuckers require clean gravel substrate for successful reproduction.

Inconnu
Stenodus leucichthys

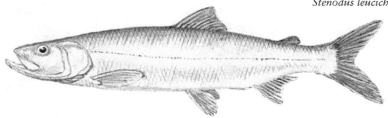

A member of the Salmonidae family and a relative of white-fish and cisco, the inconnu is a species with limited northern range. The only predatory member of the whitefish group in North America, it is highly favored by anglers as an exciting and large sportfish, but it is perhaps the least caught of North American gamefish. Its silvery coloring and tendency to leap high out of the water when hooked have earned it the nickname "Eskimo tarpon."

Identification. The general body shape of the inconnu is very similar to that of a charr or a whitefish, but the head is relatively long, pointed, and depressed on the top. Its mouth is large, and the lower jaw clearly projects outward beyond the upper jaw. The maxillary, or upper jaw bone, extends back at least as far as the middle of the eye. Small, fine teeth are found on the anterior part of the lower jaw, and on the tongue, the premaxillaries, the head of the maxillaries, the vomer, and the palatines (bones of the roof of the mouth). The tail is distinctly forked. Sheefish have large scales, a dark lateral line, and, like all salmonids, an adipose fin.

Size/Age. Inconnu are said to grow to 60 pounds. The all-tackle world record is a 53-pounder from Alaska. The largest fish may be between 25 and 35 years old.

Life history/Behavior. Spawning takes place in the late summer and the early fall, when inconnu ascend freshwater tributaries. Inland inconnu leave lakes and run up tributaries as well. In coastal regions, inconnu migrate from estuaries to river mouths after ice out, then ascend freshwater tributaries; this migration may last a few weeks in short-length rivers or months in longer ones. After spawning, they do not die but quickly migrate downstream.

Food and feeding habits. This species feeds mostly on small fish. Salmon smolts, cisco, smelt, and whitefish are among the common forage, and in coastal areas large schools of inconnu will fatten on baitfish prior to their spawning migration.

OTHER NAMES
sheefish, connie, Eskimo tarpon; Russian: *beloribitsa*.

Distribution. *In North America, inconnu are found in Alaska, from the Kuskokwim River (Bering Sea drainage) north, throughout the Yukon River in Canada, in the Mackenzie River, in Great Bear and Great Slave Lakes in Canada's Northwest Territories as far as the Anderson River near Cape Bathurst, and in isolated areas of extreme northern British Columbia. The largest North American fish occur in the vicinity of Selawik to Kotzebue, where tributaries enter into Hotham Inlet and Kotzebue Sound. In Asia, inconnu occur westward as far as the White Sea, and an isolated population inhabits the Caspian Sea and its drainage.*

Habitat. *Although generally viewed as a freshwater species, the inconnu occurs in strictly freshwater lakes and rivers and also in anadromous sea-run forms that winter in brackish deltas, bays, and tidewater areas and ascend coastal tributaries to spawn. It evidently evolved from purely freshwater fish to estuarine-anadromous fish.*

Ladyfish
Elops saurus

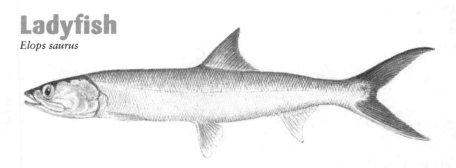

Habitat. *Ladyfish are inshore species that prefer bays and estuaries, lagoons, mangrove areas, tidal pools, and canals. They occasionally enter freshwater and are rarely found on coral reefs.*

Ladyfish are members of the small Elopidae family and are related to tarpon. They are similar in appearance to tarpon, although far smaller. Ladyfish are excellent light-tackle sportfish, commonly found in schools prowling shallow nearshore and brackish waters.

There are at least six species of ladyfish in the genus *Elops*, all of which are similar in average size, behavior, and characteristics. In the western Atlantic, the ladyfish (*E. saurus*) ranges from Cape Cod and Bermuda to the northern Gulf of Mexico and southern Brazil, although it is most common in Florida and the Caribbean. It is also known as tenpounder, as *ubarana* in Portuguese, and as *malacho* in Spanish.

In the eastern Pacific, the Pacific ladyfish (*E. affinis*) occurs from Southern California to Peru, although it is rare in northern Baja California. It is also known as machete and as *chiro* and *malacho del Pacifico* in Spanish.

Identification. The ladyfish has an elongated, slender silvery body with a blue-green back and small scales. It looks very much like a juvenile tarpon, although it can be distinguished from a tarpon by the lack of an elongated last ray on the dorsal fin. Its head is small and pointed, the mouth is terminal, and the tail is deeply forked.

Size. Some species of ladyfish may reach weights from 15 to 24 pounds and a length of 3 feet; such specimens are extremely rare, and in general these fish most commonly weigh 2 to 3 pounds. The all-tackle world record is a 5-pound, 14-ounce specimen.

Life history. These fish form large schools close to shore, although they are known to spawn offshore. Their ribbon-like larvae are very similar to those of bonefish and tarpon.

Food and feeding habits. Adults feed predominantly on fish and crustaceans. Ladyfish schools are often seen pursuing bait at the surface.

Lamprey

Sea Lamprey
Petromyzon marinus

Lampreys are one of two groups of jawless fish (the other being hagfish), which are the most primitive true vertebrates. They are members of the Petromyzontidae family. Jawless fish are fishlike vertebrates that resemble eels in form, with a cartilaginous or fibrous skeleton that has no bones. They have no paired limbs and no developed jaws or bony teeth. Their extremely slimy skin lacks scales. Fossils of lampreys have been dated back 280 million years.

The jawless, eel-like lampreys are just as ugly as their hagfish cousins in form and feeding habits; they differ in other respects, however. Hagfish are strictly marine, whereas lampreys are either totally freshwater inhabitants or, if they live in the sea, they return to freshwater rivers to spawn.

Lampreys have a large sucking disk for a mouth and a well-developed olfactory system. The mouth is filled with horny, sharp teeth that surround a filelike tongue. A lamprey's body has smooth, scaleless skin; two dorsal fins; no lateral line; no vertebrae; no swim bladder; and no paired fins. The lamprey has no prominent barbels on its snout; its eyes are well developed in the adult and visible externally; there are seven external gill openings on each side; and the nasal opening is on the upper part of the head.

Lampreys are usually parasitic. The lamprey attaches itself to the side of a live fish by using its suctorial mouth; then, by means of its horny teeth, it rasps through the victim's skin and scales and sucks the blood and body juices.

Lampreys spawn in the spring. They ascend streams where the bottom is stony or pebbly and build shallow depressions by moving stones with the aid of their suctorial mouths. Usually, the male and the female cooperate in constructing the nest. When ready to spawn, the pair stirs up the sand with vigorous body movements as the milt and the eggs are deposited at the same time. The eggs stick to particles of sand and sink to the bottom of the nest. The pair then separates and begins another nest directly above the first, thereby loosening more sand and pebbles, which flow down with the current and cover the eggs. The

OTHER NAMES

lamprey eel, stone sucker, nannie nine eyes (U.K.); Danish: *havlampret;* Dutch: *zeeprik;* Finnish: *merinahki- ainen;* French: *lamproie marine;* Italian: *lamprea di mar;* Norwegian: *havnioye;* Portuguese: *lampreia do mar;* Russian: *morskaja minoja;* Spanish: *lamprea de mar.*

procedure is repeated at short intervals until spawning is completed. Adults die after spawning.

After several days the young appear and drift downstream until they are deposited in a quiet stretch of water, where they settle down and burrow into the bottom to spend several years as larvae (called ammocetes). When they reach a few inches in length (this varies with the species), the ammocetes transform during the late summer or the fall into adultlike lampreys, complete with sucking disks and circular rows of horny teeth.

The sea lamprey is most notorious as a despoiler of valued sport and commercial fish. It ranges the western Atlantic from southern Greenland, Labrador, and the Gulf of St. Lawrence south to the Gulf of Mexico in Florida. It is landlocked in the Great Lakes, the Finger Lakes, Oneida Lake, and Lake Champlain. It breeds exclusively in freshwater.

Young lampreys, when in saltwater or en route to saltwater, are white underneath and blackish blue, silvery, or lead-colored above. Large specimens approaching maturity are usually mottled brown or dressed in different shades of yellow brown and various hues of green, red, or blue. Sometimes they appear black when the dark patches blend with each other. The ventral surface may be white, grayish, or a lighter shade of the ground color of the dorsal surface. Colors intensify during the breeding season.

Mature sea lampreys are from 2 to 2½ feet long. The maximum recorded length is nearly 4 feet, and the maximum weight 5.4 pounds.

Commonly, but erroneously, lampreys are known or referred to as "lamprey eels." They are not true eels *(see Eel, American)* of the family Anguillidae. For easy differentiation, eels possess jaws and pectoral fins; these are lacking in the lamprey.

Madtoms

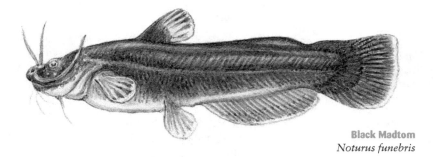

Black Madtom
Noturus funebris

Madtoms are members of the catfish *(see)* family, Ictaluridae, often referred to as bullhead catfish. Although the larger members of the catfish family have gained notoriety as sportfish, commercial fish, or food fish, the secretive and diminutive madtom escapes public attention.

These are little-known fish with interesting lifestyles. Madtoms are important links in the food webs of many streams, making it possible for large predators such as bass, wading birds, and water snakes to benefit from the stream's vast energy, represented by larval insect production. They are also a unique natural resource to North America's small streams and are endemic to the continent north of Mexico. The 40 species belonging to the family Ictaluridae occur naturally in the United States and Canada, and 27 are madtoms.

Like other members of the Ictaluridae family, madtoms possess stinging venom in their dorsal and pectoral spines. The venom originates from cells of the skin sheath over the pectoral fin. The toxicity of the venom varies but approximates that of a bee sting, although every person reacts differently to being stung.

Identification/Size. The madtom is recognized by its unique adipose fin. A non-madtom catfish has a fleshy fin protruding from its back, just ahead of the caudal fin. The adipose fin of a madtom is continuous with the caudal fin.

Madtoms belong to the genus *Noturus*, which is divided into three subgenera, *Noturus*, *Schilbeodes*, and *Rabida*, each with its own distinct appearance. The *Schilbeodes* are dull colored, generally brown or yellow brown. Those in *Rabida* have colorful markings with many bands and saddlelike pigmentation. There is only one species in the subgenus *Noturus*, the stonecat (*Noturus flavus*). The stonecat possesses the plain appearance of the *Schilbeodes*; however, no other madtoms match this species in size.

Habitat. Most anglers are probably unfamiliar with madtoms because they tend to be nocturnal, hiding under rocks, logs, and undercut banks during the day. Also, their body markings and color patterns (or lack of, depending on their preferred habitats) help camouflage them from the peering eyes of birds, water snakes, and anglers. Most madtoms prefer the cool, clear water of smaller streams, but some species are adapted to living in lakes, large streams, or muddy rivers. Where aquatic vegetation and beaver dams exist, madtoms take full advantage of their numerous niches.

Most madtoms have strong habitat preferences and thus use unique habitats. The stonecat primarily inhabits small to large rivers with rubble or boulders and lakes with gravel bars. In contrast, the black madtom prefers vegetation over gravel or sand in the clear moving water of springs, creeks, and small rivers. The margined madtom prefers rocky riffles with fast-moving water in small and medium-size rivers. Different species are even known to prefer rocks of specific sizes for cover. Because madtoms are choosy about their homes, they often have problems dealing with the degradation of their preferred habitats.

Stonecats exceed 7 inches as adults and may reach 12 inches in some locations. Madtoms range from 2½ inches to 6½ inches.

Reproduction. Madtoms start spawning about mid-April and finish spawning in mid-July. As with most fish, the commencement of spawning and the length of the spawning season depend heavily on water temperature. Madtoms usually begin spawning after the water temperature has reached 64°F and stop spawning after the water temperature exceeds 81°F. During the spawning season, adults are sexually dimorphic, which means males look different from females.

Madtoms construct nests to rear their young and provide post-spawning protection. A nest consists of an area with a pebble or gravel substrate that has been cleared of silt and debris.

Most madtoms prefer to nest under rocks; however, the speckled madtom and others have been known to nest in discarded beverage cans or bottles.

Although madtoms are small fish, they have relatively fewer and larger eggs compared to species that do not exhibit parental care. Madtom eggs may be up to 0.2 inches in diameter; they are adhesive and stick to the substrate and each other. Generally, a short time after laying the eggs, the female leaves the nest and the parental duties to the male. Eggs hatch in 8 to 10 days, depending on water temperature. After approximately 21 days of parental care, the male parent will leave the young madtoms on their own.

Food. Madtoms are crepuscular feeders, which means they feed mostly at dusk and dawn. As insectivores, they primarily feed on a diet of midge larvae, mayfly larvae, caddisfly larvae, and crayfish. Most madtoms are not as picky about their food as about their housing and will eagerly devour any available prey. Madtoms generally consume smaller amounts of stonefly, beetle, black fly, dragonfly, alder fly, and fish fly larvae. An occasional small fish (such as lamprey larvae), a spider, or zooplankton have also been found in their stomachs. When placed together, large adult madtoms have consumed small juvenile madtoms of the same species.

Madtom, Brown
Noturus phaeus

The brown madtom is a widely distributed and relatively common member of the madtoms. This diminutive catfish may be used in bait fishing for bass and is prominent in moderate- to fast-flowing water.

Identification. The brown madtom is dull colored. The upper body possesses a chocolate brown or yellowish-brown tint. The ventral side is pale. Juvenile brown madtoms, especially those collected in complex leaf debris or vegetation, may be black. These fish will adjust the intensity of their body color to simulate shades of their surroundings. The upper lip of the brown madtom protrudes beyond that of the lower lip, and the rear of the pectoral spine has six sawlike teeth.

Size/Age. Male and female brown madtoms grow at the same rate, but males reach a larger overall length because they live longer. The largest individual collected to date was a male that measured 6 inches in total length. Females live at least 3 years, while males may live 4 or 5 years. The total length of a 3-year-old fish ranges from 3.9 to 5.1 inches.

Reproduction. Spawning, as determined in northern Mississippi research, takes place from May through July.

Food. Brown madtoms exhibit crepuscular feeding, with peak feeding activity following sunset and just before sunrise. The diet, similar to other madtoms, is primarily composed of midge larvae, caddisfly larvae, and crayfish.

Distribution. *The brown madtom has a fairly wide distribution covering the following areas: Mississippi River tributaries in Kentucky, Tennessee, Mississippi, and Alabama; Tennessee River tributaries in Tennessee and Alabama; the Gulf Slope in the Sabine River drainage of Louisiana; and Bayou Teche drainage in Louisiana. It has also been reported in the Ouachita River drainage in Arkansas, probably introduced with other baitfish. In areas where brown madtoms are collected, they are usually abundant.*

Habitat. *This species is usually abundant in springs and small streams where areas of vegetation exist, in accumulations of debris, and underneath undercut banks. Madtoms in one stream in northern Mississippi preferred undercut banks to all other types of cover. Brown madtoms can be found in moderate- to fast-flowing water over small gravel or coarse sand.*

Minnow

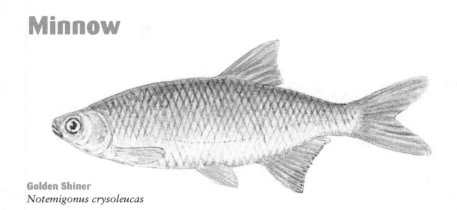

Golden Shiner
Notemigonus crysoleucas

Habitat. *The ecological habitats of minnows are as diverse as the family itself. Minnows occur in creeks, streams, rivers, swamps, ponds, lakes, and impoundments. Most minnow species, however, occur in flowing waters and do not fare well in impoundments.*

More than 2,000 species constitute the minnow, or Cyprinidae, family of freshwater fish, making it perhaps the largest family of fish. "Minnow," "shiner," and "dace" are three names commonly associated with members of this family, which also includes carp and chub.

Minnows comprise the largest family of freshwater fish in North America, having more than 300 different species. The greatest diversity in North America exists in the southeastern United States, but minnows are widely distributed from Alaska to southern Mexico and often represent a large proportion of species within regional fish faunas.

Well-known genera of native North American minnows include *Campostoma* (stonerollers), *Cyprinella* (satinfin shiners), *Gila* (Gila chub), *Luxilus* (highscale shiners), *Lythrurus* (smallscale shiners), *Nocomis* (chub), *Notropis* (true shiners), *Phoxinus* (redbelly dace), *Pimephales* (bluntnose minnows), *Ptychocheilus* (squawfish), and *Rhinichthys* (dace).

Identification. Minnows are characterized by a single dorsal fin, abdominally located pelvic fins, soft fin rays, cycloid scales, and a set of bones connecting the inner ear to the swim bladder. This last attribute, known as the Weberian apparatus, enhances minnows' ability to detect sound.

Minnows do not have teeth in their mouths but instead grind food with pharyngeal teeth located in their throats. Males of many minnow species have keratinized bumps known as tubercles on their heads, bodies, and fins. Tubercles may facilitate body contact during spawning, or they may be used in aggressive interactions between males. The large tubercles of chub and stonerollers have earned these species the nickname "hornyheads" among many anglers.

Food and feeding habits. Most species feed on aquatic insects, crustaceans, and detritus, but a few are specialized to feed on algae or plankton. Larger species, such as chub in the genus *Semotilus*, or squawfish, prey on other fish.

Size/Age. The body size and the life span of minnows vary widely. Adults of most minnow species are less than 100 millimeters long and live for 2 to 5 years. One of the smallest species is the blackmouth shiner *(Notropis melanostomus)*, which may not exceed 1.4 inches in length. At the opposite end of the spectrum is North America's largest native minnow, the Colorado squawfish *(Ptychocheilus lucius)*, which has been recorded to reach a total length of nearly 6 feet and a weight of 99 pounds. Minnows in this genus may live for more than 10 years.

Life history. Minnows exhibit a variety of life history attributes. The breeding season can be as short as 1 month or can last throughout the year. Many species reproduce between March and August, probably because warmer water temperatures are more conducive to the production of gametes and the survival of larvae. Accordingly, the length of the breeding season is generally longer for species occurring in lower latitudes. Substantial variation in reproductive behavior exists within the family.

Value. Minnows are extremely important ecologically. They transfer energy throughout aquatic ecosystems by converting their detrital, algal, and microorganismal diets into fish flesh that can be eaten by larger fish. They are also an important food source for birds and other wildlife. Minnows serve as hosts to freshwater mussel larvae (glochidia), which attach to fish gills in order to disperse and complete early development.

Nest-building minnows are sometimes referred to as "keystone species" because their presence has a strong effect on many other species in aquatic communities. Not only do their nests provide a spawning habitat for many other minnows, but the large number of eggs deposited in them may also be consumed by other species of fish and stream invertebrates.

Minnows are sought after and eaten by many anglers. In addition, they are used as bait and constitute a large proportion of the natural forage base upon which freshwater gamefish depend.

Almost all minnow species are suitable for use as bait. The golden shiner *(Notemigonus crysoluecas)* and the fathead minnow *(Pimephales promelas)* are widely sold as bait because they are easy to culture in large quantities.

Because of their abundance and the broad range of body sizes, minnows are important forage items for many game species. Given their wide distribution throughout North America, the introduction of nonnative forage fish is usually unnecessary and potentially harmful to native fish.

Minnow, Fathead

Pimephales promelas

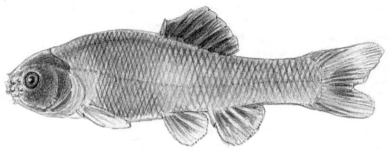

OTHER NAMES

minnow; French: *tête de boule.*

Distribution. *This species ranges widely (in part through introductions) across North America, from Quebec to the Northwest Territories and south to Alabama, Texas, and New Mexico, as well as in Mexico. It is most common in the Great Plains and scarce in mountainous regions.*

Habitat. *Fathead minnows prefer ponds and pools or slow-moving water in streams, creeks, and small rivers. They can tolerate muddy water and are occasionally found in roadside ditches.*

The fathead minnow is a small, hardy, and widely cultivated member of the Cyprinidae family of minnows that is commonly used as bait, and it is an important forage species for gamefish. It is also commonly used in toxicity studies.

Identification. The fathead minnow has a stubby, deep, compressed body with a short head that is flat on top. The snout is blunt. The mouth is small and slanted and possesses pharyngeal teeth. The body is generally dull in color, being dark olive or gray above and fading to muted yellow to white below. The scales become larger toward the tail and smaller toward the head, and the lateral line curves downward and is incomplete. There is a dark spot at the middle of the anterior dorsal rays, the caudal rays have dark outlines, and the leading edge of the pectoral fins is black. There is also a stout half-ray at the front of the dorsal fin. There are no barbels, but breeding males develop tubercles on their snouts and become darker.

Size/Age. Fathead minnows average 1½ to 3 inches long and grow to only 4 inches. Most die in their third year.

Spawning behavior. Fathead minnows have an extended spawning period, from late spring into summer. It commences when the water temperature exceeds 60°F. They are nest spawners, often creating nest sites under floating or suspended objects or beneath logs or stones, generally in 1 to 3 feet of water. Males create the nests, herd the females into them, and guard the nests until the eggs hatch; several females may deposit eggs in one nest site, and the adhesive eggs hatch in 6 to 9 days.

Food. The diet of fathead minnows is mostly algae, as well as bottom detritus, zooplankton, and insect larvae.

Mooneye
Hiodon tergisus

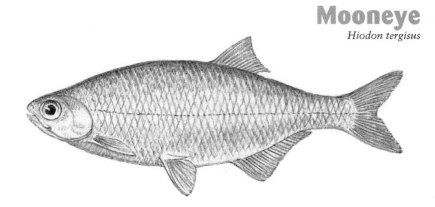

A member of the Hiodontidae family, the mooneye is a close relative and very similar in appearance to the better known goldeye *(see)*. It is most important as forage for assorted predator species. Its flesh is soft and bony and of no human food value, and it is not a target of anglers. Though often called a herring or a shad, it is neither.

Identification. The mooneye is a small fish whose compressed body is deep in proportion to its length and is covered with large, loose scales. Dark blue to blue green over the back, it is silvery on the sides and tapers to white on the belly. It has a small head and a short, bluntly rounded snout with a small terminal mouth, containing many sharp teeth on the jaws and the tongue.

The color of its eyes and the position of its anal fin distinguish it from the goldeye. The irises of the large eyes of the mooneye are silver colored (unlike the gold-colored irises of the goldeye). The mooneye's dorsal fin begins before the anal fin (the goldeye's begins opposite or behind its anal fin). The mooneye can be distinguished from the gizzard shad by not having a dorsal fin ray projection.

Size/Age. Mooneye are slightly larger on average than goldeye and are often found to be 2 pounds in weight, although their maximum attainable size is uncertain. They may live at least 10 years.

Spawning behavior. Mooneye spawn in the spring, moving up tributary rivers or streams.

Food. This species feeds on plankton, insects, and small fish. Small mooneye are preyed upon by large predators, including walleye, pike, catfish, and salmon.

Distribution. Endemic to North America, mooneye occur in the St. Lawrence-Great Lakes region (except Lake Superior), the Mississippi River drainage, and the Hudson Bay basin from Quebec to Alberta, and southward to the Gulf of Mexico. Mooneye are also present in Gulf Slope drainages from Mobile Bay, Alabama, to Lake Pontchartrain, Louisiana.

Habitat. Mooneye inhabit deep, warm, silty sections of medium and large rivers, the backwaters of shallow lakes connected to them, and impoundments.

Mosquitofish
Gambusia affinis affinis

The mosquitofish is a member of the large Poeciliidae family of livebearers, which is closely related to killifish or cyprinodonts, differing from them mainly in bringing forth its young alive, rather than laying eggs.

Also known as the North American topminnow or the western mosquitofish, this species is famous as the number-one scourge of mosquito larvae. Although there are other larvae-eating species of fish, the mosquitofish tolerates salinity and pollution levels that would kill most other species, and it produces up to 1,500 young in its lifetime.

Native to the southeastern United States, the mosquitofish has been introduced to suitable warm waters around the world since 1905, when it was experimentally introduced to Hawaii and virtually eliminated mosquitoes. As a result, *Gambusia affinis affinis* is the widest-ranging freshwater fish on earth (other species of mosquitofish have not been as successfully introduced). It has most recently been introduced in many places to help control West Nile virus.

Female mosquitofish are about 2 inches long, and the males are only half as large. The anal fin of the male is modified to form an intermittent organ for introducing sperm into the female. A mature female may produce three or four broods during one season, sometimes giving birth to 200 or more young at a time. This fish is easily raised in aquariums and is not sensitive to temperature variations, but it does not adjust well to living with other fish.

Although it has been highly effective at controlling malarial mosquitoes, the mosquitofish is not a panacea. Mosquitofish larvae cannot survive without water (as mosquito larvae can), they do not control mosquitoes in places with abundant surface vegetation to hide mosquito larvae, they may consume the young of forage and game species, and they can have adverse effects on indigenous fish species.

Mullet

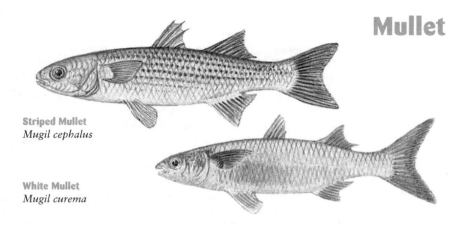

Striped Mullet
Mugil cephalus

White Mullet
Mugil curema

Mullet belong to the Mugilidae family, a group of roughly 70 species whose members range worldwide in shallow, warm seas. A few species live in freshwater and some are reared in ponds. All are good food fish, especially in smoked form, although smaller ones may be too bony to eat. Mullet roe is considered a delicacy. Mullet are important food fish for many predator species, and anglers use them alive or dead, in chunks or strips, as bait.

Identification. The striped mullet *(Mugil cephalus)* is bluish gray or green along the back, shading to silver on the sides, and white below. Also known as the black mullet, or fatback, it has indistinct horizontal black bars, or stripes, on its sides; the fins are lightly scaled at the base and unscaled above; the nose is blunt and the mouth small; and the second dorsal fin originates behind that of the anal fin. It is similar to the smaller fantail mullet *(M. gyrans)* and the white mullet *(M. curema),* both of which have black blotches at the base of their pectoral fins, a characteristic that is lacking in the striped mullet.

The fantail mullet has an olive-green back with a bluish tint, shading to silvery on the sides and white below. Its anal and pelvic fins are yellowish; there's a dark blotch at the base of the pectoral fin; the mouth has an inverted V-shape; and the second dorsal fin originates behind the anal fin.

The white mullet, also known as silver mullet, is bluish gray on the back, fading to silvery on the sides and white below. It lacks stripes; small scales extend onto its soft dorsal and anal fins; there's a dark blotch at the base of the pectoral fin; and the second dorsal fin originates behind the anal fin.

Size. The striped mullet may reach a length of 3 feet and weigh as much as 12 pounds, although the largest specimens have come from aquariums. Roe specimens in the

Distribution. The striped mullet is cosmopolitan in all warm seas worldwide and is the only member of the mullet family found off the Pacific coast of the United States. The fantail mullet occurs in the western Atlantic in Bermuda, and from Florida and the northern Gulf of Mexico to Brazil. The white mullet is found in the western Atlantic in Bermuda and from Massachusetts south to Brazil, including the Gulf of Mexico; in the eastern Atlantic from Gambia to the Congo; and in the eastern Pacific from the Gulf of California, Mexico, to Iquique, Chile.

wild are common to 3 pounds, but most striped mullet weigh closer to a pound. The fantail mullet is small and usually weighs less than a pound. The white mullet is similar in size to the fantail.

Life history/Behavior. Mullet are schooling fish found inshore in coastal environs. Many, but not all, species have the unusual habit of leaping from the water as they race along in schools. Some have stiff bodies when they jump and fall back into the water with a loud splat, which usually draws the attention of people nearby; most newcomers to mangrove coasts think these leaping fish are a sporting species or are being pursued by gamefish, although this is often not the case.

Theories abound as to why mullet jump: to escape predators, remove parasites, coordinate spawning migrations, aid respiration, and so forth. Some research has supported the respiration theory. Research on striped mullet showed that the fish uses the upper portion of the pharynx for aerial respiration, obtaining air by jumping or holding its head above the water. The research showed that the jumping frequency of this species seemed to be inversely related to dissolved oxygen concentration. The less oxygen, the more often the fish jumped.

Adult striped mullet migrate offshore in large schools to spawn; juveniles migrate inshore at about 1 inch in size, moving far up tidal creeks. Fantail mullet spawn in nearshore or inshore waters during the spring and the summer, and juveniles occur offshore. White mullet spawn offshore, and the young migrate into estuaries and along beaches.

Food and feeding habits. These mullet feed on algae, detritus, and other tiny marine forms; they pick up mud from the bottom and strain plant and animal material from it through their sievelike gill rakers and pharyngeal teeth. Indigestible materials are spit out. In most species, the stomach is gizzardlike for grinding food.

Muskellunge

Esox masquinongy

The muskellunge is the largest member of the Esocidae family of pike. Its name is derived from the native Indian word *maskinonge,* which has had numerous interpretations. Among them are deformed pike *(mashk kinonge);* ugly fish *(mas kinonge);* and large pike *(mas kenosha).* The muskellunge is strictly a North American species, native to central and eastern North America.

Identification. The muskellunge has an arrowlike body that is long and sleek. A single soft-rayed dorsal fin is located very far back near the tail. The pelvic fins are located relatively far back on the belly, about halfway between the pectoral fins and the tail, instead of directly under the pectoral fins. The mouth is large, with the maxillae reaching back at least to the middle of the eyes, and it is broad like a duck's bill but full of teeth.

The coloration and the markings on muskellunge are highly variable but usually consist of dark markings on a brownish or green background. There are numerous dark, vertical bars that may appear as vermiculations or spots, and sometimes the body has no markings. The northern pike, by comparison, has light-colored, oblong or kidney-shaped spots against a darker body, and the chain pickerel has a unique chainlike pattern on the sides, although the spaces between the "links" of the chain may be seen as large oblong spots, depending on one's point of view. The grass and the redfin pickerel look much more like the muskie in their markings, but they grow only to roughly 15 inches in length.

The muskie can also be distinguished from other *Esox* species by both cheeks and the gill cover, which are usually scaled only on the top half. In the pickerel, the cheeks and the gill cover are fully scaled; in the pike, the cheeks are fully scaled, but the gill cover is usually scaled only on the top half. Another distinction occurs in the number of pores under the lower jaw. In the muskie there are 6 to 9 pores along each side (rarely 5 or 10 on one side only). In the northern pike there are 5 along each side (rarely 3, 4, or 6 on one side only). In the pickerel, there are 4 along each side (occasionally 3 or 5 on one side only).

OTHER NAMES

maskinonge, muskallonge, mascalonge, muskie, musky, 'lunge, silver muskellunge, Great Lakes muskellunge, Ohio muskellunge, Allegheny River muskellunge, spotted muskellunge, barred muskellunge, great muskellunge, great pike, blue pike, and so on. Occasionally, it is referred to as a "jack" in some areas.

Distribution. *The muskellunge is endemic to eastern North America. It is native to the Great Lakes, Hudson Bay, and Mississippi River basins from southern Quebec to the Red River of the North in Manitoba and extends south in the Appalachians to Georgia and west to Iowa. It has been introduced (including the hybrid version) widely to Atlantic coast drainages as far as southern Virginia and elsewhere in the southern and western United States, although its representation in many of these areas is minor.*

Habitat. *Muskellunge live in medium to large rivers and in lakes of all sizes, although their preferred habitats are cool waters with large and small basins*

Muskellunge (continued)

or both deep and shallow areas. They are found in waters no more than 75 acres in size, as well as in enormous waters like Lake of the Woods, Ontario; Lake St. Clair, Michigan; or the St. Lawrence River.

They rarely venture far from cover and favor shallow, heavily vegetated waters less than 40 feet deep, but they sometimes inhabit deep water that lacks vegetation but offers ample prey.

Subtle distinctions differentiate the four variations in muskellunge coloration and marking.

Size/Age. Muskellunge are among the largest North American fish dwelling entirely in freshwater. The former all-tackle world record and current New York State record muskellunge is a 69-pound, 15-ounce fish that was caught in 1957 in the St. Lawrence River. Most muskellunge encountered by anglers weigh between 7 and 15 pounds and are less than 40 inches long; specimens exceeding 20 pounds are not uncommon, but it is hard to come by one weighing more than 30 pounds. They have been known to live between 25 and 30 years, and many fish live for 15 years, although the average life span is closer to 8 years.

Life history/Behavior. Muskies spawn in the spring in 1 to 3 feet of water, in shallow bays covered with vegetation. This occurs just after ice out, and when the water temperatures are between 49° and 59°F. They are broadcast spawners and disperse the fertilized eggs randomly. Their spawning season usually occurs after the northern pike's in areas where the two species coexist. Females grow larger than males at all ages, and both reach sexual maturity in 3 to 5 years.

Food and feeding habits. The muskie is a solitary fish that tends to stay in the same area, lurking opportunistically in thick weedbeds and waiting for prey. It is seldom a wandering, roaming fish, although it may migrate from deep to shallow environs to feed. Its diet is varied, with a preference for larger, rather than smaller, fish, as the muskie is well adapted to capturing and swallowing fish of considerable size. Yellow perch, suckers, golden shiners, and walleye are among its favorite foods, but it also consumes smallmouth bass and many other fish.

Muskellunge/Barred Variation
Dark markings, light background; pointed tail fin.

Muskellunge/Clear Variation
Light body; pointed tail fin.

Muskellunge/Spotted Variation
Dark markings, light background; pointed tail fin.

Tiger (Hybrid) Muskellunge
Dark markings, light background; rounded tail fin.

Muskellunge, Tiger

Esox masquinongy x Esox lucius

A member of the Esocidae family, the tiger muskellunge is a distinctively marked hybrid fish produced when true muskellunge *(E. masquinongy)* and northern pike *(Esox lucius)* interbreed. This occurs when the male of either species fertilizes the eggs of the female of the opposite species. This is not a common occurrence in the wild but has happened naturally in waters where both parent species occur, making it an unusual and prized catch.

The tiger muskie was believed to be a separate species until scientists succeeded in crossing a northern pike with a muskellunge, thereby discovering the tiger muskie's true origin. Deliberate crossbreeding of these species in hatcheries by fisheries managers is now much more common than is natural hybridization, and tiger muskies have been stocked in many waters where neither parent occurs naturally. Fish culturists prefer to cross a male northern pike with a female muskellunge because the eggs of the muskie are less adhesive and don't clump as badly in the hatching process.

Populations of introduced tiger muskies are naturally self-limiting because this hybrid is sterile and cannot reproduce itself. Its numbers can therefore be controlled over time. It also grows quickly and is aggressive, making it an excellent catch for anglers.

The tiger muskie has a distinctive look and should not be confused with the true muskellunge, which has been called a tiger muskie in some areas. In most respects, notably in size and appearance, the hybrid is very much like the true muskellunge, and anglers hold the naturally occurring hybrid in higher esteem than the true muskie because of its rarity, its beautiful markings, and its game nature. The true muskie may have either bars or spots on the sides or no markings at all, but it is rarely as strikingly beautiful as the tiger muskie, which has dark, wavering tigerlike stripes or bars, many of them broken, that are set against a lighter background.

OTHER NAMES

tiger muskie, norlunge, nor'lunge, hybrid muskellunge.

As is true with many hybrid fish, the body of the tiger muskie is slightly deeper than that of either comparable-length parent. The cheeks and jaws are usually spotted, with 10 to 16 pores existing on the underside of the jaws. The tips of the tail are more rounded than in the true muskie, and the fins have distinct spots. In very large specimens, the fins, especially the tail fins, appear to be much larger than for a comparable true muskie.

Naturally occurring tiger muskies in excess of 30 pounds are extremely rare, and most have come from Wisconsin lakes. A 51-pound, 3-ounce fish, caught in 1919 at Lac Vieux Desert on the Wisconsin/Michigan border, is the all-tackle world-record tiger muskie. For a time, it was thought to be a true muskellunge and thus held the world record for that species.

Methods of fishing for tiger muskies are no different than those for true muskies. Naturally occurring tiger muskies are caught incidentally by anglers fishing for true muskellunge or other fish species. Introduced muskies are caught as both targeted and incidental catches. Most are released alive, particularly those of natural origin.

Paddlefish

Polyodon spathula

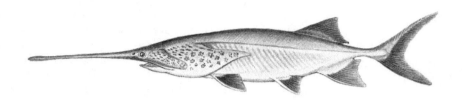

Members of the primitive Polyodontidae family of bony fish, paddlefish are distant relatives of sturgeon, whose closest living relatives are gar *(see)* and bowfin. They are large, slow-maturing, and long-lived freshwater fish of large inland rivers. They have a distinctive appearance and a prehistoric lineage that dates back hundreds of millions of years. They are not related to catfish.

There are only two known species of paddlefish. The American species *(P. spathula),* which is profiled here, is commonly referred to simply as paddlefish, lives only in the United States in the Mississippi River system and is a threatened species, although it is pursued in some areas by both commercial fishermen and recreational anglers. The other species is the Chinese paddlefish *(Psephurus gladius),* which is native to the Lower Yangtze River in China.

Paddlefish have been steadily declining in numbers, due to overexploitation in the late nineteenth and early twentieth centuries, habitat degradation (e.g., construction of dams, locks, and other migratory obstructions), and pollution. The life history of this species and its slow-maturing and intermittent spawning have contributed to its vulnerability to these activities. Paddlefish are protected in some states, and restricted fisheries exist in others. Populations of North American paddlefish that can sustain fishing pressure exist in only a few localities, and poaching is a continued threat. Poaching occurs for the purpose of securing eggs, which are substituted for sturgeon eggs and valuable when made into caviar.

Identification. The paddlefish is almost sharklike in appearance, and if its long paddle extension were cut off, it would look even more like a shark. Unlike sharks or other fish, the paddlefish has a unique, long, paddle- or spoonlike snout. The function of the snout has not been completely determined, although it is highly enervated. Paddlefish are

OTHER NAMES

spoonbill, spoonbill catfish, spoonbill cat, American paddlefish, Mississippi paddlefish, shovel-billed cat, duck-billed cat, spadefish, shovelfish.

Distribution. *The American paddlefish ranges throughout the Mississippi River drainage, from the Missouri River in Montana southward. Some populations are self-sustaining, whereas others are maintained with stocking. American paddlefish have been sent to Russia (50,000 paddlefish eggs were shipped from Missouri in the mid-1970s) in an attempt to establish the species there and to augment caviar production, which has suffered due to dwindling sturgeon populations.*

Habitat. *Paddlefish prefer low-gradient rivers, pools, backwaters, and oxbows; they also exist in flood-plain reservoirs as a result of dam building. When not spawning, they are pelagic and are found in open water.*

suspected of using their snouts to locate prey, perhaps to stir sediment on the bottom. There are two small barbels on the snout, and the underside is dotted with sensory pits.

The paddlefish also has a greatly elongated operculum flap, an extremely large basketlike mouth, long gill rakers, and a deeply forked tail with a high dorsal fin that resembles a shark fin. Adult paddlefish are toothless, but juveniles have teeth on their jaws. The color is slate gray to purplish above. They have almost white bellies, and the skin is smooth, like that of a catfish, with the only scales being on the caudal peduncles.

Size/Age. Paddlefish may live to be 25 to 30 years old. They often grow to 100 pounds, although the average fish is much smaller. Literature from the past contains reports of paddlefish that grew to more than 200 pounds. World records are not kept for this species by the International Game Fish Association (IGFA) because they are not hooked in the mouth but snagged. Nevertheless, state records show that Montana produced a 142-pound, 8-ounce fish in 1973 in the Missouri River. A 134-pounder from Missouri was over 20 years old.

Life history/Behavior. Adults migrate upstream to gravel bars in the spring, spawning in high currents with temperatures between 50°F and 60°F. They are commonly found in tailwaters below dams, which impede their upstream migration. In rivers where they are able to travel unimpeded, paddlefish may migrate significant distances.

Spawning occurs in midstream, and the adhesive eggs attach to the gravel on the bottom. When hatched, the fry are moved downstream by swift currents into deep pools with lower water velocities. Where oxbows occur, they may serve as alternate spawning sites and important nursery areas for young paddlefish, whose early growth is rapid.

Food and feeding habits. Paddlefish eat zooplankton, microscopic plants and animals that live in open water. They swim through the water with their large mouths open and strain out the zooplankton with numerous (hundreds) gill rakers. They are not bottom feeders and move about in shallow water or near the surface of slow-moving currents with favorable foraging conditions.

Perch, White

Morone americana

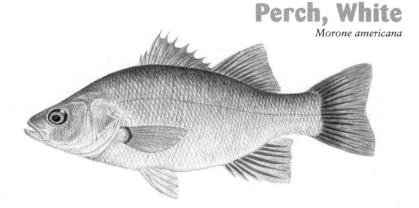

White perch are abundant in some places, rare in others, similar enough to other species to be misidentified, and underappreciated as table fare.

Identification. The white perch is not a true perch but a member of the temperate bass family and a relative of the white bass and the striped bass. It is similar in shape to the striped bass, but it has a deeper, less-rounded body and lacks the horizontal lines found on the striped bass. Although shorter, stockier, and smaller in weight than a striper, it is very similar in appearance to a white bass, except that it has no stripes. A more appropriate name for this species would probably be silver bass, and it is called by that name in some areas.

The white perch has a deep, thin body that slopes up steeply from the eye to the beginning of the dorsal fin and that is deepest under the first dorsal fin. On large, older specimens, the white perch can be nearly humpbacked at that spot. Its colors can be olive, gray green, silvery gray, dark brown, or black on the back, becoming a lighter silvery green on the sides and silvery white on the belly. The pelvic and the anal fins (both on the belly) are sometimes rosy colored. Like all members of the temperate bass family, it has two dorsal fins on the back, and the pelvic fins sit forward on the body, below the pectoral fins. The first dorsal fin has nine spines, but the second one is soft rayed. There are three spines at the front of the anal fin, and a single spine precedes the second dorsal fin and each pelvic fin. The white perch has no teeth on its tongue, its scales are relatively large, and the lateral line is complete.

Size/Age. White perch are generally small and slow-growing after attaining juvenile size. The average white perch caught by anglers weighs under a pound and is probably close to three-quarters of a pound and 9 inches in

OTHER NAMES

silver bass, silver perch, sea perch, bass, narrow-mouthed bass, bass perch, gray perch, bluenose perch, humpy; French: *bar blanc d'Amerique.*

Distribution. *White perch are found along the Atlantic coast from the southern Gulf of St. Lawrence to South Carolina and inland along the upper St. Lawrence River to the lower Great Lakes. They are present in all three Maritime Provinces, common in Lake Ontario, and especially abundant in the Hudson River and Chesapeake Bay areas. The white perch is far more coastal in occurrence than is the white bass, and most of the overlap in their distribution occurs in the area of the Great Lakes and the upper St. Lawrence River.*

Habitat. *Like its striped bass cousin, the adaptable white perch is at home in saltwater, brackish water, and freshwater. In marine waters, it is primarily found in brackish water, estuaries,*

Perch, White *(continued)*
and coastal rivers and streams, and some of the latter have sea-run populations. Some white perch remain resident in brackish bays and estuaries, whereas others roam widely in search of food.

White perch inhabit scattered freshwater lakes and ponds throughout their range, but in varied abundance. A prolific fish, they have overpopulated some ponds and small lakes and have been deemed a nuisance, especially when crowding out black bass, trout, and other species. For marine purposes, white perch are considered demersal (bottom dwelling), and in general they do tend to stay deep in their home waters, on or close to the bottom.

length. These figures can obviously vary among regions and populations. In some places, the average white perch is just 6 inches long.

These fish have a normal life span of between 5 and 7 years, but some specimens may live for 14 to 17 years. They are said to be able to grow to 19 inches and 6 pounds, but these dimensions are extremely rare; the largest white perch in angling records is a 4-pound, 12-ounce Maine fish that was caught in 1949.

Life history/Behavior. White perch are spring spawners, usually accomplishing this act when water temperatures are between 57°F and 75°F and in shallow water over many kinds of bottoms. Males and females each spawn several times in random fashion. For unknown reasons, white perch in some bodies of freshwater are extremely successful at reproduction, whereas in others they are virtually unsuccessful.

These fish are a schooling species that groups even while young and continues to stay in loose open-water schools through adulthood. They do not orient to cover and structure and tend to be deeper than yellow perch, with whom they occupy the same lakes and ponds in parts of their range.

Food and feeding habits. White perch in lakes are known to feed both during the day and at night but are generally more active in low light and nocturnally. Freshwater and saltwater populations move to surface (or inshore) waters at night, retreating to deeper water during the day.

Perch eat mostly aquatic insect larvae when they are small. As they grow, they eat many kinds of small fish, such as smelt, yellow perch, killifish, and other white perch, as well as the young of other species, particularly those that spawn after them. They also reportedly consume crabs, shrimp, and small alewives and herring.

Perch, Yellow

Perca flavescens

The most widely distributed member of the Percidae family, the yellow perch is one of the best loved and most pursued of all freshwater fish, particularly in northerly states and provinces in North America. This is due to its availability over a wide range, the general ease with which it is caught, and its delicious taste.

Identification. Unlike the white perch, which is actually a temperate bass, the yellow perch is a true perch. Although it resembles the true bass in many ways, it is more closely related to fellow Percidae family members, the walleye and the sauger. Its most striking characteristic is a colorful golden yellow body, tinged with orange-colored fins.

The yellow perch is colored a green to yellow gold and has six to eight dark, broad vertical bars that extend from the back to below the lateral line, a whitish belly, and orange lower fins during breeding season. Its body is oblong and appears humpbacked; this is the result of the deepest part of the body beginning at the first dorsal fin, then tapering slightly to the beginning of the second dorsal fin. This trait is somewhat similar in white perch, to which the yellow perch is unrelated, although both fish may inhabit the same waters.

The yellow perch is distinguished from the trout and the salmon by its lack of an adipose fin, which is ordinarily located between the dorsal and the tail fins, and from sunfish by its separate dorsal fins (connected in sunfish) and two or fewer anal fin spines (sunfish have three or more). It is distinguished from the walleye and the sauger by its lack of canine teeth and by a generally deeper body form.

Size/Age. The average yellow perch caught by anglers weighs between ¼ to ¾ pound and measures 6 to 10 inches in length. In lakes with stunted populations, the fish are on the lower end of this range, and a 10-inch fish is

OTHER NAMES

ringed perch, striped perch, coon perch, jack perch, lake perch, American perch; French: *perchaude.*

Distribution. *Yellow perch are widespread in the northern United States and Canada. They range east from Nova Scotia to the Santee River drainage in South Carolina and west throughout the Great Lakes states to the edge of British Columbia and into Washington. Small numbers extend north through Great Slave Lake almost to Great Bear Lake in Canada's Northwest Territories. They appear in nearly every state due to stocking, but they are sparsely distributed in the South, most of the West, and parts of the Midwest; they are also sparse in British Columbia and northern Canada. Although the yellow perch is a freshwater fish, Nova Scotia fisheries personnel report that it is occasionally found in brackish water along the Atlantic coast.*

Perch, Yellow (continued)

Habitat. *Yellow perch are found in a wide variety of warm and cool habitats over a vast range of territory, although they are primarily lake fish. They are occasionally found in ponds and rivers. These fish are most abundant in clear, weedy lakes that have a muck, sand, or gravel bottom. Smaller lakes and ponds usually produce smaller fish, although in very fertile lakes with moderate angling pressure, yellow perch can grow large. They inhabit open areas of most lakes and prefer temperatures between the mid-60s and the low 70s.*

usually considered fairly large. Some lakes produce perch in the 1-pound and larger class, although fish greater than 1½ pounds are infrequent. The all-tackle world-record yellow perch, taken in 1865, weighed 4 pounds, 3 ounces and is the oldest freshwater sportfish record in the books. Yellow perch can grow to 16 inches in length and can live up to 12 years.

Life history/Behavior. Yellow perch usually spawn in the early spring when the water temperature is between 45°F and 50°F. Eggs are spawned in the shallow areas of lakes or up in tributary streams in gelatinous ribbons by an adult female and are fertilized by as many as a dozen males in weedy areas several feet deep. The ribbons, which may be up to 7 feet long and several inches wide, attach to vegetation until one-quarter to one-half of the 10,000 to 48,000 eggs hatch into fry in 10 days to 3 weeks after spawning.

Yellow perch travel in schools composed of fish that are similar in size and age, and there is some evidence of the sexes dividing into separate schools. In large lakes, adults move in schools farther offshore than do the young. They move between deeper and shallow water in response to changing food supplies, seasons, and temperatures.

Because of their predaceous nature and swift breeding, overpopulation is a problem in many lakes where yellow perch have been introduced; the fish may become stunted, and other species may be adversely impacted as a result. The introduction, through natural or artificial means, of yellow perch into ponds containing trout usually results in a collapse of the trout population, and this may be true for other species of fish that were dominant before yellow perch entered.

Food and feeding habits. Young yellow perch feed on zooplankton until they have grown to several inches in length and then feed on larger zooplankton, insects, young crayfish, snails, aquatic insects, fish eggs, and small fish, including the young of their own species.

Pickerel, Chain

Esox niger

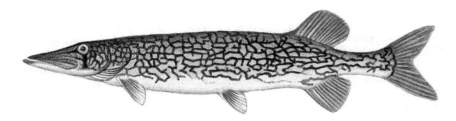

This member of the Esocidae family of pike is a lean, sporting, evil-eyed bandit, yet it is virtually neglected by most nonwinter anglers, rarely specifically pursued by open-water anglers, and often downgraded by those who catch it unintentionally while seeking more popular fish. Respectable battlers on appropriate tackle, these aggressive, available fish also offer a good chance of angling success.

Long, slimy, toothy, camouflaged in green brown and bearing chainlike markings, the chain pickerel has cold-blooded eyes and is a smaller but equally fearsome-looking version of its northern pike and muskellunge cousins. It has an unusual arrangement of bones, but the flesh is generally white, flaky, and sweet. At some times and from some places, however, the flavor is not as good. This deficit may be remedied by removing the skin before cooking. Many chain pickerel are caught through the ice.

This fish is sometimes confused with the walleye, particularly in southern Canada, where walleye are called "pickerel," but the walleye is a member of the perch family and is unlike the true chain pickerel in all respects save one: It, too, has many teeth. Chain pickerel are abundant where pike and muskies are not found or are not particularly abundant.

Identification. With its long, slender body, the chain pickerel is very similar in appearance to the northern pike and the muskellunge, especially when young. It gets its name from its markings, which appear in a reticulated, or chainlike, pattern of black lines that covers the golden to yellowish or greenish sides. The small, light-colored oval spots on the sides of the northern pike resemble the very large, light oval areas on the chain pickerel but may be distinguished by the dark background behind the pattern on the northern pike; also, the northern pike's spots never appear large in relation to the background, whereas in the chain pickerel the lighter areas are more prevalent. The chain pickerel has

OTHER NAMES

jack, pike, eastern pickerel, eastern chain pickerel, lake pickerel, reticulated pickerel, federation pickerel, mud pickerel, green pike, grass pike, black chain pike, duck-billed pike, river pike, picquerelle, water wolf.

Distribution. *This species extends along the Atlantic slope of North America from Nova Scotia to southern Florida, as well as along the Gulf Coast west to the Sabine Lake drainage in Louisiana and from the Mississippi River basin north to southwestern Kentucky and southeastern Missouri. Chain pickerel have been introduced to Lakes Ontario and Erie drainages and elsewhere. Their primary abundance is from the mid-Atlantic states northward and in Florida and Georgia.*

Habitat. *Chain pickerel inhabit the shallow, vegetated waters of lakes, swamps, streams, ponds, bogs, tidal and nontidal rivers, backwaters, and quiet pools of creeks and*

Pickerel, Chain (continued)

small to medium rivers, as well as the bays and coves of larger lakes and reservoirs. Solitary fish, they prefer water temperatures of 75º to 80ºF and are occasionally found in low-salinity estuaries, though they can tolerate a wide range of salinities. They move into deeper water during the winter and continue to feed actively.

The environs preferred by pickerel are somewhat similar to those of largemouth bass, particularly in regard to vegetation and abundant cover. Their primary hangouts are lily pads and various types of weeds, and they sometimes lie near such objects as stumps, docks, and fallen trees. Invariably, the waters with the best pickerel populations are those with abundant vegetation, much of which is found near shore.

fully scaled cheeks and gill covers. These further distinguish it from the northern pike, which usually has no scales on the bottom half of the gill cover, and from the muskellunge, which usually has no scales on the bottom half of either the gill cover or the cheek. It has only one dorsal fin, which is located very far back on the body near the caudal peduncle. There is a dark vertical bar under each eye, and the snout is shaped like a duck's bill. The lower jaw has a row of four sensory pores on each side, and the mouth is full of needle-like teeth.

Size/Age. The chain pickerel can exceed 30 inches in length and 9 pounds in weight, although the average fish is under 2 feet long and weighs less than 2 pounds. In some waters it may be even smaller. The all-tackle world record is a 9-pound, 6-ounce fish caught in Georgia in 1961. The maximum age is roughly 10, although the average is around 4. Females grow larger and live longer than males.

Pickerel, Grass and Redfin

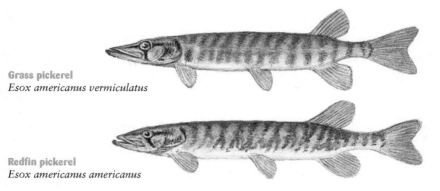

Grass pickerel
Esox americanus vermiculatus

Redfin pickerel
Esox americanus americanus

The grass pickerel and the redfin pickerel are two nearly identical subspecies of *Esox americanus,* differing only slightly in range. Because they occur only in small populations and are of small size, they have little importance as sportfish, although they are significant predators in many waters of more prominent small sportfish. The white, sweet flesh of these members of the Esocidae family is bony, but it has an excellent flavor.

Identification. Slender and cylindrical, grass and redfin pickerel look much like the chain pickerel, with the same fully scaled cheeks and gill covers. They are dark olive to brown or black above, amber to brassy white below, with 20 or more dark green to brown wavy bars along the sides. On the grass pickerel, there are pale areas between the bars that are wider than the bars. The grass pickerel is lighter in color than the redfin pickerel and has a pronounced pale midlateral stripe. The grass pickerel also has yellow-green to dusky lower fins and a long narrow snout (although shorter than the chain pickerel's), with a concave profile, whereas the redfin pickerel appropriately has red lower and caudal fins, as well as a shorter, broader snout, with a convex profile. Each has a large mouth with sharp canine teeth and several sensory pores on the lower jaw. A dark vertical bar extends down from each eye, which is more vertical in the grass pickerel than in the redfin. An easy way to distinguish the redfin from the grass pickerel is to examine the scales on the sides of the redfin, of which there are more notched or heart-shaped ones, specifically six in the area between the pelvic fins. There are up to three on the grass pickerel. Also, the redfin has more than seven of these scales between the dorsal and the anal fins, whereas the grass pickerel has four or fewer.

Size/Age. Both species seldom exceed 10 inches in length (the redfin pickerel can reach 14 inches) and three-quarters

OTHER NAMES
banded pickerel, little pickerel, mud pickerel.

Distribution. *In North America, grass pickerel range from the Great Lakes basin north to southern Ontario in Canada and to Michigan, Wisconsin, and Nebraska; they also occur in the Mississippi River and Gulf slope drainages west of the Pascagoula River in Mississippi to the Brazos River in Texas. Redfin pickerel are found in Atlantic slope drainages, from the St. Lawrence River drainage in Quebec to southern Georgia; they also occur in Gulf slope drainages from the Pascagoula River in Mississippi to Florida. Populations for both species are generally small on a local level.*

Habitat. *Grass and redfin pickerel inhabit quiet or small lakes and swamps, bays and backwaters, and sluggish pools of streams. Both prefer heavy vegetation in clear waters, but the grass pickerel favors waters with neutral to basic acidity, and the redfin inhabits comparatively acidic waters.*

of a pound in weight; the redfin pickerel generally grows faster and slightly longer than the grass pickerel. The all-tackle world record for the grass pickerel is a 1-pound Indiana fish; for the redfin pickerel, the record is a 1-pound, 15-ounce New York fish. They can live up to 8 years, although they usually live 5 years or less. Females live longer and grow larger than males.

Life history/Behavior. Reaching sexual maturity when they are roughly 2 years old and at least 5 inches long, grass and redfin pickerel spawn in the late fall, the early winter, or the spring; grass pickerel require water temperatures between 36° and 54°F, and redfin favor waters approaching 50°F. Spawning takes place in heavily vegetated, shallow areas, and the backs of the fish appear at the surface as they scatter eggs in small batches over the vegetation. Grass pickerel may produce twice as many eggs as do redfin pickerel. They do not build nests. The grass pickerel's eggs hatch in 11 to 15 days, the redfin pickerel's in 12 to 14 days, without the protection of the parents.

Food and feeding habits. Grass and redfin pickerel are largely piscivorous, feeding mainly on other fish, such as minnows, although they occasionally eat aquatic insects, small crayfish, and frogs. They will remain virtually motionless among the vegetation for hours at a time, waiting to dart out and seize a potential meal.

Pike, Northern

Esox lucius

Malevolent-looking and spear shaped, the northern pike is the namesake member of the Esocidae family of pike. It is a worthy angling quarry, one that grows fairly large, fights well, and accommodates anglers frequently enough to be of substantial interest in the areas where it is found.

Identification. The northern pike has an elongated body and head. The snout is broad and flat, shaped somewhat like a duck bill. The jaws, the roof of the mouth, the tongue, and the gill rakers are armed with numerous sharp teeth that are constantly being replaced. A single soft-rayed dorsal fin is located far back on the body.

Male and female pike are similar in appearance, and both are variable in color. A fish from a clear stream or lake will usually be light green, whereas one from a dark slough or river will be considerably darker. The underparts are whitish or yellowish. The markings on the sides form irregular rows of yellow or gold spots. Pike with a silvery or blue color variation are occasionally encountered and are known as silver pike.

The northern pike can be distinguished from its relatives by three main features. Most noticeably, the greenish or yellowish sides of these fish are covered with lighter-colored kidney-shaped horizontal spots or streaks, whereas all other species have markings (spots, bars, stripes, or reticulations) that are darker than the background color. Their markings are most likely to be confused with those of the chain pickerel. The second distinction is the scale pattern on the gill cover and the cheek. In the northern pike the cheek is fully scaled, but the bottom half of the gill cover is scaleless. In the larger muskellunge, both the bottom half of the gill cover and the bottom half of the cheek are scaleless. In the smaller pickerel, the gill cover and the cheek are both fully scaled. The third distinctive feature is the number of pores under each side of the lower jaw; there are usually 5 in the

OTHER NAMES

pike, northern, jack, jackfish, snake, great northern pike, great northern pickerel, American pike, common pike, Great Lakes pike; Danish: *gedde;* Dutch: *snoek;* Finnish: *hauki;* French: *brochet;* German: *hecht;* Hungarian: *csuka;* Italian: *luccio;* Norwegian: *gjedde;* Portuguese: *ÿlcio;* Russian: *shtschuka;* Spanish: *lucio;* Swedish: *gäddo.*

Distribution. *The northern pike is densely distributed throughout Alaska, with the exception of the offshore islands, and widespread throughout Canada and the arctic islands above Hudson Bay, being conspicuously absent from the coastal plains (most of British Columbia and the Canadian Atlantic coast east of the St. Lawrence River). In the United States, it is found south of Maine in New Hampshire, Vermont, and Massachusetts (except along the coast) and in all the Great Lakes states (although it is largely*

Pike, Northern (continued)

absent from lower Michigan and Indiana), as well as west of the Great Lakes in Minnesota, Wisconsin, Iowa, Illinois, Missouri, Nebraska, and Montana. It has been widely introduced outside this native range, even into southern and western states.

Habitat. *Although classified by biologists as a cool-water species, the northern pike exists in diverse habitats. It is especially known to inhabit the weedy parts of rivers, ponds, and lakes, but it may be found in deeper, open environs in waters without vegetation, or when the temperature gets too high in warm shallower areas. Warm shallow ponds and cold deep lakes both support pike, but large individuals have a preference for water that is in the mid-50°F range. Smaller fish are more likely to be in warm shallow water.*

northern pike (rarely 3, 4, or 6 on one side), 6 to 9 in the muskellunge (rarely 5 or 10 on one side), and 4 in smaller pickerel (occasionally 3 or 5 on one side only).

Size/Age. Pike are normally 16 to 30 inches long and weigh between 2 and 7 pounds. Females live longer and attain greater size than males. Pike up to 20 pounds are common in some Canadian and Alaskan rivers, lakes, and sloughs, and fish weighing up to 30 pounds and measuring 4 feet in length are possible. The North American record is a 46-pound, 2-ounce New York fish caught in 1940. The average life span is 7 to 10 years, but in slow-growing populations they may live up to 26 years.

Life history/Behavior. Northern pike spawn in the spring, moving into the heavily vegetated areas of lakes and rivers either just after ice out or, in some cases, prior to ice out. In many places they spawn in wetlands or marshes that will have little or no water later in the season. They are broadcast spawners, and the scattered eggs that fall to the bottom are adhesive. They usually hatch in 12 to 14 days but do so later in much colder waters. In waters that also contain muskellunge, the two species may crossbreed naturally; this occurs rarely but can happen, as muskies spawn in the same or similar environs, although usually after pike.

Food and feeding habits. Pike are voracious and opportunistic predators from the time they are mere inches long. They are solitary, lurking near weeds or other cover to ambush prey. Their diet is composed almost entirely of fish, but it may occasionally include shorebirds, small ducks, muskrats, mice, frogs, and the like. In pike waters, it is common to find scarred fish that were grabbed by but escaped the large toothy maw of a pike. Pike feed most actively during the day and are heavily sight-oriented.

Rudd

Scardinius erythrophthalmus

A prominent coarse fish, the rudd is widely sought by European anglers but is barely known to most North Americans. It is a member of the large Cyprinidae family, which includes minnows and carp, and is of similar size and color to its relative the roach.

Identification. The rudd is somewhat cylindrical, yet deep bodied. It has a moderately forked tail and an upturned mouth. The scales are strongly marked, the back is dark brown, and the sides are golden brown, tapering to a white belly. The pectoral, pelvic, and anal fins are reddish orange, and the dorsal and tail fins are dusky. The rudd has 8 to 9 dorsal rays, 10 to 11 anal rays, and eyes that are red or have a red spot. The rudd may be confused with the roach; however, the pectoral fins of the roach lack the reddish-orange color, and the body is more silvery. It is similar in appearance to the golden shiner *(see: Shiner, Golden)* but is distinguished from that species by its scaled ventral keel.

Size. The maximum size for rudd is in the 4- to 5-pound range, although fish of that nature are rare. A 2-pound rudd is typically a large one.

Life history/Behavior. Spawning takes place in heavy weeds in spring, when rudd broadcast numerous adhesive eggs, rather than construct a nest. The fry stay in schools and gather in large congregations, and they provide forage for numerous predators. Rudd remain a schooling fish as adults. Their schools generally consist of similar-size individuals.

Food and feeding habits. Rudd feed on snails, aquatic insects, and small fish and spend a lot of time in beds of vegetation. They are largely surface feeders, but they also feed on the bottom and at mid-depths. Many rudd are observed taking food from the surface or from the undersides of aquatic plants.

OTHER NAMES
European rudd; German: *rotfeder;* Italian: *scardola.*

Distribution. *Rudd range from western Europe to the Caspian and Aral Sea basins but are absent from Russia; they have been introduced to the United States.*

Habitat. *Pools, canals, lakes, and slow-running rivers with muddy bottoms are the prime locations for rudd. They spend much time in or along the edges of vegetation.*

Ruffe

Gymnocephalus cernuus

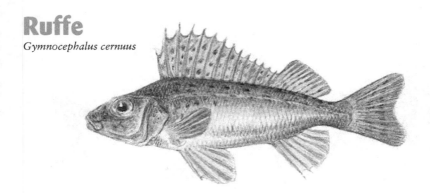

OTHER NAMES

Habitat. *The ruffe occurs in freshwater and in brackish waters with 3 to 5 parts per million salinity. It exists in a variety of lake environments, preferring turbid areas and soft bottoms without vegetation. In rivers, it prefers slower-moving water. It is more tolerant of murky and eutrophic conditions than are many other perch.*

A member of the Percidae family of perch, the ruffe was introduced into North America, evidently through ballast water discharge by transoceanic ships. It has become a considerable threat to the delicate predator-prey balance necessary to maintain flourishing fisheries in North American waters, especially in the Great Lakes. It has been reported only in Lake Superior waters but is likely to exist, or spread, elsewhere.

The species found and multiplying in Lake Superior has been identified as *Gymnocephalus cernuus.* The native range of *G. cernuus* is from France to the Kolyma River in eastern Siberia, and it has been introduced to England, Scotland, and Scandinavia.

Identification. The ruffe's body shape is very similar to that of the yellow perch, and its body markings are similar to those of the walleye. It has a spiny first dorsal fin connected to a second soft dorsal fin, two deep sharp spines on the anal fin, one sharp spine on the pelvic fins, and sharp spines on the gill cover. The dorsal fins have rows of dark spots, the eyes are large and glassy, and the mouth is small and downturned. There are no scales on its head.

Size/Age. The ruffe seldom exceeds 6 inches in length but can attain a length of 10 inches. Most female ruffe live for 7 years but may live up to 11 years. Males generally live 3 to 5 years.

Life history/Behavior. The ruffe generally matures in 2 to 3 years and spawns between mid-April and July, depending on location, temperature, and habitat. Young ruffe have a faster growth rate than many of their competitors, and adults reproduce prolifically, which allows for quick population expansion. It is a nocturnal fish, spending its days in deeper water and moving shallower to feed at night.

Food. The ruffe's primary diet is small aquatic insects and larvae, although it may consume fish eggs.

Salmon, Atlantic

Salmo salar

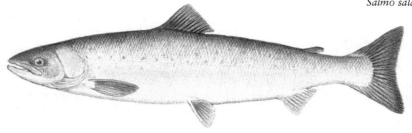

The Atlantic salmon has both anadromous and freshwater forms. The former migrate from freshwater streams to the ocean and then return to those streams to spawn, whereas the latter remain in freshwater all their lives. Called land-locked salmon or ouananiche in North America, the fresh-water form is the same species as the anadromous Atlantic salmon and shares identical characteristics, except that the freshwater fish is smaller.

Identification. Compared to the size of its body, a mature Atlantic salmon has a small head. Its body is long and slim, and in adults the caudal or tail fin is nearly square. Individuals that return to spawn prematurely (called grilse) are mostly males and have slightly forked tails. While in the sea, the Atlantic salmon is dark blue on the top of its head and back; its sides are a shiny silver, and the belly is white. The fins are dark, and there are numerous black marks in the shape of an X or Y on its head and along its body above the lateral line.

When the fish enters freshwater to spawn, it eventually becomes dull brown or yellowish. Many, particularly males, are splotched with red or have large black patches on the body and may look a lot like the brown trout *(Salmo trutta),* their closest relative. At spawning time the males are further distinguished by their elongated hooked jaws that meet only at the tips; the fins become thicker, and a heavy coat of slime covers their bodies. Post-spawn fish appear very dark, leading to the name "black salmon."

Landlocked Atlantics look the same as their anadromous counterparts, although spawning fish may be darker.

Size/Age. The Atlantic salmon can live for 8 years and is the second largest of all salmon. In North America, the largest known Atlantic salmon was a 55-pounder caught in the Grand Cascapedia River, Quebec.

Landlocked Atlantic salmon are capable of growing to between 30 and 40 pounds. A 22-pound, 11-ounce

OTHER NAMES

Sea-run fish
grilse, grilt, fiddler, Kennebec salmon; Danish and Norwegian: *laks;* Dutch: *zalm;* Finnish: *lohi;* French: *saumon Atlantique, saumon d'eau douce;* German: *lachs, las, salm;* Italian: *salmo, salmone;* Japanese: *sake masu-rui;* Portuguese: *salmao;* Russian: *losos;* Spanish: *salmón del Atlantico;* Swedish: *lax.*

Post-spawn adult fish
black salmon, slink, kelt.

Salmon living entirely in freshwater
landlocked salmon, ouananiche, grayling, lake Atlantic salmon, Sebago salmon; French: *ouananiche.*

Distribution. *In North America, numerous self-supporting runs of anadromous Atlantics exist in Canada, especially Quebec, but also in Newfoundland, New Brunswick, and Nova Scotia, although the size of these stocks is severely depleted. Self-supporting runs of Atlantic salmon in the United States are found only in Maine. Restoration*

Salmon, Atlantic (continued)

efforts have been attempted in various rivers and presently continue in the Connecticut, Pawcatuck, Merrimack, and Penobscot Rivers of New England, which is a far cry from the 28 New England rivers that once contained this species.

Although some original landlocked populations have also been extirpated, landlocked Atlantic salmon have been introduced to many waters where they did not originally exist and reintroduced to waters where they once existed. Landlocked Atlantics have been widely introduced to the Great Lakes, where the larger specimens exist today, and are widely dispersed in eastern Quebec, Newfoundland, and Labrador.

Habitat. Anadromous Atlantic salmon spend most of their lives in the ocean, ascending coastal rivers to spawn. They are found in freshwater only during their spawning runs, after engaging in extensive and complex migrations throughout their range. In coastal rivers, they primarily inhabit deep runs and pools and seldom favor fast water or riffles.

Although some landlocked salmon may exist in rivers all year, most spend the greater portion of their lives in the open water of lakes, ascending tributaries to spawn. In rivers, they inhabit deep runs and pools. In lakes they stay in cooler, deeper levels, where baitfish are abundant.

specimen from Lobstick Lake in Labrador is often cited as the largest sport-caught landlocked salmon, but these fish historically grew to 45 pounds in New York's Lake Ontario, and modern introductions in that lake and in Lake Michigan have produced numerous fish in excess of 30 pounds.

Life history/Behavior. Spawning usually occurs in gravel bottoms at the head of riffles or the tail of a pool, and in the evening or at night. Exhausted and thin, the adults often return to sea immediately before winter or remain in the stream until spring.

After roughly 3 years (but within 2 to 8 years) in freshwater, salmon parr become smolts and prepare for life in saltwater. In the spring, these parr become slimmer and turn silvery. During the spring runoff, as water temperatures rise, smolts form schools and migrate downstream at night. It is during this downstream migration that smolts "learn," or become imprinted with, the characteristics of their particular river, which will play a role in their eventual return.

Atlantic salmon will stay at sea (or in a lake) for 1 or more years and are known to travel long distances. Some Atlantics may make a spawning run only once or twice during their lifetime of roughly 8 years; others will spawn three or four times, returning in consecutive years to the same spawning grounds, and these are usually the largest fish. Atlantic salmon that are ready to spawn begin moving upriver from late spring through fall. Landlocked salmon living in lakes move up into tributary streams to spawn in a similar manner, although they usually don't do so until late summer.

Food. In rivers, salmon parr feed mainly on the immature and the adult stages of aquatic insects. In the ocean, salmon grow rapidly, feeding on crustaceans and other fish such as smelt, alewives, herring, capelin, mackerel, and cod. Landlocked salmon in lakes eat pelagic freshwater fish, primarily smelt and alewives. Neither feeds during its upstream spawning migration.

Salmon, Chinook

Oncorhynchus tshawytscha

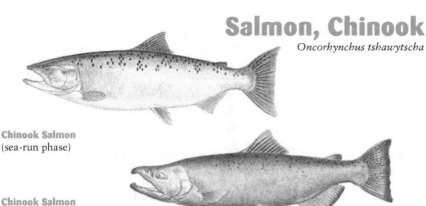

Chinook Salmon
(sea-run phase)

Chinook Salmon
(spawning male)

The chinook salmon is one of the most important sportfish and commercial fish in the world. It is the largest member of the Salmonidae family and both the largest and least-abundant member of the Pacific salmon genus *Oncorhynchus*. By nature an anadromous species, it can adapt to an entirely freshwater existence and has done so with such remarkable success in the Great Lakes of North America that it has formed the backbone of an enormous and extremely valuable sportfishery there, becoming one of the greatest fisheries transplant/management/revitalization projects of all time.

Identification. The body of the chinook salmon is elongate and somewhat compressed. The head is conical. For most of its life, the chinook's color is bluish to dark gray above, becoming silvery on the sides and the belly. There are black spots on the back, the upper sides, the top of the head, and all the fins, including both the top and the bottom half of the tail fin. Coloration changes during upstream migration; spawning chinook salmon range from red to copper to olive brown to almost black, depending on location and degree of maturation, and they undergo a radical metamorphosis. Males are more deeply colored than the females and are distinguished by their "ridgeback" condition and by their hooked nose or upper jaw, known as a kype.

One distinguishing feature of the chinook is its black mouth and gums. The very similar-looking coho salmon has a black mouth but white gums, except in the Great Lakes population, in which the gums may be gray or black.

Size. This species is the largest of all Pacific salmon; individual fish commonly exceed 30 pounds in Alaska and British Columbia and 20 pounds elsewhere. A 126-pound chinook salmon taken in a fish trap near Petersburg, Alaska, in 1949 is the largest known specimen. The all-tackle world sportfishing record is a 97-pound, 4-ounce fish, caught in

OTHER NAMES
king salmon, spring salmon, tyee, quinnat, tule, blackmouth, Sacramento River salmon, Columbia River salmon; French: *saumon chinook, saumon royal;* Japanese: *masunosuke.*

Distribution. *The chinook salmon is endemic to the Pacific Ocean and to the Bering Sea, the Okhotsk Sea, the Sea of Japan, and most of the rivers that flow into these waters. It occurs naturally from San Luis Obispo County in Southern California to the Chukchi Sea area of Alaska; the greatest concentrations are along the British Columbia coast and Alaska. In Alaska, where the chinook is the state fish, it is abundant from the southeastern panhandle to the Yukon River. Major populations return to the Yukon, the Kuskokwim, the Nushagak, the Susitna, the Kenai, the Copper, the Alsek, the Taku, and the Stikine Rivers. Important runs also occur in many smaller streams. The*

Salmon, Chinook (continued)

chinook is rare in the Arctic Ocean. Most sea-run chinook are encountered by anglers along the coasts and in spawning rivers. Scientists estimate that there are in excess of a thousand spawning populations of chinook salmon on the North American coast.

Since as early as 1872, the chinook salmon has been introduced into other waters around the world, including the Great Lakes and the Atlantic and Gulf states in the United States, some areas of Central and South America, Europe, and the South Pacific. These transplanted populations apparently failed, due to an inability to maintain self-perpetuating spawning levels, with the exceptions of South Island in New Zealand, and to some degree in the Great Lakes of the United States (which experience minimal natural reproduction, although large populations are sustained by intensive stocking). Transplanted and strictly freshwater-dwelling chinook are widely distributed throughout the Great Lakes and their tributaries in Canada and the United States, with greatest concentrations in Lakes Michigan and Ontario; these fish also exist in some large inland lakes in the United States and in other countries.

Alaska's Kenai River in 1986. Chinook transplanted to the Great Lakes commonly weigh from 15 to 30 pounds, and the largest specimens recorded weigh under 50 pounds.

Life history/Behavior. Like all species of Pacific salmon, chinook are anadromous. They hatch in freshwater rivers, spend part of their lives in the ocean, and then spawn in freshwater. Those chinook that have been transplanted to strictly freshwater environments (as in the Great Lakes) hatch in tributary rivers and streams, spend part of their lives in the open water of the lake, and then return to tributaries to spawn. In both cases, all chinook die after spawning.

Females tend to be older than males at maturity. They usually live no more than 4 to 5 years and are much larger at 2 and 3 years. Small chinook that mature after spending only one winter in the ocean or the lake are commonly referred to as "jacks" and are usually males.

The period of migration into spawning rivers and streams varies greatly. Alaskan streams normally receive a single run of chinook salmon from May through July. Streams throughout the Great Lakes primarily receive chinook from late August into October, but there are some spring runs.

Chinook salmon do not feed during their freshwater spawning migration, so their condition deteriorates gradually during the spawning run. During that time, they use stored body materials for energy and for the development of reproductive products.

Food and feeding habits. Juvenile chinook in freshwater feed on plankton, then later eat insects. In the ocean, they eat a variety of organisms, including herring, pilchards, sand lance, squid, and crustaceans. Salmon grow rapidly in the ocean and often double their weight during a single summer season.

Likewise, chinook that live entirely in freshwater feed on plankton and insects as juveniles and pelagic freshwater baitfish in the lakes. Alewives and smelt are the primary food items, and, in fact, chinook and other salmonids were introduced to the Great Lakes and other inland waters especially to help control massive populations of baitfish, which they consume voraciously. Thus, they quickly develop large, stocky bodies.

Salmon, Chum

Oncorhynchus keta

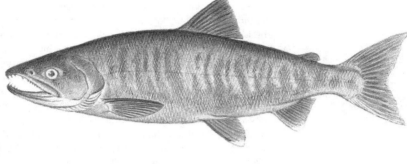

In arctic, northwestern, and interior Alaska, this member of the Salmonidae family is an important year-round source of fresh and dried fish for subsistence and personal use, although elsewhere its flesh is not favored for human consumption. Overall, it is not as popular or as desirable as other Pacific salmon. The frequently used name dog salmon reportedly originates with its prevalent use as dog food among aboriginals.

Identification. In the ocean, the slender, somewhat compressed, chum salmon is metallic greenish blue on the back, is silvery on the sides, and has a fine black speckling on the upper sides and the back but no distinct black spots. Spawning males turn dark olive or grayish; blood-red coloring and vertical bars of green and purple reach up the sides, giving the fish its "calico" appearance. It develops the typical hooked snout of Pacific salmon, and the tips of the anal and the pelvic fins are often white. The breeding male develops distinctly large front teeth, another explanation for the name "dog salmon." The color of a spawning female is essentially the same as that of a male but is less vivid, with a dark horizontal band along the lateral line. A young fish is exceptionally slender and has 6 to 14 narrow, short parr marks along the sides, located mostly above the lateral line.

The chum salmon is difficult to distinguish from the sockeye and the coho salmon, which are of similar size, without examining gills or caudal fin scale patterns; the chum salmon has fewer but larger gill rakers than do other salmon. The sockeye salmon also lacks the white marks on the fins, and the chum salmon is generally larger than the sockeye.

Life history/Behavior. The chum salmon is an anadromous fish; with the exception of a few landlocked populations, chum salmon inhabit both ocean environments and

OTHER NAMES

calico salmon, dog salmon, fall salmon, autumn salmon, chum, keta; French: *saumon keta;* Japanese: *sake, shake.*

Distribution. *Chum salmon are the most widely distributed of the Pacific salmon, native to the Pacific and Arctic Oceans, the Bering Sea, the Sea of Japan, and the Okhotsk Sea. They range south to about the Sacramento River in California and to the island of Kyushu in the Sea of Japan. In the north, they range east in the Arctic Ocean to the Mackenzie River in Canada and west to the Lena River in Siberia. In the Mackenzie, they travel all the way to the mouth of the Hay River and to the rapids below Forth Smith on the Slave River, entering both Great Bear and Great Slave Lakes and traveling through the Northwest Territories to the edge of Alberta.*

coastal streams. Spawning takes place from ages 2 to 7, most commonly at age 4 and at a weight of 5 to 10 pounds.

Like pink salmon, chum salmon are sometimes called "autumn salmon" or "fall salmon" because they are among the last salmon in the season to take their spawning run, entering river mouths after mid-June but reaching spawning grounds as late as November or December. Occasionally, there is one run of chum salmon in the summer and another in the fall in the same river; the summer-spawn fish are smaller and less likely to swim far upstream. In general, they are not strong leapers, swimming upstream only as far as the first significant barrier, although some fish in the Yukon River have been known to travel more than 2,000 miles to spawn in the Yukon Territory.

Chum salmon often spawn in the same places as do pink salmon, such as small streams and intertidal zones and in small side channels. Eggs are deposited in nests, or redds, dug by females in gravel riffles. The female guards the redd for a few days, then both sexes die.

Chum salmon enter streams in an advanced state of sexual maturity and thus do not stay in freshwater as long as do chinook, coho, and sockeye salmon, remaining for perhaps 2 to 3 weeks. Their fry do not move out to sea as quickly as do pink salmon fry in the spring. They move to saltwater estuaries in schools, remaining close to shore for a few months and waiting until fall to move into the ocean.

Size/Age. The chum salmon varies in size from 4 to more than 30 pounds, but the average weight is 10 to 15 pounds. Females are usually smaller than males. These fish can reach 40 inches in length. The all-tackle world record is a 35-pounder from British Columbia. Chum salmon can live as long as 7 years.

Food. Juvenile chum salmon in freshwater feed on plankton, then later eat insects. In the ocean, they eat a variety of organisms, including herring, pilchards, sand lance, squid, and crustaceans. Adults cease feeding in freshwater.

Salmon, Coho

Oncorhynchus kisutch

Coho Salmon
(sea-run phase)

Coho Salmon
(spawning male)

A member of the Salmonidae family, the coho salmon is an extremely adaptable fish that occurs in nearly all of the same waters as does the larger chinook salmon, but it is a more spectacular fighter and the most acrobatic of the Pacific salmon.

By nature an anadromous species, the coho can adapt to an entirely freshwater existence and has done so with remarkable success in the Great Lakes of North America.

Identification. The body of the coho salmon is elongate and somewhat compressed, and the head is conical. For most of its life (in saltwater or lake, as well as newly arrived in a spawning river), this species is a dark metallic blue or blue green above, becoming silvery on the sides and the belly. There are small black spots on the back and on the upper lobe of the caudal fin. It can be distinguished from a chinook salmon by its lack of black spots on the lower lobe of the tail, and the white or gray gums at the base of the teeth; the chinook has small black spots on both caudal lobes of the tail, and it has black gums.

Spawning adults of both sexes have dark backs and heads, and maroon to reddish sides. The male turns dusky green above and on its head, bright red on its sides, and blackish below. The female turns a pinkish red on its sides. The male develops a prominent doubled-hooked snout, called a kype, with large teeth, which make closing the mouth impossible.

Size. Coho do not attain the size of their larger chinook brethren and in most places are caught around the 4- to 8-pound mark. The all-tackle world record is a Great Lakes fish of 33 pounds, 4 ounces, caught in the Salmon River, New York, in 1989. Fish to 31 pounds have been caught in Alaska, where the average catch is 8 to 12 pounds and 24 to 30 inches long.

OTHER NAMES

silver salmon, silversides, hookbill, hooknose, sea trout, blueback; French: *saumon coho;* Japanese: *gin-zake.*

Distribution. *The coho salmon is endemic to the northern Pacific Ocean and the rivers flowing into it, from northern Japan to the Anadyr River, Russia, and from Point Hope, Alaska, on the Chukchi Sea south to Monterey Bay, California. It has been infrequently reported at sea as far south as Baja California, Mexico. Most sea-run coho are encountered along the coasts and in spawning rivers.*

The coho has been transplanted into the Great Lakes and into freshwater lakes in Alaska and along the U.S. Pacific coast, as well as into the states of Maine, Maryland, and Louisiana and the province of Alberta, Canada. Natural successful spawning has not noticeably occurred in these transplanted populations, with the possible exception of the Great Lakes in Michigan; the Great Lakes contain substantial populations of coho, which are sustained through extensive stocking.

Life history/Behavior. Like all species of Pacific salmon, coho are anadromous. They hatch in freshwater rivers, spend part of their lives in the ocean, and then spawn in freshwater. Those coho that have been transplanted to strictly freshwater environments (as in the Great Lakes) hatch in tributary rivers and streams, spend part of their lives in the open water of the lake, and then return to tributaries to spawn. All coho die after spawning.

Adult male sea-run coho salmon generally enter streams when they are either 2 or 3 years old, but adult females do not return to spawn until age 3. The timing of runs into tributaries varies. Coho salmon in Alaska enter spawning streams from July through November, usually during periods of high runoff. In California, the runs occur from September through March, and the bulk of spawning occurs from November through January. Streams throughout the Great Lakes primarily receive coho from late August into October.

Adults hold in pools before moving onto spawning grounds; spawning generally occurs at night. The female digs a nest, or redd, and deposits her eggs, which are fertilized by the male.

Food and feeding habits. Juvenile coho in freshwater feed on plankton, then later eat insects. In the ocean, coho salmon grow rapidly, feeding on a variety of organisms, including herring, pilchards, sand lance, squid, and crustaceans. Likewise, coho that live entirely in freshwater feed on plankton and insects as juveniles and on pelagic freshwater baitfish in the lakes. Alewives and smelt are the primary food items, and, in fact, coho and other salmonids were introduced to the Great Lakes and other inland waters especially to help control massive populations of baitfish, which they consume voraciously and thus quickly grow large, stocky bodies. Like all Pacific salmon, the coho does not feed once it enters freshwater on its spawning run.

Salmon, Pink

Oncorhynchus gorbuscha

Pink Salmon
(sea-run phase)

Pink Salmon
(spawning male)

An important commercial catch, the pink salmon is the smallest North American member of the Pacific salmon group of the Salmonidae family. In many Alaskan coastal fishing communities, particularly south of Kotzebue Sound, it is considered a "bread and butter" fish because of its commercial significance to fisheries and thus to local economies. It has some sportfishing value in Alaskan rivers, less so than coho or chinook salmon, but little elsewhere. The flesh is pinkish, rather than red or white, and it is mostly sold canned but is also utilized fresh, smoked, and frozen. It is valued for caviar, especially in Japan. The flesh is of most value when the fish is still an open-water inhabitant, as it deteriorates rapidly once the fish enters rivers.

Identification. The pink salmon is known as the "humpback" or "humpy" because of its distorted, extremely humpbacked appearance, which is caused by the very pronounced, laterally flattened hump that develops on the back of an adult male before spawning. This hump appears between the head and the dorsal fin and develops by the time the male enters the spawning stream, as does a hooked upper jaw, or kype.

At sea, the pink salmon is silvery in color, with a bright metallic blue above; there are many black, elongated, oval spots on the entire tail fin and large spots on the back and the adipose fin. When the pink salmon moves to spawning streams, the bright appearance of the male changes to pale red or "pink" on the sides, with brown to olive green blotches; females become olive green above with dusky bars or patches, and pale below. Young pink salmon are entirely silvery and lack the parr marks, or dark vertical bars, that the young of other salmon species have. All pink salmon have small, deeply embedded scales.

OTHER NAMES

humpback salmon, humpy, fall salmon, pink, humpback; French: *saumon rose;* Japanese: *karafutomasu, sepparimasu.*

Distribution. *Pink salmon are native to Pacific and arctic coastal waters from the Sacramento River in Northern California northeast to the Mackenzie River in the Northwest Territories, Canada.*

Pink salmon have been introduced to Newfoundland and to the western coast of Lake Superior and currently maintain populations in these locations; there have been sporadic · reports of pink salmon in Labrador, Nova Scotia, and Quebec since their introduction into Newfoundland. Introduced accidentally into Lake Superior, pink salmon are now spawning in tributaries of Lake Huron and are possibly the only isolated freshwater population to ever survive.

Salmon, Pink (continued)

Habitat. *These anadro-mous fish spend 18 months at sea and then undertake a spawning migration to the river or stream of their birth, although they sometimes use other streams. They tend to migrate as far as 40 miles inland of coastal waters, occasionally moving as far as 70 miles inland.*

Size/Age. The average pink salmon weighs 3 to 6 pounds and is 20 to 25 inches long, although these fish can grow to 15 pounds and 30 inches. The all-tackle world record is a 14-pound, 13-ounce specimen from Washington. Pink salmon live for only 2 years.

Life history/Behavior. Pink salmon are often referred to as "autumn salmon" or "fall salmon" because of their late spawning runs; these occur from July through mid-October in Alaska. Females dig a series of nests, or redds, depositing hundreds to thousands of eggs, which hatch from late December through February. Young become free-swimming in the early spring soon after hatching, often returning to sea in the company of young chum and sockeye salmon. Adults die soon after spawning. Pink salmon can hybridize with chum salmon.

Almost all pink salmon mature in 2 years, which means that odd-year and even-year populations are separate and essentially unrelated.

Food and feeding habits. While in freshwater on spawning runs, sea-run pink salmon may eat insects, although they often do not feed at all. At sea, they feed primarily on plankton, as well as on crustaceans, small fish, and squid. They do not feed during the spawning run.

Salmon, Sockeye

Oncorhynchus nerka

Sockeye Salmon
(spawning male)

Kokanee Salmon

A member of the Salmonidae family, the sockeye is like some other members of the Pacific salmon group, in having both anadromous and freshwater forms. The former migrate from freshwater streams to the ocean and then return to those streams to spawn, whereas the latter remain in freshwater all their lives. Called kokanee, the freshwater form was once thought to be the subspecies *O. kennerlyi* but is now accepted as the same species with characteristics identical to that of the anadromous sockeye, although it is a smaller fish. It occurred naturally in some waters in the drainages of the Pacific and has been spread through stocking to many other waters. Kokanee can be fine gamefish and excellent food fish; sockeye salmon are predominantly prized more for their food value than for sport, however, as the upstream migrants are not aggressive at taking bait or lures.

Identification. The sockeye is the slimmest and most streamlined of Pacific salmon, particularly immature and pre-spawning fish, which are elongate and somewhat later-ally compressed. They are metallic green-blue on the back and the top of their heads, iridescent silver on the sides, and white or silvery on the bellies. Some fine black speckling may occur on their backs, but large spots are absent.

Breeding males develop humped backs and elongated, hooked jaws filled with sharp, enlarged teeth. Both sexes turn brilliant to dark red on their backs and sides, pale to olive green on their heads and upper jaws, and white on the lower jaws. The totally red body distinguishes the sockeye from the otherwise similar chum salmon, and the lack of large distinct spots distinguishes it from the remaining three Pacific salmon of North America. The number and the shape of gill rakers on the first gill arch further distinguish the sockeye from the chum salmon; the sockeye salmon has 28 to 40 long, slender, rough or serrated closely set rakers

OTHER NAMES

sockeye, red salmon, blue-back salmon, big redfish; French: *saumon nerka;* Japanese: *benizake, himemasu.* The landlocked form is called kokanee salmon, Kennerly's salmon, kokanee, landlocked sockeye, kickininee, little redfish, silver trout; French: *kokani.*

Distribution. *The sockeye salmon is native to the northern Pacific Ocean and its tributaries from northern Hokkaido, Japan, to the Anadyr River, Russia, and from the Sacramento River, California, to Point Hope, Alaska. Kokanee exist in Japan, Russia, Alaska, at least three western provinces in Canada, seven western U.S. states, and three eastern states.*

Habitat. *Sockeye salmon are anadromous, living in the sea and entering fresh-water to spawn. They mainly enter rivers and streams that have lakes at their source. Young fish may inhabit lakes for as many as*

4 years before returning to the ocean. Kokanee occur almost exclusively in freshwater lakes, migrating to tributaries in the fall to spawn (or to outlet areas or shoreline gravel in waters without suitable spawning streams).

on the first arch, whereas the chum salmon has 19 to 26 short, stout, smooth rakers.

Kokanee are smaller but otherwise identical to sea-run sockeye in coloration; they undergo the same changes as sockeye do when spawning.

Size. Adult sockeye usually weigh between 4 and 8 pounds. The all-tackle world record is an Alaskan fish that weighed 15 pounds, 3 ounces. Kokanee are much smaller; in many places they do not grow much over 14 inches or 1 pound, especially where the plankton food resource is low or where many other species compete for it; the all-tackle world record is a British Columbia fish that weighed 9 pounds, 6 ounces.

Life history/Behavior. Sockeye salmon return to their natal streams to spawn after spending 1 to 4 years in the ocean. They enter freshwater systems from the ocean during the summer months or the fall, some having traveled thousands of miles. Most populations show little variation in their arrival time on the spawning grounds from year to year; kokanee spawn from August through February, sockeye from July through December.

Eggs hatch during the winter, and the young alevins remain in the gravel, living off the material stored in their yolk sacs until early spring. At this time they emerge from the gravel as fry and move into rearing areas. In systems with lakes, juveniles usually spend 1 to 3 years in freshwater before migrating to the ocean in the spring as smolts weighing only a few ounces. In systems without lakes, however, many juveniles migrate to the ocean soon after emerging from the gravel.

Although most sockeye salmon production results from the spawning of wild populations, some runs have been developed or enhanced through human effort.

Food and feeding habits. Anadromous salmon rarely feed after entering freshwater, although young fish will feed mainly on plankton and insects. In the ocean, sockeye salmon feed on plankton, plus on crustacean larvae, on larval and small adult fish, and occasionally on squid. Kokanee feed mainly on plankton but also on insects and bottom organisms.

Sauger

Stizostedion canadense

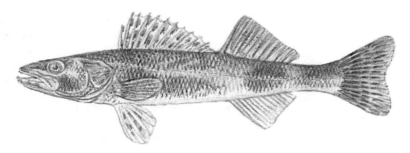

A member of the perch family, the sauger is a smaller, slimmer relative of the walleye, which it closely resembles. It is an important commercial species in some places, especially in Canada, and a gamefish that is often overlooked in some parts of its range. Most of the commercial Canadian catch is taken in Manitoba, where fishing with gillnets and pound nets occurs in the summer, the autumn, and the winter. Sauger are marketed almost entirely as fresh and frozen fillets, and much of the catch is exported to the United States. Their flesh is slightly softer, sweeter, and finer in texture than that of the walleye, but this difference is generally indistinguishable to most people, and commercially, they are sold as one and the same fish.

Identification. The sauger's body is slender and almost cylindrical, and the head is long and cone shaped. The back and the sides are a dull brown or olive gray flecked with yellow and shading to white over the belly. There are three or four dark saddle-shaped blotches on the back and the sides. It is easily distinguished from the smooth-cheeked walleye by the presence of rough scales on its cheeks and two or three rows of distinct black spots on the membranes of its spiny dorsal fin, by the absence of a large blotch on the anterior portion of its spinous dorsal fin, and by the absence of a white tip on its tail. The eyes are large and glossy, and the teeth are large and sharp.

Size/Age. Sauger are commonly caught at sizes ranging from 10 to 16 inches and up to 1½ pounds. Specimens exceeding 22 inches and 5 pounds are rare. The maximum size is about 9 pounds, and the all-tackle world record is an 8-pound, 12-ounce fish caught in North Dakota in 1971. The life span is 10 to 12 years.

Life history/Behavior. Male sauger mature at age 2, females at ages 3 or 4. They spawn when the water

OTHER NAMES

sand pickerel, sand pike, blue pickerel, pike, gray pike, blue pike, river pike, pike-perch, spotfin pike, jack, jack fish, jack salmon; French: *doré noir.*

Distribution. *This species has a general distribution in mid-central North America from Quebec to Tennessee and Arkansas, and northwesterly through Montana to about central Alberta. Between Alberta and Quebec it occurs in southern Saskatchewan, Manitoba, and Ontario and throughout the Great Lakes to James Bay. It does not occur east of the Appalachians or much south of Tennessee, except in a few drainages where it has been introduced, principally from the Carolinas through the lower coastal states to as far south as Texas on the lower Gulf of Mexico.*

Habitat. *Habitat preferences of the sauger tend to large, turbid, shallow lakes and large, silty, slow-flowing rivers. It is more tolerant of muddy water and swifter*

Sauger   **173**

Sauger (continued)
current than walleye, and it prefers water temperatures between 62° and 72°F. It is often found in tailwaters below dams and along rocky riprap. Eddies near turbulent water are often staging and feeding areas. Gravel bars and points are prominent holding locations in lakes.

temperature is between 41° and 46°F. Adults enter backwaters or tributaries or congregate in tailwaters and search for gravel or rock substrate where they can deposit their eggs. In large river systems, the upstream spawning run can cover 100 to 200 miles, although it will be just a short distance from reservoirs into tributaries. In waters where they occur with walleye, they will usually spawn immediately after walleye. Sauger can naturally interbreed with walleye, producing a fish called a saugeye. Sauger grow more slowly than do walleye, however, and are primarily a river fish that locates near the bottom on a variety of bottom types. Like walleye, the sauger is a schooling species.

Food and feeding habits. Sauger feed on such small fish as shad, sunfish, and minnows, as well as on crayfish, leeches, and insects. Most feeding occurs over rocky gravel bottoms or along sparsely weeded sandy bottoms.

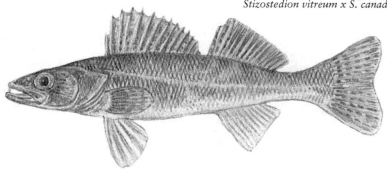

The saugeye is a hybrid fish resulting from the interbreeding of walleye and sauger. It occurs naturally, although infrequently, where the two species mix together. Most populations are produced in hatcheries and are usually stocked in locations where neither parent species has been able to maintain a population. In some literature, it is identified as *Stizostedion vitreum x S. canadense,* which refers to a cross between a female walleye and a male sauger. The meat of the saugeye is similar to that of its parents, making it excellent table fare.

Identification. The body of the saugeye is more similar to that of a walleye than to that of a sauger, although the dorsal fin is sometimes spotted (it is on the sauger and is not on the walleye). It also has saddlelike markings on the back and the sides, as the sauger does, and the caudal fin has a white border on its lower lobe, as that of the walleye does. The saugeye also has a dark blotch on the membranes of the spiny dorsal fin. The body may have a yellowish cast.

Size/Age. This fish grows rapidly and has the potential to reach the intermediate sizes, although not the overall size, that walleye typically attain. The all-tackle world record is a 12-pound, 13-ounce fish from Ohio. Typical saugeye are about 15 inches in length and they normally range from 10 to 24 inches.

Spawning behavior. Unlike some hybrid species, saugeye are not sterile and do have the ability to produce offspring with either parent stock. Spawning occurs in tributaries or in tailwater areas when the temperature is between 40° and 50°F.

Food. Small fish are the primary food for saugeye. Shad are especially favored in many lakes and rivers.

Distribution. *The saugeye has been introduced to waters in the United States from western Ohio, Kentucky, and Tennessee to the eastern Dakotas and southward to Oklahoma.*

Habitat. *Like their sauger parent, saugeye are more tolerant of muddy or turbid water than are walleye and seem better suited to impoundments that receive a high rate of water exchange (which increases turbidity). The introduction of saugeye to new waters, however, is still in its early stages.*

Shad, Alabama

Alosa alabamae

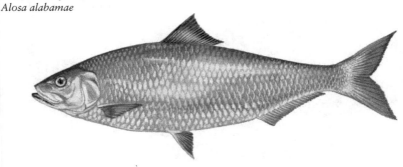

OTHER NAMES

Gulf shad, Ohio shad.

Distribution. *This species occurs in the northern Gulf of Mexico from the Mississippi Delta and Louisiana eastward to the Choctawhatchee River in Florida; it also occurs in rivers from Iowa to Arkansas and across West Virginia.*

Habitat/Life history. *The Alabama shad is a schooling species that spends most of its life in the ocean; when mature, it returns from early spring through the summer to rivers and streams to spawn, inhabiting open water of medium to large rivers. Young shad descend rivers in autumn.*

This member of the Clupeidae family of herring and shad is an anadromous species virtually ignored by anglers. It does have some commercial significance, however.

Identification. A silvery fish like its other relatives, the Alabama shad has a large terminal mouth with upper and lower jaws of almost equal length. Its tongue has a single median row of small teeth, there is no lateral line, the posterior of the dorsal fin lacks an elongated slender filament, and there are 18 or fewer anal rays. In general, it is nearly identical to the larger-growing American shad, but the adult fish has 42 to 48 gill rakers on the lower limb of the first gill arch.

Size. The Alabama shad can grow to just over 20 inches but is usually under 15 inches long.

Food/Angling. The feeding habits of this species at sea are unknown but are presumably similar to those of hickory and American shad. The Alabama shad is anadromous and only a potential angling target during upriver spawning migrations, during which time it does not feed. This smallish shad is a largely incidental catch and a rare deliberate angling target.

Shad, American
Alosa sapidissima

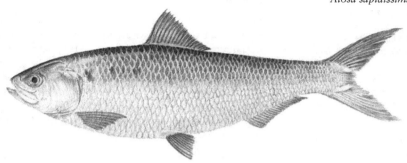

Frequently referred to simply as "shad," this species is an anadromous member of the Clupeidae family of herring and shad and, it is highly regarded as a gamefish due to its strong fighting and jumping characteristics. American shad spawning runs provide a popular but seasonal sportfishery on both coasts of the United States, although these fish receive scant attention in Canada. The white, flaky flesh of this shad is full of bones but makes good table fare if prepared with patience and care; the scientific name *sapidissima* means "most delicious," an appropriate appellation for a fish that supports a considerable commercial fishery and whose roe is considered a delicacy and commands a premium price.

Other North American shad to which it is closely or distantly related include the smaller hickory shad, a western Atlantic species whose range overlaps with the American shad, and the Alabama shad of the Gulf Coast.

Identification. The laterally compressed, fairly deep body of the American shad is silvery white with some green to dark blue along the back, frequently with a metallic shine. The coloring darkens slightly when the fish enters freshwater to spawn. There is a large black spot directly behind the top of the gill cover, followed by several spots that become smaller and less distinct toward the tail; sometimes there are up to three rows of these dark spots, one under the other. The American shad has large, easily shed scales, as well as modified scales called scutes, which form a distinct ridge or cutting edge along the belly. It has a single dorsal fin in the middle of the back, the tail is deeply forked, and there are soft fin rays and long anal fins. It has weak teeth or no teeth at all.

Bearing a close resemblance to the hickory shad, the American shad is distinguished by the way its lower jaw fits easily into a deep, V-shaped notch under the upper jaw,

OTHER NAMES

poor man's salmon, common shad, Atlantic shad, Connecticut River shad, North River shad, Potomac shad, Susquehanna shad, white shad, Delaware shad, alose; French: *alose savoureuse.*

Distribution. *The endemic range of this species is east of the Appalachians along the Atlantic coast of North America from Sand Hill River, Labrador, to the St. Johns River, Florida; practically every significant coastal river along the western Atlantic seaboard has supported a distinct spawning population at one time or another. Important sportfisheries currently exist in the Connecticut and Delaware Rivers. The Hudson River has historically had major runs, but sportfishing for shad in this deep, wide river is negligible, although it has in the past been commercially significant. The Susquehanna has been undergoing restoration of its runs. In 1871, American shad were introduced into the Sacramento River in California* *and today are found up and down the Pacific coast, ranging from Bahia de Todos Santos in upper Baja California, Mexico, to Cook Inlet, Alaska, and the Kamchatka Peninsula. Most sportfishing occurs in the U.S. portion of this range, and a major run occurs in the Columbia River.*

Habitat. *American shad spend most of their lives in the ocean, ascending coastal rivers to spawn. They are found in freshwater only during their spawning runs and cannot tolerate cold waters below 41°F. Predominant in more northerly climates, American shad engage in extensive and complex migrations throughout their range, relying on their acute sense of homing for navigation. In coastal rivers, they primarily inhabit deep runs and pools.*

whereas the lower jaw of the hickory shad protrudes noticeably beyond the upper jaw.

Size/Age. The normal size of American shad is 2 to 5 pounds, but specimens weighing up to 8 pounds are not uncommon when fish are abundant. They reach a maximum of 2½ feet and possibly 13½ pounds. The all-tackle world record is an 11-pound, 4-ounce fish taken from Massachusetts waters in 1994. Although American shad can live to age 13, few live past age 7. Females (called roe fish or hens) grow more quickly and generally larger than males (called bucks).

Life history/Behavior. Most fish spawn for the first time when they weigh 3 to 5 pounds. Males reach sexual maturity at age 3 to 4, females at age 4 to 5. When water temperatures range from 41° to 73°F, the fish swim upriver and as far inland as 300 miles. Peak migrations occur when the water temperature is in the 50s. These migrations usually take place in April in southern rivers and through July in northern regions, even beginning as early as mid-November in Florida.

Most spawning activity takes place in deep areas with moderate to strong currents, particularly during the night, when water temperatures are in the mid-60s. A single female is accompanied by several males, swimming close to the surface and splashing and rolling as tens of thousands of eggs are laid. The nonadhesive eggs drift with the current, gradually sinking and then hatching from 3 to 12 days later. Post-spawning adults attempt to return to the sea after spawning; many die immediately after spawning, whereas others have been known to live long enough to spawn as many as seven times.

Food and feeding habits. American shad primarily feed on plankton, swimming with their mouths open and gill covers extended while straining the water; they also eat small crustaceans, insects, fish eggs, algae, and small fish. They cease feeding during upstream spawning migration but resume during their relatively quick downstream post-spawning migration.

Shad, Gizzard

Dorosoma cepedianum

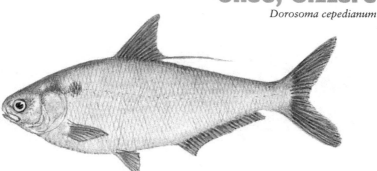

A member of the Clupeidae family of herring and shad, the gizzard shad is important forage for large fish. However, its rapid growth rate causes it to exceed a consumable size for most predators early on in its life. It is often labeled a nuisance fish by anglers and biologists, due to large die-offs, which happen because the species is especially susceptible to drastic changes in temperature and low concentrations of oxygen.

Identification. The gizzard shad is one of two freshwater members of the herring family that has a distinctively long, slender last ray on its dorsal fin. The body is silver blue on the back and silver white underneath, with either blue-and-green or gold reflections on the head and the flanks; occasionally, there are six to eight horizontal dark stripes on the back, starting behind a large purple blue or black shoulder spot (which is faint or absent in large adults). The gizzard shad also has dusky fins, a blunt snout, a subterminal mouth, and a deep notch at the center of the upper jaw.

Size/Age. Growing to a maximum of 20½ inches and averaging about 10 inches in length, this species commonly reaches more than a pound in weight but has grown to over 4 pounds. Most gizzard shad die before they reach age 7, although they can live up to 10 years.

Life history. Gizzard shad occur in schools and are first able to spawn when 2 to 3 years old or 7 to 13 inches long. They breed near the surface in freshwater from March through August, when water temperatures range from 50° to 70°F. They roam open waters in search of plankton, which occurs at various levels, according to the season and conditions.

Food and feeding habits. Gizzard shad are filter feeders that strain microscopic organisms from the water or pick through mud and organic matter on the bottom.

Shad, Hickory

Alosa mediocris

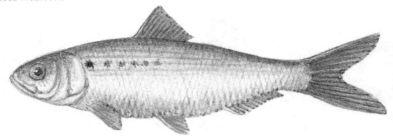

OTHER NAMES

shad herring, hickory jack, freshwater taylor, fall herring, bonejack.

Distribution. *Found only along the Atlantic coast of North America, the hickory shad ranges from the Kenduskeag River, Maine, to the St. Johns River, Florida. It is most common in the Southeast and in the mid-Atlantic regions. This species overlaps with American shad and ascends some of the same rivers when spawning.*

Habitat. *The hickory shad is a schooling species that spends most of its life in the ocean; when mature, it returns in the early spring through the summer to rivers and streams to spawn, inhabiting open water of medium to large rivers. Young shad descend rivers in the autumn.*

A member of the Clupeidae family of herring *(see)* and shad, the hickory shad is of significant recreational interest, being a friskier although smaller cousin of the American shad *(see: Shad, American)*. It is also of commercial value, particularly its roe.

Identification. Gray green on the back and fading to silver on the sides, the hickory shad has clear fins, with the exception of the dusky dorsal and caudal fins, which are occasionally black edged. It has a strongly oblique mouth, a lower jaw that projects noticeably beyond its upper jaw, and a cheek that is longer than or about equal to its depth. There is a blue-black spot near the upper edge of the gill cover, followed by a clump of indistinct dusky spots that extends below the dorsal fin. There are also teeth on the lower jaw and 18 to 23 rakers on the lower limb of the first gill arch.

Size. The hickory shad can reach almost 2 feet in length and averages 1 to 3 pounds in weight. It can weigh as much as 6 pounds.

Life history/Behavior. Hickory shad mature when they are 2 years old and about 12 inches long. Adults ascend coastal rivers during the spring. Preferred water temperatures range from 55° to 69°F, but the lower end of that range seems to trigger the spawning urge. Young fish remain in rivers, estuaries, and backwaters, migrating to the sea by the fall or early winter.

Food and feeding habits. At sea, hickory shad feed on small fish, as well as on squid, small crabs, other crustaceans, and fish eggs. They are not pursued or caught by anglers in places where they do feed but are pursued and caught when migrating upriver in natal waters when they do not feed.

Shad, Threadfin

Dorosoma petenense

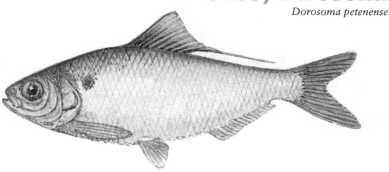

A well-known forage fish and a member of the Clupeidae family of herring and shad, the threadfin shad rarely grows larger than 5 inches long, remaining small enough to be one of the most important open-water forage species for prominent freshwater gamefish, especially bass and stripers.

Identification. The threadfin shad is silvery with a deeply compressed body and is most easily recognized by the elongated, thin last ray on its dorsal fin. It has a small, dark shoulder spot, and its upper jaw does not project past the lower jaw. It is similar in appearance to other herring, including the similar-size but more northerly ranging alewives and the larger gizzard shad, with which it shares overlapping ranges and many of the same waters. It is distinguished from gizzard shad of similar size by its more pointed snout, terminal mouth, black dots on its chin and the bottom of the mouth, and yellow fins.

Size. This species is commonly found at 2½ to 4 inches long and can attain a maximum length of 9 inches. Many threadfins do not live longer than 2 years, although they can live as long as 4 or more years.

Life history/Behavior. Threadfin shad spawn in the spring and the autumn near or over plants or other objects. They are prolific but short-lived and are highly susceptible to winter kill from extreme cold temperatures, which helps keep their numbers in check.

Food and feeding habits. Threadfins are filter feeders that primarily consume plankton and organic detritus in open water; they occasionally feed on fish larvae and on the organic material found on or over sandy or silty bottoms. In reservoirs and large lakes, these fish are constantly on the move, searching for and feeding on minute plankton, the location and the level of which will vary seasonally and according to various factors.

OTHER NAMES
shad, threadfin.

Distribution. *Threadfin shad occur throughout the Mississippi River basin, from the Ohio River of Kentucky and southern Indiana southwest to Oklahoma and south to Texas and Florida, as well as in other Gulf of Mexico drainages and Atlantic drainages in Florida. They are also present in rivers in Guatemala and Honduras. They have been introduced as a forage species in Hawaii and the western United States and to other areas in the mainland United States.*

Habitat. *Occasionally found in the brackish waters of estuaries and bays, threadfin shad are mainly a freshwater fish occurring in large rivers, reservoirs, lakes, and backwaters, where they principally inhabit open-water environs.*

Shiner, Common

Luxilus cornutus

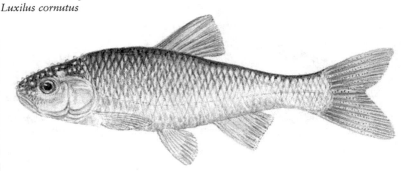

OTHER NAMES

shiner.

Distribution. *This species occurs throughout the Mississippi River, the Hudson Bay, the Great Lakes, and the Atlantic basins from Nova Scotia to Saskatchewan, south to Missouri and Virginia.*

Habitat. *Common shiners are most prevalent in small to moderate-size streams, preferring areas that are clear and without fast-moving water. They will tolerate a small amount of silt but not muddy water.*

The common shiner is an abundant minnow of the Cyprinidae family that is commonly used as a baitfish. It has been known to hybridize with striped shiners.

Identification. The common shiner is silvery with a deep compressed body, a dusky dorsal stripe, large eyes, diamond-shaped scales that flake off easily, and nine anal rays. It has no barbels and no dark lateral stripe, but there is a dark stripe along the middle of the generally olive-colored back. During the spawning season, males develop blue backs and red or pink bodies, with pinkish fins, and display large tubercles on their heads, their pectoral fins, and anterior parts of their bodies.

Size. Common shiners are usually 3 to 4 inches long but can grow to 8 inches.

Spawning behavior. Common shiners spawn in the late spring in water temperatures ranging from 60° to 65°F. They are diverse spawners, preferring to use the nests of other minnows such as chub and fallfish, but they also spawn over gravel or in excavated depressions in gravel or sand. Groups of males gather at the spawning site and vie for position at the upstream end of the nesting area. Spawning occurs when the male wraps his body around a female and drives her toward the nest. Because they often spawn in nests constructed by other minnow species, hybridization is common.

Food. Common shiners feed mainly on insects and insect larvae, but their diet may also include plant material, fish eggs, and small fish.

Shiner, Emerald

Notropis atherinoides

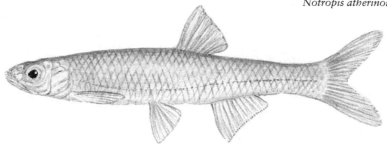

The emerald shiner is one of many shiners that are members of the minnow, or Cyprinidae, family. These fish are important forage for predator species and are frequently used as bait by anglers. Unlike most minnows, however, the emerald shiner is a pelagic big-water species and is abundant in large rivers and in lakes within its range.

Identification. The emerald shiner is a slender, elongated fish with a pale and silvery slab-sided body; it is faintly iridescent green on the top, fading to silver or white on the belly. Juveniles appear semitransparent. Other characteristics include a faint lateral band, a short and fairly pointed snout, large eyes, and usually 11 anal fin rays. It has no barbels. During the spawning season, males develop very small tubercles on the fins but have no breeding colors.

Size/Age. Emerald shiners are commonly 3 to 4 inches long and seldom grow to more than 5 inches long. They typically live for only 3 years.

Spawning behavior. Spawning occurs when water temperatures reach about 75°F and may be continued over an extended period, lasting from late spring through midsummer in some places. Unlike many other shiners, this species spawns in midwater in groups. It is also prone to cyclical abundance.

Food. A pelagic species, emerald shiners feed on plankton, zooplankton, blue-green algae, diatoms, and insect larvae.

OTHER NAMES
buckeye, shiner, lake shiner, lake emerald shiner, common emerald shiner; French: *mémé émeraude.*

Distribution. *This species has a wide range, from the St. Lawrence and the Hudson River basins west to the Mackenzie River drainage of the Northwest Territories and south throughout the Great Lakes and the Mississippi River drainages, to the Gulf Coast from Texas to Alabama. It is probably the most abundant fish in the Mississippi River and other large rivers, and is also prominent in the Great Lakes, as well as in other large lakes.*

Habitat. *Emerald shiners travel in large schools in midwater and near-surface areas. They roam in large lakes and are common in the pools of big rivers. They are known to move vertically toward the surface at night and to deeper water in daylight.*

Shiner, Golden

Notemigonus crysoleucas

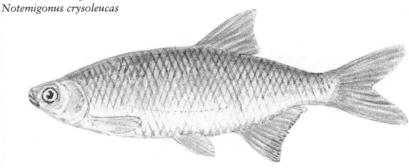

OTHER NAMES

roach, shad roach, shiner, pond shiner.

Distribution. This species is widely distributed east of the Rockies in the central and eastern United States, ranging from Quebec to Saskatchewan in the north, and to Florida, Texas, and Mexico in the south. It has been introduced elsewhere, including Arizona, California, and Washington.

Habitat. Slow-water fish, golden shiners are prevalent in lakes, ponds, backwaters, and the slower parts of streams and small to medium rivers. They are common in weedy, clean, quiet, and shallow waters.

The golden shiner is a prominent and widespread minnow of the Cyprinidae family. These fish are important forage species for predators and are widely used in various sizes as bait by anglers.

Identification. The golden shiner has a deep, compressed body that is generally golden yellow or brass colored in turbid water, varying to more silvery in clear water. The fins are yellow green but become reddish in large spawning adults. The mouth is small and upturned with a slightly pointed snout, and there is a distinctive fleshy, scaleless keel along the belly from the pelvic to the anal fin. The dusky lateral line of the golden shiner noticeably dips down in the middle of the body, and the caudal fin is moderately forked. The color of the fins is more pronounced during breeding season; the breeding male develops fine tubercles on the dorsal surface of the head and the body. The golden shiner has 7 to 9 dorsal rays and 8 to 19 anal rays.

Size/Age. Golden shiners can grow to 10½ to 12 inches in length, although the average size varies with the environment. Many northerly waters are likely to produce smaller fish on average, and 3 to 5 inches is the norm in many places. These fish reportedly live for up to 10 years.

Spawning behavior. Golden shiners reach sexual maturity in their second year when they are usually 2½ to 3½ inches long, and spawn over an extended period, commencing in the spring when water temperatures exceed 68°F. They do not prepare nests, as many other shiners and minnows do; rather, they scatter adhesive eggs over algae and other aquatic vegetation and do not exhibit parental care.

Food. The food of golden shiners consists of plankton, algae, insects, and small fish; they feed in midwater and at or near the surface.

Shiner, Striped

Luxilus chrysocephalus

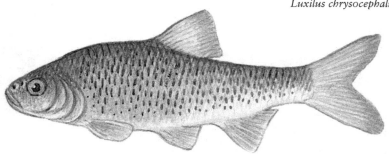

The striped shiner is a common and widespread minnow of the Cyprinidae family that is familiar to anglers who use it as bait or observe it spawning over the gravel nests built by other minnows. Two subspecies are recognized: *Luxilus chrysocephalus chrysocephalus* and *L. c. isolepis*.

Identification. The striped shiner is a silvery, laterally compressed minnow with large eyes and a terminal mouth. The exposed portion of its scales near the anterior lateral line is much more deep than it is wide. Anterior portions of scales are darkly pigmented, giving a crescent-shaped appearance to the sides.

Several parallel stripes run along each side of the upper body and converge posterior to the dorsal fin. *L. c. chrysocephalus* has wavy stripes, whereas *L. c. isolepis* has straight stripes. Other characteristics include 8 to 10 anal fin rays and a complete lateral line with 36 to 42 scales. The nuptial male develops a rosy pink color on its head, its body, and the margins of all fins and has tubercles on the head, the snout, the lower jaw, and the pectoral fins.

Size/Age. Adults can exceed 8 inches in length, but most are less than 5 inches long; they can live up to 6 years.

Spawning behavior. Striped shiners reach sexual maturity in their second year. Adult males are larger than females. Spawning occurs from late spring to early summer in water temperatures ranging from 61° to 81°F.

Striped shiners are classified as pit spawners. Males excavate small pits on the top of chub nests or directly on the stream bottom and aggressively defend these pits while attempting to secure females for spawning. Because of their tendency to spawn over chub nests, striped shiners often hybridize with chub and with other minnows that use nests.

Food. Striped shiners feed mainly on insects, but their diet may also include detritus, algae, fish eggs, crayfish, and small fish.

Distribution. *The subspecies L. c. chrysocephalus extends throughout drainages of the lower Mississippi River and the Gulf Coast; L. c. isolepis occurs in drainages of the Great Lakes and the Mississippi River basins north of the Red River in Arkansas.*

Habitat. *Striped shiners occur in water bodies ranging from small streams to small rivers but are most abundant in small to medium streams. Their preferred habitats are pools, runs, and backwaters of flowing streams. They are more common in free-flowing streams with clear or slightly turbid water.*

Smelt, Rainbow
Osmerus mordax

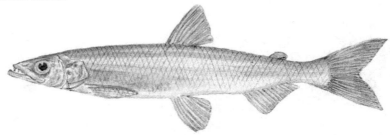

OTHER NAMES

American smelt, frostfish, leefish, toothed smelt, freshwater smelt; French: *éperlan du nord.*

Distribution. *The rainbow smelt is widely distributed throughout eastern and western North America, inhabiting coastal waters, as well as countless inland freshwater lakes. On the Atlantic coast, rainbow smelt range from New Jersey in the south to Hamilton Inlet, Labrador, in the north. Their inland habitats include lakes in northeastern states and provinces, as well as throughout the Great Lakes from the St. Lawrence River to Lake Superior.*

Habitat. *The rainbow smelt is a pelagic schooling species, inhabiting inshore coastal regions and the midwaters of lakes. Because it is sensitive to both light and warmer temperatures, schools of rainbow smelt tend to concentrate near the bottom of lakes and coastal waters during daylight hours.*

One of the most prominent members of the Osmeridae family of smelt, the rainbow smelt is an important forage species for predatory fish and a principal target for inland and coastal commercial fishing. It is the subject of some recreational activity, particularly via dipnetting in the spring during spawning runs and ice fishing for landlocked populations in some lakes.

The rainbow smelt is a close relative of the eulachon of the Pacific, the pond smelt *(Hypomesus olidus)* of the western Arctic, the capelin of the Atlantic, and the European smelt *(Osmerus eperlanus).*

Originally an anadromous coastal species, rainbow smelt were first stocked inland in 1906, in streams and lakes feeding Lake Michigan, in order to provide forage for salmonids. Eventually, large rainbow smelt populations were found in all the Great Lakes, especially Lake Erie. There is some evidence that the rainbow smelt inhabiting Lake Ontario were not a result of these stockings but of an independent movement from Lake Champlain stocks.

Commercial fishing for rainbow smelt was primarily centered on the Atlantic coast until the middle of the twentieth century; in 1948, an experimental gillnet fishery was established in the Great Lakes and became increasingly successful. Gradually, the Great Lakes fishery exceeded Atlantic coast ventures in terms of the weight of total landings and their market value. Coastal anadromous rainbow smelt, however, are more highly valued—fetching more than twice the price—than inland smelt and are considered to be of superior food quality. Anglers target rainbow smelt strictly as a food fish, and this species generates extensive efforts in the Great Lakes and the coastal areas of the Maritime Provinces and the northeastern United States.

Identification. The rainbow smelt is a slender, silver fish, with a pale green or olive-green back. Fresh from the water, the sides of the fish take on a purple, blue, or pink iridescent hue. The scales on the rainbow smelt are large and easily detached, and at spawning time those on the males develop small tubercles, resembling tiny buttons that serve as a mark of their sex. The lower jaw of the fish projects beyond the upper one, and the entire mouth extends beyond the middle of the eye. On the tip of the tongue are large teeth. One large dorsal fin is located about halfway along the back, and behind that is a small adipose fin.

Size/Age. Most rainbow smelt are less than 8 inches long, although some coastal specimens measuring 14 inches have been found in the coastal waters of the Maritimes and in Lake Ontario. They may live for at least 6 years.

Life history. In the spring, both anadromous and land-locked adult rainbow smelt migrate upstream to freshwater spawning grounds. In some rivers, rainbow smelt start their upstream migration before the spring thaw has begun. Spawners reach the tide head in the main tributaries when the water temperature is only 39° to 41°F. In the Great Lakes, migration begins shortly after ice out, when the water temperature is at least 46°F. They enter smaller streams when the temperature is 43° to 45°F.

Rainbow smelt remain at spawning sites for a number of days. Shortly after spawning, many males die. Surviving males and females remain for about 5 to 10 days before migrating downstream.

Some rainbow smelt are mature at 2 years of age and all are mature at age 3. Fecundity varies from one area to another, and anadromous populations are more fecund than are landlocked populations.

Spawning occurs mainly at night, typically over a gravelly bottom. The eggs are adhesive and stick to the gravel or other bottom objects.

Rainbow smelt restricted to small inland lakes are usually smaller than they are elsewhere, and often do not exceed 4 inches in length.

Food. Zooplankton, insect larvae, aquatic worms, and small fish constitute the diet of rainbow smelt, with zooplankton being predominant.

Snook

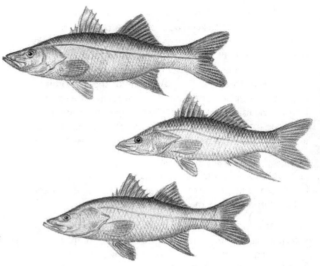

Fat Snook
*Centropomus
parallelus*

Swordspine Snook
Centropomus ensiferus

Tarpon Snook
Centropomus pectinatus

Distribution. *In the western Atlantic, all three species
are present and are most
abundant in southern
Florida, although sword-
spine and tarpon snook are
rare on Florida's west coast.
Fat and swordspine snook
occur around the Greater
and Lesser Antilles, whereas
fat snook also extend down
the southeastern coast of
the Gulf of Mexico and the
continental Caribbean
coasts to Santos, Brazil.
Swordspine snook occur
down the continental
Caribbean coasts of Central
and South America to Rio de
Janeiro, Brazil. Tarpon
snook are found in the West
Indies and from Mexico to
Brazil. They are also*

These three species of snook are all small, similar-looking fish with almost identical ranges and habits but are less prominent than their larger relative the common snook. As members of the Centropomidae family, which includes the Nile perch and the barramundi, they are excellent table fish with delicate, white, flaky meat and are good gamefish, despite their small size.

There are believed to be 12 species of snook, 6 of which occur in the western Atlantic and 6 in the eastern Pacific, although no single species occurs in both oceans. A good deal is known about these three smaller Atlantic-occurring species and about the common snook, but not about the others, especially those in the Pacific, which include such large-growing species as the Pacific black snook *(C. nigrescens;* commonly called black snook) and the Pacific white snook *(C. viridis),* as well as the smaller Pacific blackfin snook *(C. medius).*

Identification. Snook in general are distinctive in appearance, with characteristic protruding lower jaws and particularly prominent black lateral lines running from the gill covers to the tails.

The fat snook has a deeper body than the other snook do, although it is not strongly compressed. Coloration varies, depending on the area the fish inhabits, but the fat snook is frequently yellow brown or green brown on the back and silvery on the sides, and the lateral line is weakly outlined in black. The mouth reaches to or beyond the center of the eye, and it has the smallest scales of all the snook. There are 15 to 16 rays in the pectoral fin, 6 soft rays in the anal fin, and 10 to 13 gill rakers.

The swordspine snook is the smallest snook and is named for its very long second anal spine, which usually extends to or farther than the area below the base of the tail. With a slightly concave profile, it is yellow green or brown green on the back and silvery on the belly, and it has a prominent lateral line outlined in black. It has the largest scales of all the snook, as well as 15 to 16 rays in the pectoral fin, 6 soft rays in the anal fin, and 13 to 16 gill rakers.

The tarpon snook is distinctive, having 7 anal fin rays, when all other snook have 6. It also has a distinguishing upturned or tarponlike snout and a compressed, flat-sided body. The prominent black lateral line extends through the tail. The pelvic fin is orange yellow with a blackish edge, and the tips of the pelvic fins reach past the anus. There are 14 rays in the pectoral fin, 7 soft rays in the anal fin, and 15 to 18 gill rakers.

Size/Age. The fat snook rarely reaches more than 20 inches in length, although it is said to attain a length of 2½ feet. The swordspine and the tarpon snook are usually less than 1 pound in weight or 12 inches in length. The all-tackle world records for the fat and the tarpon snook are, respectively, 9 pounds, 5 ounces, and 3 pounds, 2 ounces, both taken in Florida. Snook have a life span of at least 7 years.

Food. These species feed on fish and crustaceans.

reported on the Pacific coast from Mexico to Colombia.

Habitat/Behavior. *Snook inhabit the coastal waters of estuaries and lagoons, moving between freshwater and saltwater seasonally but always remaining close to shore and to estuaries. Fat and swordspine snook prefer very low salinity water or freshwater, whereas the tarpon snook is most common in shaded lakes with brackish waters. Fat snook occur more often in interior waters than do other snook (instead of estuarine waters), and all three species use mangrove shorelines as nursery grounds. Snook are usually sexually mature by their third year.*

Snook, Common

Centropomus undecimalis

OTHER NAMES

linesider, robalo, sergeant fish, snook; Portuguese: *robalo;* Spanish: *robalo, robalito.*

Distribution. *In the western Atlantic, common snook are found primarily in southern Florida, as well as off the southeastern coast of the Gulf of Mexico. They are also occasionally encountered off North Carolina and Texas. The largest snook in Florida, exceeding 30 pounds, are caught chiefly in East Coast bays and inlets from Vero Beach south to Miami, but their most abundant populations are on the West Coast, from Boca Grande south throughout the Everglades region, including Florida Bay.*

The range of the Pacific black snook is in the eastern Pacific, primarily from Baja California, Mexico, to Colombia. The range of the Pacific white snook is similar, extending from Baja California to Peru.

Habitat. *Snook inhabit warm, shallow coastal*

The common snook is the most abundant and wide-ranging of the snook and is a member of the Centropomidae family, which also includes such prized species as the Nile perch and the barramundi.

In all, there are believed to be 12 species of snook, 6 of which occur in the western Atlantic and 6 in the eastern Pacific, although no single species occurs in both oceans. Large-growing Pacific species with similar traits, although less common, include the Pacific black snook (*C. nigrescens,* commonly known as the black snook) and the Pacific white snook (*C. viridis*).

Identification. A silvery fish with a yellow green or olive tint, the common snook has a body that is streamlined and slender, with a distinct black lateral line running from the top of its gills to the end of its forked tail. It has a sloping forehead; a long, concave snout; and a large mouth with brushlike teeth and a protruding lower jaw. The fins are occasionally bright yellow, although the pelvic fin is usually pale, unlike the orange-yellow, black-tipped pelvic fin of the tarpon snook. The common snook has a high, divided dorsal fin, as well as small scales that run from about 70 to 77 along the lateral line to the base of the tail. It has relatively short anal spines that do not reach the base of the tail when pressed against the body; there are usually 6 soft rays in the anal fin. There are also 15 to 16 rays in the pectoral fins and 7 to 9 gill rakers on the first arch.

Size/Age. The common snook grows much larger than do other Atlantic-range snook, averaging 1½ to 2½ feet or 5 to 8 pounds, although it can reach 4 feet and 50 pounds. Females are almost always larger than males, although growth rates are variable. The all-tackle world record is a 53-pound, 10-ounce fish. Common snook can live for more than 20 years.

Snook, Common (continued)

The Pacific black snook attains similar sizes and is believed to reach 60 pounds; a 57-pound, 12-ounce specimen is the all-tackle world record for this species. The Pacific white snook also grows large, and a 47½-pound specimen from Cabo San Lucas, Mexico, is the all-tackle world record.

Life history/Behavior. Common snook congregate at mouths of passes and rivers during the spawning season, returning to the same spawning sites each summer. Spawning grounds include significant passes and inlets of the Atlantic Ocean and the Gulf of Mexico, such as Sebastian, Ft. Pierce, St. Lucie, Jupiter, and Lake Worth inlets on the east coast and Hurricane, Clearwater, and John's passes on the west coast. Common snook also spawn inside Tampa Bay, around passes to the secondary embankments of Miquel Bay, Terra Ceia Bay, and Riviera Bay. The season extends from April through November, but activity peaks between May and July; more intense spawning occurs during new or full moon phases.

Common snook are protandric hermaphrodites—they can change their sex from male to female; this change usually happens between the ages of 2 and 7 and between the lengths of 17 to 30 inches. Within a group of common snook, sex reversal is brought about by a change in the size of individuals; that is, if a group that loses its largest fish has lost females, some males may undergo sex reversal to fill the absence, a process that takes from 60 to 90 days.

Food and feeding habits. Carnivorous predators that ambush their prey as currents sweep food into their vicinity, snook feed on both freshwater and saltwater fish, shrimp, crabs, and larger crustaceans.

waters and are able to tolerate freshwater and saltwater. They are most common along continental shores, preferring fast-moving tides and relying on the shelter of estuaries, lagoons, mangrove areas, and brackish streams, as well as freshwater canals and rivers, usually at depths of less than 65 feet. Occasionally, they occur in small groups over grassy flats and shallow patch reefs and may be found at the mouths of tributaries and along the ocean side of shores near tributaries. Snook cannot tolerate water temperatures below 60°F; in winter, they stay in protected, stable-temperature areas such as those under bridges, in ship channels, in turning basins, in warmwater outflows near power plants, and in the upper reaches of estuaries.

Splake

Salvelinus namaycush x Salvelinus fontinalis

OTHER NAMES

wendigo.

Distribution. *Splake inhabit Lakes Superior and Huron in the Great Lakes and various midsize lakes in selected states, from Colorado, Utah, and Idaho in the western United States to northern New York and Maine in the east.*

A member of the charr group of the Salmonidae family, the splake is a distinctively marked hybrid fish produced in a hatchery by crossing a true lake trout female *(S. Namaycush)* and a true brook trout male *(S. fontinalis)*. This interbreeding does not occur in nature but is initiated by humans and results in a fertile hybrid species capable of reproducing.

Identification. The splake is difficult to identify externally because it resembles different aspects of both parents. The body shape is intermediate between the heavier lake trout and the slimmer brook trout. The shape of the tail is also intermediate. It is not as deeply forked as that of the lake trout and more closely resembles the slightly indented tail of the brook trout. In coloration and markings, the splake more closely resembles the brook trout. It has vermiculations like brook trout, red-orange ventral fins, and yellowish spots along its flanks.

Size. Splake do not grow as large as lake trout, but they do grow larger than brook trout. Most splake weigh a few pounds, although those from bigger waters with a large forage base may be in the 8- to 12-pound class. The all-tackle world record weighed 20 pounds, 11 ounces.

Life history/Behavior. Although they can reproduce, not all splake do, and some populations lack a suitable habitat for spawning, which is generally rocky reefs near deep water. They also are capable of back-crossing (hybrids mating with parent species), which has occurred in hatcheries but evidently not in the wild. Spawning occurs in the fall, usually in October, on rocky reefs. In the spring, splake are often near tributaries or on gravel shoals, and in the summer they seek deep water.

Food. This omnivorous species eats smelt, white perch, yellow perch, crayfish, insects, sculpin, and other fish.

Squawfish, Northern

Ptychocheilus oregonensis

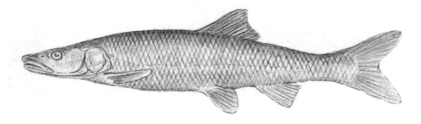

The northern squawfish is a large-growing member of the Cyprinidae family of minnows that is often caught in northwestern North America trout and salmon waters. Yet it is not actively sought and is viewed as a threat to more popular species. Related fish include the Colorado squawfish *(P. lucius)*, the Sacramento squawfish *(P. grandis)*, and the Umpqua squawfish *(P. umpquae)*, which have limited distribution in their respective river systems. The Colorado squawfish, which is endangered, is North America's largest native minnow and can grow to 6 feet.

Identification. The northern squawfish's mouth is terminal and large, extending back past the front edge of the eye. The head is somewhat conical and flattened between the eyes, and the body is slender and barely compressed. All fins are clear, with no spots or coloration, and there are 9 to 10 rays in the dorsal fin and 8 rays in the anal fin. The caudal fin is deeply forked. Its coloring is usually dark green or greenish brown above and lighter and often silvery on the sides, and it has a whitish belly. The spawning male takes on a yellowish or yellow-orange color and develops tubercles on the head, the back, and some fins.

Size/Age. This species can live 10 years and can grow to 25 inches, although it has been reported to attain lengths between 3 and 4 feet. Common sizes are in the 7- to 10-inch range.

Food. The diet of northern squawfish is terrestrial insects, aquatic insect larvae, plankton, crustaceans, small fish, and fish eggs. Large individuals especially prey on small fish and are considered serious predators of juvenile salmonids. In the Columbia River, fisheries managers undertake efforts to control squawfish numbers to minimize this problem.

OTHER NAMES
squawfish, Columbia River dace, Columbia squawfish; French: *sauvagesse du nord.*

Distribution. *Northern squawfish occur in North America in the Pacific drainages from the Nass River in British Columbia to the Columbia River in Nevada, in the Harney River basin in Oregon, and in the Peace River system (Arctic basin) in British Columbia and Alberta.*

Habitat. *Northern squawfish inhabit lakes, ponds, and runs of small to large rivers.*

Steelhead

Oncorhynchus mykiss

Distribution. *The original steelhead range in North America extended from Alaska's Kenai Peninsula to the Baja Peninsula in Mexico, and far inland in coastal rivers. Northern California, Oregon, Washington, southern Alaska, and especially British Columbia have had significant steelhead populations. Overfishing, pollution, dams, other habitat alterations, and additional factors have adversely affected many native runs of steelhead, as they have impacted Pacific salmon stocks. Some coastal runs are depressed, if not threatened. Steelhead are also native to the eastern Pacific and portions of Asia and have been widely introduced throughout the Great Lakes in North America, where they are primarily supported through hatchery production, as well as to other waters in North America and on other continents.*

The term "steelhead" refers to the anadromous form of rainbow trout, and the fish known as steelhead bears the same scientific name as rainbow trout. Most scientific evaluations of rainbow trout list the steelhead as a form of rainbow trout. There are no major physical differences between a steelhead and a rainbow trout, although the nature of their differing lifestyles results in subtle differences in shape and general appearance and a greater difference in color. Technically, the steelhead is a rainbow trout that migrates to sea as a juvenile and returns to freshwater as an adult to spawn, a process known as anadromy. Pacific salmon do this too, although steelhead (and rainbow trout) are positively separated from the various Pacific salmon species by having 8 to 12 rays in the anal fin. Steelhead may exist both in coastal environments and in large inland lake-river systems. The appearance and behavior of both forms of steelhead are largely the same.

Identification. Steelhead are generally more slender and streamlined than rainbow trout. Coloration on the back is basically a blue green, shading to olive with black, regularly spaced spots. The black spots also cover both lobes of the tail. The black coloration fades over the lateral line to a silver-white coloration that blends more toward white on the stomach. Steelhead fresh from the ocean or an inland lake are much more silvery than the resident rainbow is. On steelhead, the typical colors and spots of the trout appear to be coming from beneath a dominant silvery sheen, which gradually fades when the fish are in rivers.

Steelhead have white leading edges on their anal, pectoral, and pelvic fins. A spawning fish develops a distinct pink to red striplike coloration that blends along the sides, both above and below the lateral line. On steelhead, coloration gradually fades following spawning to the more characteristic silvery color that the fish display during their ocean and lake journey.

Size/Age. Steelhead grow much larger on average than rainbow trout do and are capable of exceeding 40 pounds. The all-tackle world record is for a 42-pound, 2-ounce Alaskan fish caught in 1970. Steelhead are typically caught from 5 to 12 pounds, and fish exceeding 15 pounds are not uncommon in some waters. Most fish returning to rivers are 5 to 6 years old, and they can live for 8 years.

Life history/Behavior. Each spring, 6-inch-long steelhead smolts leave their natal streams to begin an ocean journey that few survive. Over a period of 1 to 3 years, steelhead move hundreds of miles or more from their parent stream. Most populations of steelhead reappear in rivers in the fall; called fall-run steelhead, they enter freshwater systems as adults from August into the winter. Some river systems have spring-run steelhead, which end their ocean journeys in mid-April, May, and June; bright, shiny spring-run fish may be mixed with well-marked resident rainbows that have spent the entire winter waiting for the spring spawning period. Still other populations return to their home stream in July and are known as summer steelhead. Spring and summer runs are much less common.

Spawning takes place in the winter and the spring. Unlike salmon, steelhead commonly spawn more than once, and fish exceeding 28 inches are almost always repeat spawners. The ragged and spent spawners move slowly downstream to the sea, and their spawning rainbow colors of spring return to a bright silvery hue.

Steelhead of the Great Lakes and inland systems have a similar life history, although their appearance in or near tributaries varies, depending on their origins. Most migrate into tributaries from late fall through early spring, spawning in the late winter or the early spring. Summer-run fish, called Skamania steelhead, appear near shore and in tributaries in the summer months.

Food and feeding habits. Steelhead in the ocean consume squid, crustaceans, and small fish. In large lakes, they primarily consume pelagic baitfish such as alewives and smelt. When making spawning runs in rivers and streams, they do not feed.

Sticklebacks

Ninespine Stickleback
Pungitius pungitius

Sticklebacks are small, slim members of the Gasterosteidae family that are rarely more than 3 inches long and are confined to the Northern Hemisphere, occurring most abundantly in North America. They are primarily freshwater fish, but some also occur in brackish or shallow inshore waters of seas. The family contains seven genera, nine species, and several subspecies; they are of minimal forage value for predatory fish and are little used as bait, but they have a distinctive appearance and unusual courtship and spawning behaviors.

The stickleback gets its name from the short, stout spines in its first dorsal fin, the number of spines generally identifying the species. Each family member has from 3 to 26 well-developed isolated dorsal spines, preceding a normal dorsal fin having 6 to 14 rays. Almost every species also has a spine at the leading edge of the anal fin and each pelvic fin. The body lacks scales, but in most species it is armored along the sides with bony plates.

Several species of sticklebacks are kept in aquariums. They swim with short spurts of speed, then pause. This makes them interesting to watch, as does their spawning ritual, which people are unlikely to observe in the wild. At spawning time, the males adopt courtship colors, with the bellies bright red in some and velvety black in others. Each male builds a nest among the stems of aquatic plants; the nest is hollow inside but completely covered on the top, the bottom, and the sides, with stems held together with a secretion of sticky threads. Once the nest has been built, the male searches for a female and drives her toward the nest, nipping at her fins and chasing after her if she turns the wrong way.

As soon as the female has laid her eggs, she leaves the nest, sometimes squirming out through the bottom. The male enters the nest immediately and fertilizes the eggs.

Sticklebacks *(continued)*

Often he may go out again and get one or two other females to lay eggs in the nest. Some males build several nests at the same time. The eggs hatch in a week or less. While the eggs are incubating, the males of most species aerate them by fanning currents of water through the nests (the male of one species builds a nest with two holes in the top and sucks water from one of the holes to cause circulation over the eggs). After the eggs hatch, the male tends the fry for several days, generally trying to keep them near the nest.

One of the common species in North America is the brook stickleback *(Culaea inconstans)*, found in streams from southern Ohio westward to Montana and northward, and throughout southern Canada from Nova Scotia to eastern British Columbia. It is generally less than 3½ inches long. The five or six spines on its back are completely separate from one another, rather than joined by a membrane, and the caudal peduncle is especially slender. Like most sticklebacks, it is quarrelsome and guards its territory, particularly its nest, from intruders.

The threespine stickleback *(Gasterosteus aculeatus)* occurs in northern Eurasia and North America, living in both brackish water and freshwater. A number of subspecies are recognized. The ninespine stickleback *(Pungitius pungitius)*, found in northern Europe, China, Japan, and northern North America, is dark brown, and the male becomes a rich black during the courtship and spawning periods. The fifteenspine stickleback *(Spinachia spinachia)* is a European saltwater species restricted to northwestern Europe. The fourspine stickleback *(Apeltes quadracus)* is found only along the eastern coast of North America, from North Carolina to the Gulf of St. Lawrence. The blackspotted or twospine stickleback *(G. wheatlandi)* is another western Atlantic species.

Stonecat

Noturus flavus

Distribution. *The stonecat has a widespread distribution. It exists in the Great Lakes, the St. Lawrence River, drainages of Hudson Bay, and the Mississippi River basin. It can be found from the Hudson River drainage of New York, west to the Red River drainage of Hudson Bay. It is found in drainages of the Mississippi River basin from Quebec to Alberta, southerly to northern Alabama and Mississippi, and westerly to northeastern Oklahoma.*

Habitat. *Generally, the stonecat inhabits riffles of medium to large rivers in places with many large rocks. It also occurs in lakes where currents or wave action produces streamlike conditions. In the main channels of large rivers, it has been found in swift water over sand substrate.*

The stonecat is a widely distributed and relatively common member of the madtoms. It is the largest madtom in body size, is the species with the longest life span, and has a lower relative fecundity than other madtoms. It may be used for bait, especially in bass fishing.

Identification. Stonecats are olive, yellowish, or slate colored on the upper half of their bodies and are the only madtoms that exceed 7 inches in total length. The stonecat has backward extensions from the sides of the toothpatch on the roof of its mouth. In most cases, the stonecat has a patch on its nape, a white spot at the rear of the dorsal fin base, and another white spot on the upper edge of the caudal fin. There are either no or a few weak teeth on the rear of the pectoral spine.

Size/Age. Of 261 specimens collected from Missouri and Illinois streams, the largest specimens were a 7-inch male and a 6.4-inch female. Growth is fastest in the first year of life. Individuals up to 5.3 inches are at least 3 years of age. Individuals greater than 6.5 inches are 4 years and older. The largest and oldest stonecat ever collected was 12.25 inches in total length and 9 years old.

Spawning behavior. Females mature at 3 to 4 years of age and a mean standard length of 4.7 inches. Clutches are guarded by males under large flat rocks in pools or crests of riffles. Rocks used as spawning cover averaged 200 square inches and were found in water averaging 34 inches deep.

Food. Mayfly larvae are important food for all sizes of stonecat. Excluding those specimens greater than 4.7 inches in standard length, all stonecats consume stonefly, caddisfly, and midge larvae. Stonecats less than 3.1 inches in standard length consume blackfly larvae, whereas larger stonecats consume more crayfish. Like most typical madtoms, stonecats consume a variety of organisms that are only infrequent prey, including fish eggs, worms, amphipods, and chilopods.

Stoneroller, Central
Campostoma anomalum

The central stoneroller is a member of the Cyprinidae family of minnows. It is a hardy species that provides important forage for gamefish and is commonly used as bait.

Identification. The central stoneroller has a thick and barely compressed torpedo-shaped body that is dull gray with a brassy tint and a pale golden stripe along the upper sides. It has an unusual appearance due to its subterminal mouth and a hard cartilaginous ridge on the lower jaw. The mouth formation and the lower ridge enable the central stoneroller to scrape algae and other minute organisms off rocks. There are dark brown to black blotches on the back and the sides of large specimens, the caudal fin is moderately forked, and the lateral line is nearly straight. A breeding male exhibits large tubercles on the top of the head and the upper scales almost to the base of the tail, and there are small tubercles on the pectoral rays and the first dorsal ray; it also has an orange cast, with orange and black anal and dorsal fins.

Size. This species grows to 8½ inches but is usually 4 to 6 inches long.

Spawning behavior. The male central stoneroller primarily builds pit nests by carrying pebbles in its mouth or disturbing the upstream gravel to float pebbles downstream. Nests are communal and are constructed in gravel areas at the top of riffles. They are relatively shallow and are built in quiet areas, those with moderate current, or where there is overhanging protection. Spawning occurs in the spring, and males defend their territories and aggressively challenge other males.

OTHER NAMES
stoneroller, minnow, hornyhead, knottyhead.

Distribution. *The central stoneroller ranges widely in the eastern and central United States and southern Canada in the Atlantic, Great Lakes, Hudson Bay, and Mississippi River basins, from New York to North Dakota and south to Georgia and Texas and northern Mexico. It is least common in the Great Plains.*

Habitat. *Central stonerollers prefer clean riffles, runs, and pools with current in streams, creeks, and small to medium rivers.*

Sturgeon

Green Sturgeon
Acipenser medirostris

Sturgeon are large, slow-maturing, long-lived, and primitive fish found in large inland and coastal rivers, as well as in some lakes. They are contemporary species of ancient lineages; fossil remains of sturgeon and related paddlefish have been dated to early in the Triassic period of the Mesozoic era (230 to 265 million years ago), making them contemporaries of dinosaurs and causing them to be referred to as "living fossils."

Best known for the black caviar made from their eggs, sturgeon and paddlefish are members of the order *Acipenseriformes,* but at some distant point they separated from a common ancestor. As a result, sturgeon are members of the family Acipenseridae, and paddlefish are members of Polyodontidae. Both are considered bony fish; however, they have a mostly cartilaginous skeleton. Their closest living relatives are gar and bowfin.

Like paddlefish, sturgeon are distinctive in appearance. Each species possesses a heterocercal tail (the upper lobe is larger than the lower), a spiral valve intestine, a spiracle (aperture for breathing), an upper jaw that is not fused with the cranium, and a cartilaginous backbone as an adult. The sturgeon have five rows of bony scutes (scalelike plates), a bottom-oriented, extendible, hoselike mouth with fleshy lips; four barbels; an extended snout; and a teardrop-shaped body.

Species. In North America, there are nine recognized species. White sturgeon *(Acipenser transmontanus)* and green sturgeon *(A. medirostris)* occur on the West Coast of North America. White sturgeon occur in lower and upper waters, sometimes hundreds of miles inland. Green sturgeon are usually found in the lower areas of estuaries. Atlantic sturgeon *(A. oxyrinchus oxyrinchus)* and shortnose sturgeon *(A. brevirostrum)* live on the East Coast. The lake sturgeon *(A. fulvescens)* occurs in the Great Lakes and the upper Mississippi river system. Shovelnose sturgeon *(Scaphirhynchus platorhynchus)* and pallid sturgeon *(S. albus)*

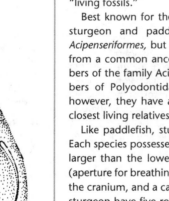

The mouth and barbels of a shovelnose sturgeon.

Sturgeon *(continued)*

are found in the Mississippi River system. The Alabama sturgeon *(S. suttkusi)* is endemic to the Mobile River drainage in Alabama. The gulf sturgeon *(A. oxyrinchus desotoi),* a subspecies of the Atlantic sturgeon, occurs frequently in all Gulf drainages from Tampa Bay, Florida, west to Mermantau River, Louisiana.

Life history. Members of the genus *Scaphirhynchus,* as well as the lake sturgeon, are potamodromous. They live in rivers or lakes, respectively, and migrate upstream into smaller tributaries or rivers to spawn. Their migratory patterns are similar to those of paddlefish.

Adult sturgeon of the genus *Acipenser,* with the lone exception of lake sturgeon, are anadromous. They typically winter in the ocean, migrating into coastal rivers as the water warms above 54°F. Sturgeon also use peak river discharge in the spring as a cue for migratory behavior. Most sturgeon stage in brackish water for a few days before migrating upstream or out to the ocean. They then migrate hundreds of miles upstream to reach gravel bars and spawn in high-velocity currents. Several males spawn with each female, and the eggs adhere to the gravel. The eggs hatch, and the fry are carried downstream to areas with slower water velocity. Adults then move downstream to summer habitats, where they remain until the fall.

Early growth is rapid, and juveniles may reach their adult size in as few as 3 years. Sturgeon often do not mature until 6 years of age, and in some areas they do not mature until age 10 or 12. Sturgeon spawn intermittently, every 2 to 6 years, depending on the species.

Most sturgeon are opportunistic feeders. Juveniles primarily eat aquatic invertebrates, whereas subadults may also consume mollusks, fish, and crayfish. Some species, such as white sturgeon, are good predators and willingly prey on other fish. Migrating adults of *Acipenser,* except white and lake sturgeon, typically do not feed while in freshwater.

Sturgeon are most often found on or near the bottom. They are typically concentrated in deep pools that occur in river bends. During migration (spring and fall), juveniles and adults inhabit deep pools that occur in brackish water along the freshwater-saltwater interface of coastal rivers.

Sturgeon, Atlantic

Acipenser oxyrinchus

OTHER NAMES

sturgeon, common sturgeon, sea sturgeon, Albany beef; French: *esturgeon noir d'Amerique.*

Distribution. *This species ranges along the northwestern and the western Atlantic coast in North America from the Hamilton River in Labrador, Canada, to northeastern Florida. It is currently more populous in the Hudson River, New York, than in other parts of its range, although it is not abundant there.*

Habitat. *The habitats of Atlantic sturgeon are primarily the estuaries and bays of large rivers and deep pools of rivers when inland; in the ocean they inhabit shallow waters of the continental shelf.*

The Atlantic sturgeon is a member of the Acipenseridae family of sturgeon and primarily a fish of the East Coast of North America. It has been used as a high-quality food fish and as a source of caviar since colonial days; it was so abundant in portions of its range that in 1675, canoeists in Delaware Bay were warned to beware of 14- to 18-foot sturgeon that floated like submerged logs in tidal tributaries.

Like many other sturgeon, the Atlantic sturgeon is anadromous, living much of its life in brackish or saltwater and spawning in freshwater rivers. This species and other sturgeon are relatively slow growing and mature late in life, making them vulnerable to overexploitation. Dam construction, water pollution, and other changes in habitat, in addition to commercial overfishing, caused continued declines throughout the twentieth century. The Atlantic sturgeon is a threatened species today.

There is virtually no sportfishery for Atlantic sturgeon, due to their low numbers and harvest restrictions. If populations were high, a recreational fishery would undoubtedly exist, similar to that for the white sturgeon in the Pacific Northwest. A limited directed commercial fishery still occurs for them, however, and a large portion of the landings are bycatch, due to developing ocean fisheries. These practices continue to threaten recovery efforts.

Most fisheries are now closed in compliance with the Atlantic sturgeon management plan of the Atlantic States Marine Fisheries Commission, but the outlook is still poor, and much needs to be done to bring about even a modest growth in populations.

Identification. The Atlantic sturgeon is dark brown or olive green with a white belly. The head is protractile and has a long flat snout with four barbels on the underside. Five rows of scutes (bony, scalelike plates) extend along the length of the body; one is along the back, and two each are along the sides and the belly. The centers of the scutes along the back and the sides are light, making them stand out in contrast to the darker surrounding color. These scutes are set extremely close together, and the bases of most overlap. The Atlantic sturgeon is distinguished from the similar shortnose by a longer snout.

Size/Age. Atlantic sturgeon may live as long as 60 years. They can attain a size of 14 feet and weigh more than 800 pounds. An 811-pounder is the largest known specimen. Fish exceeding 200 pounds, however, are rare today.

Life history/Behavior. Spawning migrations to freshwater last from late winter through early summer, occurring later in the year at higher latitudes. Although it matures late in life, the Atlantic sturgeon is highly fecund, with total egg production proportional to its body size (a 9-foot, 245-pound female, about 30 years old, produced 61 pounds of roe). Nevertheless, it has a low reproduction rate, as females spawn only once every 3 to 5 years, and juvenile mortality is high. Furthermore, females do not mature until ages 7 to 10 in the southern part of their range and ages 22 to 28 in the most northern part of their range; these late maturations complicate management efforts, especially because the fish are at sea for long periods, until they return to natal waters to spawn.

Juvenile sturgeon remain in freshwater for their first summer of life and then migrate to deeper, more brackish water in winter. The juveniles migrate to and from freshwater for a number of years before joining the adult migration pattern. Tagging studies have demonstrated that Atlantic sturgeon migrate extensively both north and south of their natal river systems.

Food and feeding habits. Juveniles and adults are bottom-feeding scavengers, consuming a variety of crustaceans, bivalves, and worm prey, as well as insect larvae and small fish.

Sturgeon, Lake

Acipenser fulvescens

Distribution. *Lake sturgeon occur in the St. Lawrence waterway and the Great Lakes. They are found in the Hudson Bay and the Mississippi River basins from Quebec to Alberta and southward to Alabama and Louisiana, including Lake Winnipeg, Manitoba, and its tributaries. They are rare in the Ohio and the middle Mississippi River basins. Lake sturgeon numbers are a fraction of what they once were throughout this range, and the species does not occur in some parts of its former range; some stocking efforts have been undertaken.*

Habitat. *Lake sturgeon are primarily freshwater fish, occurring in large lakes and rivers, usually 15 to 30 feet deep. They are found over mud, sand, or gravel bottoms but may (rarely) occur in brackish water.*

A member of the Acipenseridae family of sturgeon, the lake sturgeon was an important part of aboriginal culture in North America. In some cultures, spring ceremonial festivities were held at lake sturgeon spawning sites. Around 1855, a market for caviar was developed, which in turn spurred a market for smoked fish around 1860. Caviar and smoked meat from lake sturgeon were also important exports to Europe. By 1910, however, lake sturgeon fisheries had been overexploited through the Great Lakes region. Overfishing, the building of dams, habitation alteration, and pollution have since impeded the lake sturgeon's recovery in most areas.

For waterways with declining or extirpated populations (that is, Lake Winnipeg, Lake Erie, and Lake Ontario), lake sturgeon are being successfully raised in hatcheries for stocking. Current research shows, however, that brood stock should be taken from the water body where hatchery-raised fish will be released; yet brood stock is also rare in areas where stocking may be helpful. These populations will require a great deal of time and improved conditions before they can recover fully. Lake sturgeon have responded positively to changes in dam discharges that facilitate or imitate river conditions. Signs of this include increased spawning activity.

Identification. The somewhat torpedo-shaped lake sturgeon has a spiracle, and the upper lobe of the caudal fin is longer than the lower lobe. The anal fin origin is behind the dorsal fin origin. The fish exhibits an olive-brown coloring, and the scutes (bony scalelike plates) on the back and along the side are the same color as the skin. There are 9 to 17 scutes on the back, 29 to 42 scutes along the sides, and 25 to 30 anal rays. There are 4 barbels on the underside of the mouth.

Size/Age. Lake sturgeon may reach 9 feet in length and have been reported to weigh between 200 and 300 pounds, although fish of 100 pounds are extremely large today, and most are in the 40-pound range and about 4 feet long. The life expectancy of lake sturgeon varies, according to different reports, but at one time it was believed to be 80 to 100 years or more. A specimen caught in 1952 was reputed to have been 152 years old, but older specimens of the modern era have ranged only to 38 years old.

Life history/Behavior. Males mature around 14 to 16 years of age and females near 24 to 26 years of age. As adults, lake sturgeon migrate as far as 125 miles to spawn. They sometimes leap out of the water during spawning and fall with a loud splash.

Spawning sturgeon migrate in the fall and then overwinter at the spawning sites. Spawning peaks in April at temperatures of 48° to 58°F; a secondary spawning probably follows in May. They spawn on gravel bars or below dams or other obstructions, in swift, shallow water, sometimes in a spectacular commotion of thrashing, rolling, and leaping. Six to eight males spawn with each female. They broadcast their eggs and sperm over large substrate such as boulders, and the eggs adhere to the substrate. Eggs hatch at 8 to 14 days of fertilization and drift downstream to more placid waters during the night. As is typical for most sturgeon, early growth is rapid. Mature females spawn only once every several years.

Food and feeding habits. Lake sturgeon feed in freshwater, typically on the bottom. In Lake Winnebago, young lake sturgeon feed primarily on midge larvae, larvae of some moths with aquatic life phases, and water fleas. Mayfly nymphs and mollusks are also important components of the lake sturgeon's diet. The amount of fish consumed by lake sturgeon varies by location, ranging from little or none to 25 percent of the diet. In some areas, small fish are a preferred bait.

Sturgeon, Shovelnose
Scaphirhynchus platorinchus

OTHER NAMES

sturgeon, hackleback sturgeon.

Distribution. *The shovelnose occurs in much the same range as the lake sturgeon, although not in the Great Lakes. Its range is the Mississippi River basin from western Pennsylvania to Montana and south to Louisiana; the Mobile Bay drainage in Alabama and Mississippi; and the upper Rio Grande in New Mexico.*

Habitat. *This species prefers the fast currents of large rivers with sand or gravel bottoms but can live in muddy waters.*

A member of the Acipenseridae family of sturgeon, the shovelnose is a small species and the most abundant sturgeon in the Mississippi and Missouri Rivers and tributaries. The shovelnose is rarely encountered by anglers but has historically had commercial value. Because shovelnose sturgeon are nearly identical to pallid sturgeon *(S. albus),* a federally endangered species, some localities do not allow commercial or recreational fishing for shovelnose.

Identification. The shovelnose sturgeon has a broad, flat head with an extended spadelike snout. There are four barbels under the snout, the two middle ones being almost as long as the outside barbels. All four are located in a straight line in front of the mouth. The body is brown to gray in color, with five rows of scutes (bony scalelike plates). The upper lobe of the caudal fin is longer than the lower lobe and has a threadlike extension, which may be worn off in older individuals. There are scales under the body and also on the caudal peduncle.

Size/Age. The average size of adult shovelnose sturgeon is about 20 inches and 1½ pounds. A large specimen is about 5 pounds; they rarely exceed 3 feet or 6 pounds in weight but reportedly may grow to 10 pounds. The shovelnose is smaller than the pallid sturgeon, which is also found in the Mississippi River system.

Spawning behavior. Spawning begins at 5 to 7 years of age and occurs over sand and gravel in large channels with fast currents.

Food. The shovelnose feeds entirely on the bottom on the larvae of aquatic insects, which constitute the bulk of its diet. It may occasionally eat small fish.

Sturgeon, White

Acipenser transmontanus

A member of the Acipenseridae family of sturgeon, the white sturgeon is the largest fish occurring in freshwater in North America. In some areas, populations have recovered sufficiently since their decline in the early 1900s to support important recreational and commercial fisheries. Fisheries for white sturgeon occur in California, Washington, Oregon, and Idaho. Regulations vary from catch-and-release to slot limits. Peak fishing seasons vary among locations and span the entire calendar year. White sturgeon are listed as federally endangered in the Kootenai River, where the population has declined to critical levels due to dam operations and poor water quality from mining operations. Recent improvements in dam operations and water quality have allowed white sturgeon to begin spawning again in that river, and it is hoped that this population will not be extirpated.

Identification. The white sturgeon has a moderately blunt snout as an adult, barbels closer to the snout tip than to the mouth, and no obvious scutes (bony scalelike plates) behind the dorsal and anal fins. The fish is gray to pale olive on its upper body and white to pale gray on its ventral side. It has 28 to 30 anal rays, 11 to 14 scutes on its back, and 38 to 48 scutes along the sides.

Size/Age. White sturgeon have been reported at more than 100 years old; most of the oldest individuals of the current era are roughly 40 to 60 years old. Accounts of historic landings of white sturgeon report maximum weights of between 1,300 and 2,000 pounds and a length of 20 feet. At least three white sturgeon caught in the nineteenth century reportedly exceeded 1,500 pounds, and the largest-known rod-and-reel catch was a Columbia River specimen of 1,285 pounds. Fish under 6 feet long and weighing 60 to 70 pounds are commonly caught today, and fish from 6 to 9 feet long and weighing 200 to 500 pounds are possible, certainly in the Hell's Canyon section of the Snake River.

OTHER NAMES
sturgeon, Columbia sturgeon, Oregon sturgeon, Pacific sturgeon, Sacramento sturgeon; French: *esturgeon blanc.*

Distribution. *White sturgeon are limited to the Pacific shores of North America from the Aleutian Islands, Alaska, to Monterey Bay, California, although they move far inland to spawn. In Canada, this fish is found in the Fraser River system; the Columbia River above Revelstoke, British Columbia; Duncan Lake, Vancouver Island; and possibly Okanagan Lake and other coastal drainages. The white sturgeon is landlocked in the upper Columbia River drainage and Montana. In Idaho, the white sturgeon occurs in the Snake River downstream from Shoshone Falls and in the Clearwater and the Salmon Rivers. An isolated stock occurs in the Kootenai River drainage. In Montana, the white sturgeon appears in the Kootenai River. Genetic studies of Northwest populations have suggested that distinct subpopulations may be present*

Sturgeon, White (continued)

within the species, range. Some of the most reliable sportfisheries occur in the lower Columbia River, in the Snake River in Idaho, and in California's San Francisco Bay.

Habitat. The habitats of white sturgeon are primarily the estuaries and bays of large rivers, and the deep pools of rivers when inland.

Life history/Behavior. White sturgeon are anadromous, migrating from the ocean into freshwater to spawn; populations that are landlocked due to dams also show seasonal movements. Spawning typically occurs from April through early July, when water temperatures are 50° to 64°F, during the highest daily flows of the river. Spawning occurs in swift water. When hatched, yolk-sac larvae drift to deep water with slower currents, where they grow rapidly, sometimes 15 inches or more in the first year. Females typically mature when 16 to 35 years of age, at roughly 47 inches in fork length.

Food and feeding habits. Young-of-year fish prey on amphipods, chironomid larvae, eulachon eggs, and other benthic organisms. Juveniles additionally consume bivalves. Adults are piscivorous and do feed in freshwater. Common baits include pile worms, ghost shrimp, grass shrimp, squawfish, and carp.

Sucker

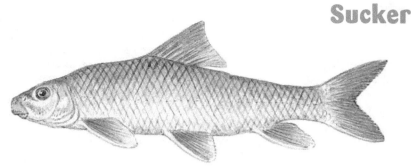

Northern Redhorse
Maxostoma macrolepidotum

Suckers are medium-size fish that are well known to many anglers for their large lips. They belong to the family Catostomidae, which is closely related to the minnows.

Identification. Suckers are most easily distinguished by their inferior mouths and large fleshy lips. They have no barbels like catfish, no hardened spines in their dorsal or anal fins like perch and sunfish, and no adipose fins like trout. Suckers are robust fish, slightly laterally compressed. Most suckers are medium-size fish, but they range in adult size from only 6 inches (Roanoke hogsucker, *Hypentelium roanokense*) to more than 33 pounds (buffalo).

Most suckers are not bright or distinctive in color. Many have an almost metallic sheen in shades of gold, green, purple, or white. Their coloration becomes more intense during reproduction, when many species darken in color and develop lateral stripes. Reproductive adults also develop hardened tubercles on their anal and caudal fins and heads. Young suckers typically have a more distinct color pattern, with several saddles on their backs and dark blotches on their sides for camouflage.

Life history. Suckers inhabit all types of freshwater habitats, including rivers, lakes, and small streams. Most river species live in moderately fast-run habitats with moderate depths. The biggest suckers live in large lakes and deep pools in larger rivers. Because of their large size, suckers do not need to seek cover from predators, so they often coexist with bass and trout in deep pools. Despite popular belief, suckers are not fish that inhabit dirty, silty waters. In fact, most suckers require very clean substrate and are not tolerant of low dissolved oxygen.

Food. With inferior mouths and large, fleshy lips, suckers are well adapted to feeding on the bottom of streams or lakes. Most species suck up substrate and sift out small

Distribution. *Suckers are widespread, distributed all across North America from the Arctic Circle down well into Mexico and from the East Coast to the West Coast. The white sucker (Catostomus commersoni) is one of the most widely distributed fish in North America.*

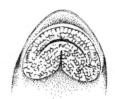

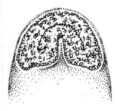

Sensory pores around the mouths of suckers, including the white sucker (top) and northern sucker (bottom), help these bottom scroungers find food.

invertebrates and other organic materials. The most common foods are insects and worms, although some suckers are specialized for feeding on snails, vegetation, or crustaceans. Several species will also feed on detritus and will scrape algae from rocks. Suckers that feed on detritus, like the white sucker *(see: Sucker, White)*, are the most widespread and abundant. Chubsuckers (genus *Erimyzon)* are midwater plankton feeders.

Age. Most suckers are moderately long lived, and the average life span is 8 to 15 years.

Spawning behavior. Suckers become sexually mature at 2 to 3 years. A majority spawns in early spring, although some species continue into early summer. Many larger species make long migrations to the headwaters of rivers to spawn. They may come from farther down in the river or from adjacent lakes. These species spawn upstream, then the larvae hatch and drift downstream to recolonize lower stream reaches. Suckers typically need clean gravel substrate in which to spawn. This type of habitat usually occurs at the tail ends of pools, in riffles, and in gravel bars.

Most sucker species spawn in large aggregations. Several males may spawn with the same female at the same time. Many suckers spawn in a trio, with a female flanked by two smaller males. The males align next to the female in a suitable location in a riffle or pool tail. Then all three individuals shake violently as sperm and eggs are released. This shaking allows the fish to dig down into the substrate and bury the newly deposited eggs. Only one species of sucker, the river redhorse *(Moxostoma carinatum),* actually prepares a redd as trout do, but many do move around much gravel as they dig into the stream bottom. Suckers produce many small eggs and provide little or no parental care.

Value. The real value of suckers is in their ecological role. They utilize food resources such as snails, detritus, and algae that would otherwise go largely unused. This gives them an important role in the ecosystems in which they live, processing nutrients and resources that benefit other species.

Sucker, White
Catostomus commersoni

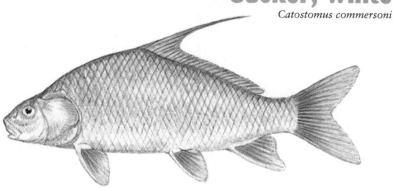

This is one of the most widespread and abundant suckers, found only in North America.

Identification. White suckers are inconspicuously colored, usually in drab hues of white, yellow, and pink. The upper half of the fish is typically more darkly colored than the lower half. Although an adult has little dark pigmentation, a juvenile has three lateral black blotches halfway up the side of the body: one between the dorsal fin and opercle, one below the dorsal fin, and one on the caudal peduncle. The body is elongate and nearly circular in cross-section. The white sucker has rather small scales that get larger near the posterior.

Age/Size. The white sucker is a medium-size fish, reaching up to 18 inches or more in length and up to 8 pounds in weight. The largest individuals may be as old as 17 years, but the normal life expectancy is between 12 and 15 years. Sexual maturity is reached at about the same time in both sexes. The first spawning occurs between 3 and 5 years of age, depending on the region.

Life history/Spawning behavior. White suckers make long upstream spawning migrations in the early spring. The spawning season may extend from late March into early July in some areas. Upstream migration may be triggered by increasing water temperature or stream flow that occurs during this time of year. The suckers move into deep pools and congregate before spawning. They then gather and spawn in areas of clean gravel substrate. Males and females line up next to each other on the bottom of the stream, then shake violently, releasing eggs and sperm as they bury the eggs in the substrate. In lakes, they perform this activity in shallow shoals or may move upstream into rivers. White suckers darken in coloration during spawning. The male becomes olive colored on the upper portion of the body and may develop a pinkish lateral stripe.

OTHER NAMES
black sucker, black mullet, brook sucker, carp, common sucker, common white sucker, eastern sucker, mud sucker, fine scaled sucker, grey sucker, mullet; French: *meunier noir, cyprin-sucet.*

Distribution. The white sucker is one of the most widely distributed suckers in North America. It ranges from Canada south to the southern Appalachian Mountains and west into Utah and Idaho. Its range has expanded from bait bucket transfers when anglers release unused baitfish.

Habitat. The white sucker is a habitat generalist, living in all types of freshwater environs. It occurs in lakes, rivers, ponds, reservoirs, and even some small streams. It can exist in fairly degraded systems, being tolerant of some turbidity, pollution, siltation, and eutrophication. In rivers, adults frequently inhabit deep pools, whereas juveniles live in stream margins and backwaters.

Food and feeding behavior. Like most suckers, this species feeds on a variety of benthic organisms and organic nutrients. Its primary diet includes burrowing insect larvae that are sucked up and sifted in its gill rakers. Midge larvae, small crustaceans, algae, and detritus are the most common foods.

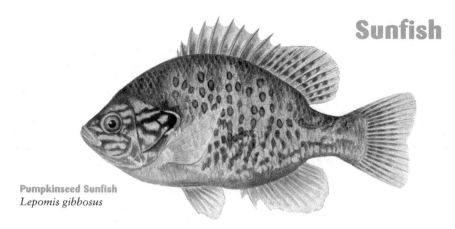

Sunfish

Pumpkinseed Sunfish
Lepomis gibbosus

Scientifically, sunfish are members of the Centrarchidae (meaning "nest building") family. Although this family is typically categorized as including sunfish only, some scientists include sunfish and bass. The terminology and cross-usage of some words attributed to the various species have made for a good deal of confusion among nonscientists.

Centrarchids number some 30 strictly freshwater species of North America and include three generalized subdivisions: black bass, crappie, and true sunfish. All of these are warmwater species with similar or overlapping habitats. Each species has rough scales and two dorsal fins that are united, the first of which is heavily spined. The anal fins all have three or more spines, and the tail is typically broad. Nearly all are nest spawners, with nests built by the males, who also guard the nests and the young briefly. All are carnivorous, and the larger members prey on small fish.

Black bass belong to the genus *Micropterus;* they have more elongated bodies than do other centrarchids and include the largest and most famous family member, the largemouth bass. The crappie belongs to the genus *Pomoxis;* it has a longer anal fin, generally equal in length at the base to its dorsal fin, than any of the other centrarchids, and is capable of larger growth than most of the sunfish. There are two species of crappie; however, a smaller crappielike species, the flier *(Centrarchus macropterus),* is sometimes lumped with crappie by ichthyologists, even though it is generally grouped with sunfish by the public.

The largest group of centrarchids is the true sunfish. Most of the species are small and not of much angling interest, although they are of great importance in their respective environments as forage for larger predators and for the foraging they do themselves. True sunfish do not include the pygmy sunfish of the Elassomatidae family.

The larger-growing and more widely distributed sunfish are extremely popular with anglers throughout the United States and provide countless hours of angling enjoyment. They are widely valued for their excellent white, flaky flesh. Their abundance and high rates of reproduction generally allow for liberal recreational harvest; commercial fishing for these species is illegal in all places where they are found.

The various sunfish and crappie are all considered panfish, which is a nontechnical generic group term for small freshwater fish that are widely utilized for food, as well as sport.

The most wide-ranging and best-known true sunfish is the bluegill; it and many other species of sunfish are colloquially known as "bream." Other popular species of sunfish are the green, the pumpkinseed, the redbreast, and the redear; the warmouth; and the rock bass. In some places, anglers may encounter such sunfish as the Sacramento perch *(Archoplites interruptus)*; the Roanoke bass; the orangespotted sunfish *(Lepomis humilis)*; the mud sunfish; and the spotted sunfish *(Lepomis punctatus)*.

Sunfish are tolerant of diverse and warm environments and have proven very adaptable. They have been widely introduced elsewhere in North America, sometimes deliberately and others by accident, and have also been introduced to Europe and Africa. In some places they are kept in balance by angling and natural predation, but in others they become overpopulated, resulting in stunting.

The generally shallow habitats of true sunfish permit angling by shore-based anglers, making them collectively the number-one warmwater pursuit of nonboating anglers. They are characteristically strong, although not flashy, fighters for their size, making them a pleasing catch on light spinning, spincasting, and fly tackle, as well as with reel-less poles.

Sunfish, Green

Lepomis cyanellus

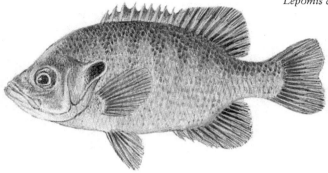

The green sunfish is a widespread and commonly caught member of the Centrarchidae family. It has white, flaky flesh and is a good food fish.

Identification. The green sunfish has a slender, thick body; a fairly long snout; and a large mouth, with the upper jaw extending beneath the pupil of the eye; it resembles the warmouth and the smallmouth bass. It has short, rounded pectoral fins, connected dorsal fins, and an extended gill cover flap, or "ear lobe," which is black and has a light red, pink, or yellow edge. The body is usually brown to olive or bluish green with a bronze to emerald-green sheen, fading to yellow green on the lower sides and yellow or white on the belly. An adult fish has a large black spot at the rear of the second dorsal and the anal fin bases, and breeding males have yellow or orange edges on the second dorsal, the caudal, and the anal fins.

Size. The average length is 4 inches, ranging usually from 2 to 8 inches and reaching a maximum of 12 inches, which is extremely rare. Most weigh less than a half pound. The all-tackle world record is a 2-pound, 2-ounce fish taken in Missouri in 1971.

Spawning behavior. This species becomes sexually mature at 2 years old, spawning from April through August, when water temperatures range from 68° to 84°F. Males build saucer-shaped nests in water usually less than 1 foot deep and often in areas sheltered by rocks or logs. The yellow, adhesive eggs are guarded by the male until they hatch in 3 to 5 days. Green sunfish spawn simultaneously with other species of *Lepomis,* and hybridization is not uncommon.

Food. Green sunfish prefer dragonfly and mayfly nymphs, caddisfly larvae, midges, freshwater shrimp, and beetles and will occasionally eat small fish such as mosquitofish.

OTHER NAMES

green perch, black perch, pond perch, creek perch, sand bass, bluespotted sunfish, rubbertail.

Distribution. In North America, green sunfish occur from New York and Ontario through the Great Lakes and the Hudson Bay basins to Minnesota and South Dakota, and south to the Gulf of Mexico. They also occur from the Escambia River in Florida and Mobile Bay in Georgia and Alabama to the Rio Grande in Texas, as well as in northern Mexico.

Habitat. Green sunfish prefer warm, still pools and backwaters of sluggish streams, as well as ponds and small shallow lakes. Often found near vegetation, they are known to establish territory near the water's edge under brush, rocks, or exposed roots. They often become stunted in ponds.

Sunfish, Longear

Lepomis megalotis

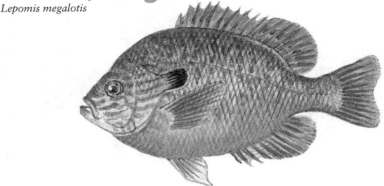

OTHER NAMES

longear.

Distribution. *Similar in range to the green sunfish, the longear sunfish occurs in east-central North America, west of the Appalachian Mountains from southern Quebec and western New York throughout the Mississippi Valley, and westward through Minnesota and Nebraska and south into Texas, as well as along Gulf Coast drainages to western Florida.*

Habitat. *This species inhabits rocky and sandy pools of headwaters, creeks, and small to medium rivers, as well as ponds, bays, lakes, and reservoirs; it is usually found near vegetation and is generally absent from downstream and lowland waters.*

Similar in size and general appearance to the pumpkinseed and a member of the Centrarchidae family of sunfish, the longear sunfish is a small, excellent gamefish on light tackle, although in many places it is generally too small to be avidly sought. The white and sweet flesh is excellent to eat.

Identification. With a stout body, the longear sunfish is not as compressed as the bluegill or the pumpkinseed, its close relatives. It is one of the most colorful sunfish, particularly the breeding male, which is dark red above and bright orange below, marbled, and spotted with blue. The longear generally has red eyes, orange to red median fins, and a blue-black pelvic fin. There are wavy blue lines on the cheeks and the opercles, and the long, flexible, black ear flaps are generally edged with a light blue, white, or orange line. The longear sunfish has short and rounded pectoral fins, which usually do not reach past the eyes when they are bent forward. It has a fairly large mouth, and the upper jaw extends under each eye pupil.

Size. The longear sunfish may grow to 9½ inches, averaging 3 to 4 inches and just a few ounces. The all-tackle world record is a 1-pound, 12-ounce fish, taken in New Mexico in 1985.

Spawning behavior. Spawning takes place from late May to mid-August, when water temperatures range in the upper 70s and lower 80s Fahrenheit, with longear sunfish that are at least 1 to 2 years old moving to gravel bottoms. Males build shallow, saucer-shaped nests in water 8 inches to 2 feet in depth, guarding the eggs until they hatch about a week after being deposited. Many nests are usually found close together.

Food. Longear sunfish feed primarily on aquatic insects but also on worms, crayfish, and fish eggs off the bottom.

Sunfish, Mud

Acantharchus pomotis

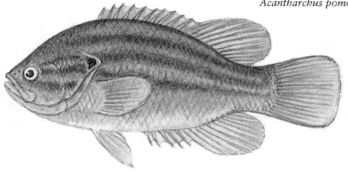

Strongly resembling the rock bass in general color and shape, the mud sunfish is not actually a member of the *Lepomis* sunfish genus, although it is called a sunfish. It has a rectangular, compressed body that is dusky reddish brown on the back and pale brownish underneath. The lateral-line scales are pale, and along the arch of the lateral line is a broad irregular stripe of dark scales about three scale rows wide. Below the lateral line are two straight dark bands, each two scale rows wide, and an incomplete third, lower stripe one scale wide. It is distinguished from the similar rock bass by the shape of the tail, which is round in the mud sunfish and forked in the rock bass. Also, young mud sunfish have wavy dark lines along the sides, whereas young rock bass have a checkerboard pattern of squarish blotches. The mud sunfish may reach a maximum of 6½ inches.

In North America, mud sunfish are widely distributed in the Atlantic Coastal Plain and the lower Piedmont drainages from the Hudson River in New York to the St. Johns River in Florida, and in Gulf Coastal Plain drainages of northern Florida and southern Georgia from the Suwanee River to the St. Marks River. They usually occur over mud or silt in vegetated lakes, pools, and backwaters of creeks and in small to medium rivers. Adult fish are frequently seen resting head down in vegetation.

This species is generally an incidental catch for anglers.

Sunfish, Pumpkinseed

Lepomis gibbosus

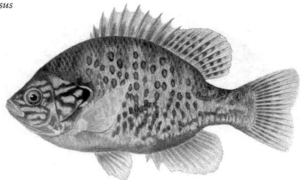

OTHER NAMES

bream, common sunfish, round sunfish, pond perch, pumpkinseed, punky, speckled perch, sun bass, sunfish, sunny, yellow sunfish.

Distribution. *Although pumpkinseeds occur from Washington and Oregon in western North America to New Brunswick, Canada, they are most abundant in the northeastern United States. Their range extends as far south as Georgia on the east and includes most of the United States, except for the south-central and southwestern regions. It includes Ontario and southern Quebec.*

Habitat. *Pumpkinseed sunfish inhabit quiet and vegetated lakes, ponds, and pools of creeks and small rivers, with a preference for weed patches, docks, logs, and other cover close to shore.*

The pumpkinseed is one of the most common and brightly colored members of the Centrarchidae family of sunfish. Although small on average, it is especially popular and good to eat.

Identification. A brilliantly colored fish, the adult pumpkinseed is olive green, spotted with blue and orange and streaked with gold along the lower sides; there are dusky chainlike bars on the side of juveniles and adult females. A bright red or orange spot is located on the back edge of the short, black ear flap. Many bold dark-brown wavy lines or orange spots cover the second dorsal, the caudal, and the anal fins, and there are wavy blue lines on the cheeks. The pumpkinseed has long, pointed pectoral fins that usually extend far past the eyes when bent forward. It has a small mouth, with the upper jaw not extending under the pupils of the eyes.

Size/Age. Most pumpkinseed sunfish are 4 to 6 inches long, but some reach a length of 12 inches and are believed to live to age 10. The all-tackle world record is a 1-pound, 6-ounce fish taken in New York in 1985.

Spawning behavior. Males and females reach sexual maturity at 2 years, spawning during the spring and the summer when waters are in the mid-60°F range. Males construct nests in water less than 5 feet deep, often near shore and aquatic vegetation; the circular nests are 4 to 16 inches in diameter and are built separately or in small groups. Eggs hatch in about 3 days, and the male guards the young for a week or more. There is frequent hybridization between this and other fish in the genus *Lepomis*.

Food. Pumpkinseed sunfish feed on a variety of small foods, including crustaceans, dragonfly and mayfly nymphs, ants, small salamanders, mollusks, midge larvae, snails, water beetles, and small fish.

Sunfish, Redbreast

Lepomis auritus

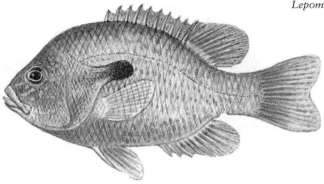

The redbreast sunfish is the most abundant sunfish in Atlantic Coastal Plain streams. Like other members of the Centrarchidae family of sunfish, it is a good fighter for its size and excellent to eat.

Identification. The body of the redbreast sunfish is deep and compressed but rather elongate for a sunfish. It is olive above, fading to bluish-bronze below; in the spawning season, males have bright orange-red bellies while females are pale orange underneath. There are several light blue streaks radiating from the mouth, and the gill rakers are short and stiff. The lobe or flap on the gill cover is usually long and narrow in adult males and blue-black or completely black all the way to the tip. The pectoral fins are short and roundish, and the opercular flaps are soft and flexible.

Size. Redbreast sunfish grow at a slow rate and may reach lengths of 6 to 8 inches, although they can attain 11 to 12 inches and weigh about a pound. The all-tackle world record is a 1-pound, 12-ounce fish from Florida in 1984.

Spawning behavior. Redbreasts spawn in the spring and the summer when they are 2 to 3 years old and as small as 4 inches long. Spawning peaks when water temperatures range from 68° to 82°F. Males build nests in water 1 to 2 feet deep near stumps, logs, rocks, or other protected areas over a sand or gravel bottom; the nests are 30 to 36 inches in diameter and 6 to 8 inches deep.

Food. Their primary food is aquatic insects, but redbreasts also feed on snails, crayfish, small fish, and occasionally on organic bottom matter.

OTHER NAMES
longear sunfish, redbreast bream, robin, redbelly, sun perch, yellowbelly sunfish.

Distribution. Generally occurring in rivers across the United States and Canada, the original distribution of redbreast sunfish is the Atlantic slope of North America from New Brunswick, Canada, to central Florida, and westward to the Appalachian Mountains; the range now extends to parts of Texas, Oklahoma, Arkansas, and Kentucky. They have been introduced to waters in Mexico, Puerto Rico, and Italy, where they are considered a nuisance due to stunting.

Habitat. Redbreast sunfish inhabit rocky and sandy pools of creeks and small to medium rivers. They prefer the deeper sections of streams and vegetated lake margins.

Sunfish, Redear

Lepomis microlophus

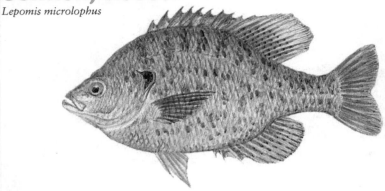

OTHER NAMES

shellcracker, stump-knocker, yellow bream, bream.

Distribution. *Native to North America, redear sunfish are found from about the Savannah River in South Carolina to the Nueces River in Texas, north toward the Mississippi River basin to southern Indiana and Illinois, with some populations in western states. They have been introduced to waters in Africa and Latin America.*

Habitat. *Redear sunfish inhabit ponds, swamps, lakes, and vegetated pools of small to medium rivers; they prefer warm, clear, and quiet waters.*

The redear sunfish is a popular sportfish that reaches a relatively large size and can be caught in large numbers. Like other members of the Centrarchidae family of sunfish, it is good to eat, with white, flaky meat.

Identification. Light golden-green above, the redear sunfish is roundish and laterally compressed; an adult has dusky gray spots on the sides, whereas a juvenile has bars. It is white to yellow on the belly, with mostly clear fins, and the breeding male is brassy gold with dusky pelvic fins. The redear sunfish has a fairly pointed snout and a small mouth, with blunted molaform teeth that make shell cracking possible. It has connected dorsal fins and long, pointed pectoral fins that extend far beyond the eyes when bent forward. The ear flaps are short and black, with a bright red or orange spot or a light margin at the edges.

Size/Age. The redear sunfish can reach large sizes, although it averages under a half pound and about 9 inches. The all-tackle world record is a 5-pound, 7-ounce fish taken in South Carolina in 1998. It can live up to 8 years.

Spawning behavior. Some redear sunfish are able to spawn when they are only 5 inches long and 1 year old, although most do so after they are age 2 or older. Spawning occurs when waters reach 70°F and extends through early fall. Males build and guard shallow circular nests, often built in colonies near vegetation in 2- to 8-foot depths.

Food. An opportunistic bottom feeder, the redear sunfish forages mostly during the day on aquatic snails, which gives it its common name, "shellcracker." These fish also feed on midge larvae, amphipods, mayfly and dragonfly nymphs, clams, fish eggs, and crayfish.

Tarpon
Megalops atlanticus

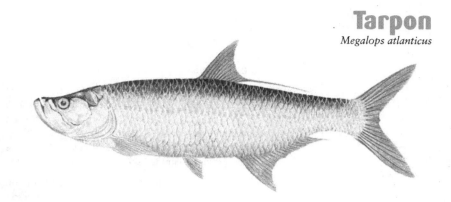

The largest member of the small Elopidae family, the tarpon is one of the world's premier saltwater gamefish. A species of warm tropical waters, it would probably be recognized as the greatest gamefish in the world if it also occurred in temperate waters and was available to all anglers. It presents the foremost qualities that anglers seek in sportfish—it is very large, very strong, challenging to hook and land, often a target of sight fishing and casting in shallow water, and a spectacular leaper when hooked.

Also known as the Atlantic tarpon, this species is sometimes scientifically identified as *Tarpon atlanticus;* it is a relative of the ladyfish and of a similar but much smaller species, the Indo-Pacific tarpon *(Megalops cyprinoides),* also known as oxeye tarpon or oxeye herring. In prehistoric times, there were many more species of tarpon; today, there are just these two.

A hardy giant that can survive in a variety of habitats and salinities, the tarpon can even gulp air for extended periods when not enough oxygen is present in the water to sustain it. Despite its popularity among anglers, many aspects of this extremely long-lived fish's life cycle and behavior remain a mystery. This especially includes its migratory habits.

Identification. The tarpon's body is compressed and covered with extremely large platelike scales and a deeply forked tail fin. Its back is greenish or bluish, varying in darkness from silvery to almost black. The sides and the belly are brilliant silver. Underwater, tarpon appear to shimmer like huge gray ghosts as they swim sedately by. This appearance, along with their impressive size, is likely responsible for their nickname, "silver king." Inland, brackish-water tarpon frequently have a golden or brownish color because of tannic acid.

The huge mouth of the tarpon has a projecting, upturned lower jaw that contains an elongated bony plate. A single, short dorsal fin originates just behind the origin of

OTHER NAMES

silver king, Atlantic tarpon, cuffum; French: *tarpon argenté;* Italian: *tarpone;* Portuguese: *camurupi, peixe-prata-do-atlântico, tarpao;* Spanish: *pez lagarto.*

Distribution. *Because tarpon are sensitive to cold water, their range is generally limited to temperate climates. Atlantic tarpon have been reported as far north as Nova Scotia and also off the coast of Ireland, although they prefer tropical and subtropical waters. In the western Atlantic, they are most common from Virginia to central Brazil and throughout the Caribbean Sea and the Gulf of Mexico.*

Habitat. *Tarpon are most abundant in estuaries and coastal waters but also occur in freshwater lakes and rivers, in offshore marine waters, and occasionally on coral reefs. Adults often patrol the coral reefs of the Florida Keys. In Costa Rica and Nicaragua, anglers frequently catch*

Tarpon (continued)
*tarpon in freshwater lakes
and rivers miles from the
coast.*

the pelvic fin and consists of 12 to 16 soft rays (no spines), the last of which is greatly elongated. The anal fin has 19 to 25 soft rays. The lateral line is straight, even along the anterior portion, with a scale count of 41 to 48.

Size/Age. Most angler-caught Atlantic tarpon are in the range of 40 to 50 pounds, but many from 60 to 100 pounds are encountered. Fish exceeding 150 pounds are rare in the western Atlantic.

Some Atlantic tarpon live as long as 55 years. Most of the tarpon caught in the Florida fishery are 15 to 30 years old.

Life history/Behavior. In May and June, Atlantic tarpon in the western Atlantic begin gathering together in staging areas near the coast in preparation for the journey to their offshore spawning grounds. Although no one knows exactly where tarpon spawn, tarpon larvae only a few days old have been collected as far as 125 miles offshore in the Gulf of Mexico. Spawning in Florida occurs mainly in May, June, and July.

Juvenile tarpon make their way into marshes and mangrove swamps, where they will spend the remainder of the first year of their lives, often showing a preference for stagnant pools. They grow rapidly and are roughly a foot long within 1 to 2 years.

Although tarpon can tolerate water of various salinities, they are vulnerable to cold snaps and become stressed when water temperatures fall below 55°F. Adults can often seek refuge from the cold in deep holes and channels, but young fish are less able to escape cold waters.

Food. Tarpon often travel in schools with other tarpon and are opportunistic eaters that feed on a variety of fish and crabs.

Tilapia

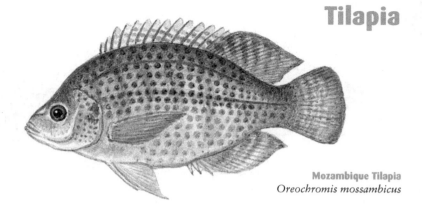

Mozambique Tilapia
Oreochromis mossambicus

Tilapia are native to Africa and the Middle East and have been widely introduced around the world for food production. They are abundant in many Mexican lakes, where they were introduced and are commercially netted by the hundreds of thousands, and are found in some southern U.S. waters, most notably Florida.

Perhaps the most well-known member of this group is the Mozambique tilapia *(Oreochromis mossambicus),* which has been widely cultivated in fish ponds.

The tilapia is generally small with a moderately deep and compressed body. It has a long dorsal fin, the anterior of which is spiny; a single nostril on each side of the snout; and an interrupted lateral line, which may be in either two or three parts. It is distinguished from the bluegill by the absence of a dark blue or black opercular flap.

In freshwater, they are primarily algae and plant feeders. Many are mouthbrooders, although some build spawning nests, which they guard after the eggs hatch. Most are small, although some reportedly can grow as large as 20 pounds, and they are schooling species.

Despite their abundance, tilapia have little to no sportfishing value in most areas where they have been introduced, although they are valuable food fish. Tilapia have had mixed value in some areas where they have been introduced, crowding out some native species, stunting and breeding rapidly, and sometimes producing large crops of very small individuals, but also providing forage for larger predators, especially largemouth bass.

Habitat. *Tilapia thrive in warm, weedy waters of sluggish streams, canals, irrigation ditches, ponds, and lakes. Most tilapia are strictly freshwater fish, but some have adapted to brackish or saltwater environments, and some can tolerate environments with an extremely high temperature and very low oxygen.*
Tilapia are members of the Cichlidae family, which is well known to aquarium hobbyists. There are approximately 1,300 cichlid species and 100 tilapia species.

Trout

Rainbow Trout
Oncorhynchus mykiss

Habitat/Distribution. Like most members of the Salmonidae family, trout are in some way associated with cold, often rushing waters and high oxygen demands. Some—including the brown trout, the cutthroat, and the rainbow—have forms that are also tied to the sea and spend a portion of their lives there. The Pacific salmon, the Atlantic salmon, and the arctic charr are all examples of this. All trout spawn in freshwater and most require cold running water.

Some trout, especially the brown, have a lineage of historical, cultural, and angling significance, especially in Europe. All are good table fare and esteemed sportfish. They include species with a limited range, especially various strains and isolated populations that are little known to most people, and species that have been distributed virtually around the world. Rainbow trout are likely the most widely spread gamefish worldwide and have become important food fish

The word "trout" is used to describe various related members of the Salmonidae family, which also includes salmon, charr, whitefish, and grayling. As a group, these fish are endemic to freshwaters of the temperate and cool regions of the Northern Hemisphere but have been introduced widely outside their native range. Species that are commonly referred to as trout occur not only in the true trout genus *Salmo*, but also in the Pacific salmon genus *Oncorhynchus* and the charr genus *Salvelinus*, which complicates both a definition and an explanation of what a trout is.

Species. Among the most popular and widely known species of fish that are called trout are brook trout, brown trout, cutthroat trout, rainbow trout, and lake trout; these have many strains, sea-run forms, and hybrid versions.

Some taxonomists would argue that the brown trout is the only true trout, as it was the first of its kind described by Linnaeus, the father of modern taxonomy, and that other fish species have been labeled trout (especially in North America) largely because of their similar body form. This issue is best left to scientists, but from a technical standpoint it should be noted that such commonly known species as lake trout and brook trout are actually members of the charr group. So is the lesser-known bull trout. Likewise, the rainbow trout and its anadromous steelhead variation, which was once placed in the trout genus, is now a member of the Pacific salmon group, as are the cutthroat trout, the lesser-known golden trout, and the Apache trout.

Identification. As a rather primitive group of fish, trout lack spines in the fins. Most of the soft rays in the fins are branched. The pelvic fins are situated far back on the trout's body—in the "hip" region, where the legs of amphibians articulate with the body. This placement contrasts with the location of the pelvic fins in many other species, like the largemouth bass, for example, whose pelvic fins are so far forward, they are almost directly beneath the pectoral fins. Other indications of the trout's primitive nature are the possession of an adipose fin and a primitive air bladder.

Trout as a group are among the most distinguished-looking and prettiest freshwater fish. Some are especially colorful, particularly in spawning mode, and most have distinctive body markings, although there are great variations, depending on the environment. Within each species there is considerable variation in color and markings from one river to another, as well as between river and lake populations. The brown trout found deep in a lake, for example, are more silvery and rather bland, compared to brown trout caught in a rich limestone stream; so great is the difference that the casual observer would not assume that the two were the same species.

Issues. Like nearly all members of the Salmonidae family, trout have suffered from changes wrought by humans. These include overfishing, pollution, habitat alteration, factors that have caused a warming of waters, hatchery impacts, and competition from exotic species.

Some native populations of the various trout and their subspecies or strains have declined dramatically or have even been extirpated, although others have declined and recovered or expanded. Competition between species, especially between native and introduced trout, or between trout and other introduced species, has often been a great problem.

Each of the major trout species is of great interest to anglers, although rainbow trout and brown trout have the greatest following because of their suitability to diverse habitats and wide international distribution. Trout are generally associated with river and stream fishing, especially wading and casting activities, although a great many anglers pursue these fish from various types of boats in large rivers and lakes, making it possible to fish for them in a multitude of ways.

through aquaculture production. As a group, trout are among the most widely cultivated fish, perhaps second only to carp, which are the mainstay of fish farming in China. Trout have been widely planted to supplement existing stocks, reintroduce species to waters where natural populations were extirpated, or introduce them to waters where they did not previously exist.

Trout, Apache

Oncorhynchus apache

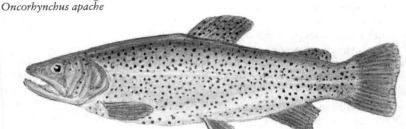

OTHER NAMES

Arizona trout.

Distribution. *The Apache trout occurs in the upper Salt River and the Little Colorado River systems (the Colorado River drainage) in Arizona. It exists in the West Fork of the Black River and a few small impoundments, such as Lee Valley Lake, and the largest population is on the Fort Apache Indian Reservation.*

Habitat. *Apache trout inhabit clear, cool mountain headwaters of streams and creeks above 7,500 feet and mountain lakes. They are dependent on pool development, shade-giving streamside vegetation, and undercut banks for cover and are capable of tolerating a range of temperatures.*

A member of the Salmonidae family, the Apache trout is Arizona's state fish and was once so abundant that early pioneers caught and salted large numbers of them as a winter meat source. Since those times, a 95-percent reduction in range has resulted from hybridization with rainbow trout, brook trout, and other trout. The Apache trout was among the first fish species protected when the Endangered Species Act of 1973 was enacted, and it is currently listed as "threatened" or "likely to become endangered in the near future."

Identification. The Apache trout is a striking fish, with yellow to golden sides, an adipose fin, and a large dark spot behind each eye. The head, the back, the sides, and the fins have evenly spaced dark spots, and the dorsal, the pelvic, and the anal fins are white tipped. The underside of the head is orange to yellowish-orange, with a complete lateral line of 112 to 124 scales.

Size. Adult fish usually range from 8 to 15 inches in length, although they can reach 18 inches. The all-tackle world record is a 5-pound, 3-ounce fish taken in Arizona in 1991.

Life history/Behavior. Depending on the geographic elevation, spawning occurs between March and mid-June; the higher the elevation, the later spawning occurs, beginning when water temperatures reach 46°F. Females lay between 100 and 4,000 eggs in nests (called redds) at the downstream ends of pools; the lower egg counts occur in wild stream populations and the higher counts in hatcheries.

Food. As with other trout that live in flowing water, Apache trout eat both aquatic and terrestrial insects such as mayflies, caddisflies, and grasshoppers.

Trout, Blueback

Salvelinus alpinus oquassa

This member of the charr family was once classified as a separate species, with the scientific name *Salvelinus oquassa.* A landlocked, or nonanadromous, charr, it was reclassified as a subspecies of the arctic charr *(S. alpinus oquassa),* along with its close relatives the Sunapee trout and the Quebec red trout. The blueback trout of Rangeley Lakes, Maine, were once extremely abundant but are now extinct; however, bluebacks are abundant in a few other waters of this state, and there is open-water fishing for them.

Trout, Brook

Salvelinus fontinalis

OTHER NAMES

Eastern brook trout, speckled trout, native, spotted trout, speckled charr, brook charr, salter, coaster, squaretail, brookie, aurora trout, mountain trout; French: *truite mouchetée.*

Distribution. *Brook trout populations still exist over much of the species' original distribution. Their range covers all of the northeastern United States, the Canadian Maritimes, Labrador, and Newfoundland, and they exist in all the Quebec and Ontario rivers and streams that enter Hudson and James Bays. The 96° longitudinal line, where it crosses into Minnesota, is the natural western limit of brook trout in the United States, although they have been introduced elsewhere and as far west as California. The most southerly brook trout distribution is the headwaters of the Chattahoochee River in Georgia.*

Habitat. *Compared to all other charr, as well as to salmon and trout, brook*

Brook trout are technically not true trout but are closely related to trout; they are charr and members of a family composed of lake trout, bull trout, bluebacked trout, Dolly Varden, and arctic charr. As a native North American fish, and a sensitive one that has been displaced in some habitats as the result of fish stocking or water degradation, the brook trout has long been a favorite of stream and pond anglers, especially in the northeastern region of North America.

Identification. Brook trout have a coloration and patterns so unique that there is seldom any confusion with other fish, especially when one is looking at a native specimen (which will be richer and more brightly marked and colored than a hatchery specimen). Three external features allow immediate separation of the brook trout from either the brown or the rainbow trout or other charr. White pipings on the outer edges of all but the caudal (tail) fin identify it as a charr. On the interior of the white leading edges on the fins is a narrow black stripe. Body spots of a true trout are on a light background but are reversed in all charr. Trout have large scales easily seen by the eye, whereas charr have very small scales. The feature that is wholly unique to the brook trout is the wormlike wavy lines, called vermiculations, on the back and the head. These appear on the dorsal, the adipose, and the caudal fins like a series of tiger stripes.

Like all salmonids, the brook trout sports a vestigial adipose fin on its back. It also has paired pectoral and pelvic fins and a singular anal fin, just posterior of the vent.

Coloration can vary greatly, depending on the environment, ranging from a light, metallic blue in fish that enter saltwater (which are called salters) or in fish that leave natal streams and spend part of the year in large, deep, clear lakes (which are called coasters), to dark brown and yellowish bodies in trout trapped behind beaver dams or in high mountain ponds. In both sexes, body colors intensify during spawning and are more pronounced in males.

Size/Age. Brook trout are not a long-lived fish, generally surviving into their fourth or fifth year, although some fish have lived to at least 10 years of age. In most environs, the average brook trout caught is between 7 and 10 inches long and weighs considerably less than a pound. In many of their small-water natural habitats, the conditions do not exist to foster large sizes. A brook trout exceeding 12 inches in most northeastern waters is a sizable fish, and one exceeding 2 pounds is uncommon. Nevertheless, brook trout are capable of reaching larger sizes; a 14-pound, 8-ounce brook trout caught in 1916 is the all-tackle world record for the species, and that individual measured 31 inches in length.

Life history/Behavior. Brook trout spawn in the late fall and the early winter. Immature and small, adult brook trout are likely to stay in a stream even when access to a lake or a pond is nearby because stream habitats offer more protection from predators. During summer months, larger brook trout typically inhabit the lake, which has larger food items, and move to rivers or streams only to spawn.

Some populations of brook trout migrate to sea for short periods. They move downstream and upstream in the spring or the early summer and remain in estuaries and ocean areas where food is plentiful. After roughly 2 months, they return to freshwater. Not all fish in a population migrate, nor do they necessarily do so every year. Sea-run brook trout live longer and grow larger than strictly freshwater brook trout.

Food and feeding habits. Brook trout from 4 to 8 inches long feed mainly on aquatic and terrestrial insects. Between 8 and 12 inches, they begin feeding on small fish. Large trout, particularly in northern waters during the summer, are known to eat small mammals (mice, voles, shrews, and lemmings) that find their way into the water.

trout are the least specialized in their habitat demands. This allows them to live in a great variety of environments, with a wide range of tolerances. They inhabit small trickles, rivulets, creeks, and beaver ponds. They live in larger streams and any lake, from the Great Lakes to little lakes and ponds, to small rivers and big rivers with tumbling falls and rapids. Because of a unique organ (the glomerulus) in their kidneys, they are anadromous and can move into riverine estuaries and are at home in brackish streams that feel the surge of tides, in a purely saline bay, or even the oceans themselves. They are, however, the classic example of a coldwater species and thrive best in the northern half of the Northern Hemisphere.

Trout, Brown

Salmo trutta

OTHER NAMES

Brown trout (all forms)
German brown, German trout, German brown trout, Loch Leven trout, European brown trout, English trout, von Behr trout, brownie, sea trout, lake trout, brook trout, river trout.

River and stream
brown trout
Danish: *baekørred;* Finnish: *tammukka, purotaimen;* French: *truite commune;* German: *bachforelle;* Norwegian: *bekkaure;* Polish: *pstrag potokowy;* Russian: *forel strumkova;* Swedish: *bäcköring.*

Brown trout in lakes
Danish: *søørred;* Finnish: *jarvitaimen;* French: *truite de lac;* German: *seeforelle;* Polish: *troc jeziorowa;* Russian: *forel ozernaya.*

Sea trout, or sea-run
brown trout
Danish: *havørred;* Dutch: *zeeforel;* French: *truite de mer;* Gaelic: *breac;* German: *meerforelle;* Italian: *salmo trota;* Norwegian: *aure orret;* Russian: *losos taimen;* Spanish: *trucha marina;* Swedish: *öring.*

Distribution. *The brown trout is found in rivers and lakes in much of North*

One of the most adaptable members of the Salmonidae family, the brown trout was the first species of trout described by Linnaeus, the father of modern taxonomy.

The species called *Salmo trutta* (meaning, respectively, "salmon" and "trout") is the backbone of natural and hatchery-maintained trout fisheries on six continents and is one of the world's premier sportfish, but it takes on many forms—river, lake, and sea-run—in many diverse environments, and is greatly varied in its appearance.

Identification. The brown trout gets its common name from the typical olive-green, brown, or golden brown hue of its body. The belly is white or yellowish, and dark spots, sometimes encircled by a pale halo, are plentiful on the back and the sides. Spotting can be found on the head and the fins along the back, and rusty red spots also occur on the sides. There is a small adipose fin, sometimes with a reddish hue, ahead of the tail. Sea-run brown trout have a more silvery coloration, and the spotting is less visible. Residents of large lake systems, especially the Great Lakes of North America, have a silvery coloration as well, dark spots without halos, and no colored spots.

Size/Age. Brown trout are capable of living up to 18 years, but most live no more than 12 years; sea trout can spend as long as 9 years in the sea. Most river and stream fish are only 9 to 14 inches long and weigh up to 4 or 5 pounds, rarely growing more than double that weight, although there are some notable exceptions. Big river and lake specimens can grow to huge sizes. The North American record, caught in 1992, is 40 pounds, 4 ounces.

Life history/Behavior. Brown trout spawn in the fall and the early winter (October through February) in rivers or tributaries of lakes or large rivers. They return to the stream where they were born, choosing spawning sites that are spring-fed headwaters, the head of a riffle, or the tail of a pool. Selected sites have good water flows through the gravel bottom. The female uses her body to excavate a nest (redd) in the gravel. She and the male may spawn there several times. Females cover their eggs with gravel after spawning, and the adults return downstream. The eggs develop slowly over the winter, hatching in the spring. A good flow of clean, well-oxygenated water is necessary for successful egg development.

Yearling brown trout move into cobble and riffle areas. Adults are found in still deeper waters and are most active at night. They mature in their third to fifth year and many become repeat spawners. Apart from moving upstream to spawn, adults tend to stay in the same place in a river, with very little movement to other stream areas. Others move to or from estuaries in the spring or the fall.

In sea-run populations, brown trout spend 2 to 3 years in freshwater, then migrate downstream to spend one or two growing seasons in coastal waters near river mouths and estuaries, where they feed on small fish and crustaceans. Most return to their home streams to spawn. In lakes, brown trout seek out levels of preferred temperature and are deep during the summer months and shallower in the spring and the fall, when the water is cooler. After ice out, they are in shallow and nearshore areas, often around warmer tributaries, but move deeper as the surface level warms.

Food. Brown trout are carnivores and consume aquatic and terrestrial insects, worms, crustaceans, mollusks, fish, salamanders, and even tadpoles or frogs. In small streams their diet may be largely insects, but in larger flows or where there is plenty of baitfish, it also includes assorted small fish. In large lakes, the primary diet is other fish, especially abundant pelagic schooling species, such as alewives; small fish are a primary food for sea trout.

America, with the exception of the most southerly American states, the most northerly Canadian regions, and Alaska. It is also found in some coastal rivers from Long Island, New York, to the Maritime Provinces and Quebec.

Habitat. *Brown trout prefer cool, clear rivers and lakes with temperatures of 54° to 65°F. They can survive and thrive in 65° to 75°F conditions, which are warmer than most other trout can tolerate, but in streams they do best where the summer temperature is less than 68°F. In streams and rivers, they are wary and elusive fish that look for cover more than does any other salmonid, hiding in undercut banks, stream debris, surface turbulence, rocks, and deep pools. They also take shelter under overhanging vegetation.*

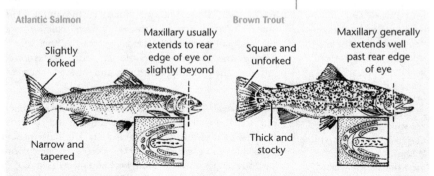

The most obvious differences between adult Atlantic salmon and brown trout are apparent in the head and tail areas. The vomerine teeth, which are inside the upper jaw, are depicted in the insets. On the salmon, these teeth are small and extremely sparse and appear in a straight row on the shaft; on the brown trout, they are well developed and form a zigzag on the shaft.

Trout, Cutthroat

Oncorhynchus clarki

OTHER NAMES

cut, native trout, coastal cutthroat, Clark's trout, red-throated trout, short-tailed trout, lake trout, sea trout, brook trout, native trout, Yellowstone cutthroat, Snake River cutthroat, Lahontan cutthroat, Rio Grande cutthroat, Colorado cutthroat, Utah cutthroat, Paiute cutthroat, harvest trout, blackspotted trout; French: *truite fardée*.

Distribution. *Cutthroat trout are the most widely distributed of all the western trout of North America, which is proven by the many names that refer to rivers, states, or drainages where unique forms occur. The coastal cutthroat trout normally does not exist more than 100 miles inland. It is known from the Eel River, California, north to Prince William Sound, Alaska. Inland nonanadromous forms occur from southern Alberta, Canada, to as far south as New Mexico, as far east as Colorado and most of Montana, and west as far*

The term "cutthroat throat" and its scientific designation *O. clarki*—the species name in honor of Captain Clark of the Lewis and Clark expedition—is more like a name for a family tree than for a single species of fish. According to some scientific estimates, there are 14 subspecies, hybrids, and variations, forming what has been called an ichthyological jigsaw puzzle of fish that are endemic to western North America. All of these are members of the Salmonidae family of salmon, trout, whitefish, and grayling, and were reclassified from the trout genus *Salmo* to the Pacific salmon genus *Oncorhynchus*.

Of the 14 species, all but one inhabit only freshwater rivers, lakes, and streams; the exception is the coastal cutthroat trout *(O. clarki clarki)*, which has both freshwater and anadromous forms; for unknown reasons, some fish migrate to sea, whereas others stay in freshwater. The coastal cutthroat is fairly well distributed and available to anglers and is one of the more prominent cutthroat species, in addition to the West Slope (intermountain) cutthroat *(O. clarki lewisi)*, the Yellowstone cutthroat *(O. clarki bouvieri)*, and the Lahontan cutthroat *(O. clarki henshawi)*. Other species include the Bonneville cutthroat, the blackspotted cutthroat, the greenback cutthroat, and the Rio Grande cutthroat.

Identification. This is a highly variable fish, in coloration and size. The characteristic that gives the inland cutthroat its name is the yellow, orange, or red streak or slash mark in the skin fold on each side under the lower jaw. The color of the body ranges from cadmium blue and silvery (sea-run) to olive green or yellowish green. There may be red on the sides of the head, the front part of the body, and the belly. In some specimens there may be a narrow pink streak along the sides, but not as broad as in the rainbow trout. The body is covered with black spots, which extend onto the dorsal, the adipose, and the tail fins. On the tail, which is slightly forked, the spots radiate evenly outward.

Coastal cutthroat coloration also varies with habitat and life history. Resident fish living in bog ponds are typically from 6 to 16 inches long, are golden yellow with dark spots on the body and the dorsal and the caudal fin, and have a vivid red slash mark under the jaw. Free-swimming residents in large landlocked lakes can exceed 24 inches, are uniformly silver with black spots, and have rosy gill covers and a faint slash mark. Sea-run cutthroat are seldom more than 18 inches long; they have bluish silver with dark or olive backs and less conspicuous black spots; the characteristic slash is a faint yellow.

Size/Age. The largest form (or subspecies) of *O. clarki* was once the Lahontan cutthroat, which was native to the Lahontan drainage system of Nevada and California, and is now nearly extinct. The smallest cutthroat occurs only in upper Silver King Creek, California, and does not exceed 12 inches. Coastal anadromous cutthroat have been recorded to 17 pounds but average under 5 pounds, whereas most inland specimens seldom exceed 5 pounds. Most cutthroat live 4 to 7 years, and they have a maximum life span of at least 12 years.

Life history/Behavior. Cutthroat trout are late-winter or early-spring spawners, although sea-run fish typically ascend rivers from late summer through the fall of the year prior to spawning. They spawn in small, isolated headwater streams. The female makes one or more nests; eggs hatch in 6 to 7 weeks. Later, the young occupy beaver ponds, sloughs, or lakes. In lakes, smaller inland and nonanadromous coastal cutthroat trout hide among lily pads, sunken logs, or rubble, from which they dart out and seize insects and small fish. Some fish abandon this "sit and wait" feeding strategy when they reach about 14 inches and become cruisers, pursuing and eating other fish. Cutthroat that adapt this feeding strategy can grow from 24 to 28 inches and weigh 8 pounds.

Food. Inland cutthroat mostly consume insects and small fish. Coastal cutthroat eat various small fish, shrimp, sandworms, and squid.

as Alberta and eastern California. A small, disjunct population that may have been transplanted occurs in northern Baja California, Mexico. The species has been transplanted to other locations, including the east coast of Quebec, Canada, and Europe.

Habitat. Inland cutthroat and resident (nonanadromous) coastal cutthroat live in a wide variety of cold-water habitats, from small headwater tributaries, mountain streams, and bog ponds to large lakes and rivers. During their spawning migration, sea-run cutthroat are usually found in river or stream systems with accessible lakes; otherwise, they stay in saltwater near shore and their natal tributaries. In some watersheds, both anadromous and resident coastal cutthroat occur together.

Trout, Gila
Oncorhynchus gilae

Along with the Apache trout *(see: Trout, Apache),* the Gila is one of two native trout in Arizona, both severely threatened. Because of interbreeding with rainbow trout *(see: Trout, Rainbow)* and a similarity in appearance to cutthroat trout *(see: Trout, Cutthroat),* it wasn't identified as a separate species until 1950.

A member of the Salmonidae family, the Gila trout is an olive-yellow to brassy fish, with small irregular black spots across its upper body, head, and dorsal and caudal fins. These markings protect the fish from predators. There is an indistinct rose stripe along each side, as well as a yellow "cutthroat" mark under the lower jaw and white or yellow tips on the dorsal, the anal, and the pelvic fins.

Growing to 18 inches, the Gila trout was originally found in tributaries of the Verde River in Arizona and still lives in small numbers in the headwaters of the Gila River in New Mexico. It prefers clear, cool mountain creeks above 7,800 feet in elevation and feeds on both aquatic and terrestrial invertebrates.

Trout, Golden

Oncorhynchus aguabonita

California's state fish, the golden trout is classified as two recognizable subspecies, *O. aguabonita aguabonita* of California's South Fork of the Kern River and Golden Trout Creek, and *O. aguabonita gilberti* of the main Kern and the Little Kern Rivers; an area of warm water where the South Fork joins the Kern apparently serves as a natural barrier separating the two subspecies.

Identification. The golden trout is considered one of the most beautiful of freshwater gamefish because of its striking coloration and markings; it has a bright red to red-orange belly and cheeks, with golden lower sides, a red-orange lateral streak, and a deep olive-green back. The sides have 10 parr marks centered on the lateral line, and the golden trout is the only salmonid in which these marks remain prominent throughout life. The tail is a brilliant golden yellow and is covered with large black spots that are also scattered across the back and the upper sides, as well as on the dorsal fins; the front part of the body may have spots above the lateral line on the back and the top of the head, but not always.

Size/Age. The golden trout grows slowly, usually weighing less than a pound, and is capable of reaching 7 years of age. The all-tackle world record is an 11-pound Wyoming fish taken in 1948.

Life history/Behavior. Spawning takes place when water temperatures reach about 50°F in early to midsummer. Stream dwellers spawn in their native streams or small tributaries, and lake dwellers spawn in inlets or outlets. Females dig several nests (redds), generally at the tail of a pool, depositing eggs in each and returning to their home pools or lakes afterward.

Food and feeding habits. Golden trout feed primarily on small crustaceans and adult and immature insects, especially caddisflies and midges.

OTHER NAMES
French: *truite dorée*.

Distribution. Golden trout occur in the upper Kern River basin in Tulare and Kern Counties in California and have been introduced into Canada, as well as into the states of Washington, Idaho, and Wyoming, which have developed self-sustaining populations.

Habitat. Golden trout inhabit clear, cool headwaters, creeks, and lakes at elevations above 6,890 feet.

Trout, Lake

Salvelinus namaycush

OTHER NAMES

laker, mackinaw, Great
Lakes trout or charr,
salmon trout, landlocked
salmon, gray trout, great
gray trout, mountain
trout, tongue, togue,
namaycush or masamay-
cush, siscowet, fat trout,
paperbelly, bank trout,
bumper, humper; Cree:
*namekus, nemakos,
nemeks;* French: *touladi;*
Inuit: *iluuraq, isuuraq.*

Distribution. *The natural
range of the lake trout is
across the northern region of
North America. It occurs
from Quebec, the Maritime
Provinces, and Labrador in
the east, southerly through
New York, and west across
the north-central United
States and all of Canada to
British Columbia and Alaska
in the west. It is widely distributed in the Nunavut, the
Yukon, and the Northwest
Territories and in the northern sections of other Canadian provinces, including the
arctic islands. It has been
introduced to northern deep
lakes elsewhere in the United
States and reintroduced to*

The lake trout is one of the largest members of the Salmonidae family, which encompasses salmon, trout, charr, and
whitefish. This fish is not actually a "trout" but a charr, and
thus a close relative of the brook trout and the arctic charr.

The lake trout was once associated with many variations,
some of which have been termed subspecies or strains;
some of these no longer exist, and others are deep dwellers
that are not commonly known to anglers. The siscowet or
siscoet (which has been listed by some sources as *S. siscoet*)
is one of these; a deep-dwelling (reportedly from 300 to 600
feet) fish of Lake Superior, it is known as the fat lake trout to
commercial fishermen because of its extremely oily flesh.

Identification. The lake trout has the same moderately
elongated shape as does the trout and the salmon. Its tail is
moderately forked, more so than those of other charr; its
scales are minute; and it has several rows of strong teeth,
which are weak, less numerous, or absent in other charr. Its
head is generally large, although fast-growing stocked fish
will have small heads in relation to body size, and there is an
adipose fin.

Like other charr, the lake trout has white leading edges
on all its lower fins and light colored spots on a dark background. The body is typically grayish to brownish, with
white or nearly white spots that extend onto the dorsal, the
adipose, and the caudal fins. There are no red, black, or
haloed spots of any kind.

Coloration is highly variable. Lighter specimens are often
the deep-dwelling fish of light-colored southerly lakes with
alewife and smelt forage bases; darker specimens, including
some with reddish and orange tones, come from less fertile,
tannin-colored northern lakes.

Size/Age. The all-tackle world record is a 72-pound fish
caught in 1995 at Great Bear Lake, Northwest Territories,

although a 74-pounder was caught there in 2001. A 102-pound lake trout was netted in Lake Athabasca, Saskatchewan, in 1961.

In most of its range, a 20-pound lake trout is a very large specimen and is considered a trophy catch; fish from 30 to 45 pounds are caught every season in a few far-northern waters, most of them being released. The average angler catch in most places weighs 4 to 10 pounds.

Lake trout growth and ages vary from place to place, depending on diet, water temperature, altitude, and genetics. Lake trout in the cold, deep, infertile waters of the north are capable of long life spans. In the more southerly portions of their range, however, they grow more quickly but do not live as long, and in most places they do not live longer than 20 years.

Life history/Behavior. Lake trout generally spend their entire lives in lakes, staying deep and often near the bottom at cool levels. They often orient to structure, cluster at tributaries, and wander in search of food, and although they are not school species like some of their forage, they are usually found in groups, often of like-size individuals.

Spawning takes place in the late summer or the early fall over clean, rocky lake bottoms. Rocky shoals or reefs are prominent spawning sites. Unlike other salmonids, lake trout do not make nests. Spawning usually takes place at night, with peak activity occurring after dusk. Eggs hatch early in the following spring. In some populations, spawning occurs every year, whereas in others spawning may occur every other year or less frequently.

Food. The diet of lake trout varies with the age and the size of the fish, the locality, and the food available. Food items commonly include zooplankton, insect larvae, small crustaceans, clams, snails, leeches, and various species of fish, including their own kind. Lake trout feed extensively on such other fish as whitefish, grayling, sticklebacks, suckers, and sculpin in the far north or cisco, smelt, and alewives elsewhere.

some parts of its native range, including the Great Lakes in North America.

Habitat. *Overall, and especially in the southern portions of its range or where introduced south of its native range, the lake trout is an inhabitant of cool waters of large, deep lakes. In far-northern regions it may occur in lakes that are generally shallow and that remain cold all season long, and it may occur in either the shallow or the deep portions of lakes that have large expanses of deep water. It is also found in large deep rivers or in the lower reaches of rivers, especially in the far north, although it may sometimes move into the tributaries of large southerly lakes to forage. It rarely inhabits brackish water.*

Trout, Rainbow

Oncorhynchus mykiss

OTHER NAMES

steelhead, rainbow, 'bow, redsides, Kamloops, red-band trout, Eagle Lake trout, Kern River trout, Shasta trout, San Gorgonio trout, Nelson trout, Whitney trout, silver trout; Danish: *regnbueørred;* Finnish: *kirjolohi;* French: *truite-arc-en-ciel;* German: *regenbogenforelle;* Italian: *trota iridea;* Japanese: *nijimasu;* Russian: *forel raduzhnaya;* Spanish: *trucha arco iris;* Swedish: *regnbåge;* Turkish: *alabalik türü.*

Distribution. *The rainbow trout is native to the West Coast of North America from southern Alaska to Durango, Mexico, and inland as far as central Alberta in Canada and Idaho and Nevada in the United States. It has been extensively introduced across the lower Canadian provinces, throughout the Great Lakes region and the northeastern United States to the Atlantic coast and south through the Appalachians to northern Georgia and Alabama, in*

The rainbow trout is one of the most widely distributed freshwater fish and the one member of the Salmonidae family that presently has global distribution. Endemic to western North America, it was reclassified from the trout genus *Salmo* to the Pacific salmon genus *Oncorhynchus* (it was formerly identified as *Salmo gairdneri*) and occurs in both freshwater resident and anadromous, or sea-run, races *(see: Steelhead).* One landlocked variety of rainbow trout from the interior of British Columbia is called the Kamloops trout, a genetically large strain called Gerrard trout exists in British Columbia's Kootenay Lake and its Lardeau River tributary, and there are many other variations (as well as hatchery-created hybrids) of rainbows known.

Identification. The rainbow trout possesses the typical elongated and streamlined salmonid form, although body shape and coloration vary widely and reflect habitat, age, sex, and degree of maturity. The body shape may range from slender to thick. The back may shade from blue-green to olive. There is a reddish-pink band along each side about the midline that may range from faint to radiant. The lower sides are usually silver, fading to pure white beneath.

The rainbow has numerous prominent black spots that may cover the entire body or may be more abundant near the tail. The spots characteristically extend onto the dorsal fin, the adipose fin, and the tail. Those on the tail radiate outward in an even, orderly pattern. Spots may be present on any of the lower fins. Rainbow trout are positively identified by the 8 to 12 rays in the anal fin, a mouth that does not extend past the back of the eye, and the lack of teeth at the base of the tongue.

Coloration varies greatly with size, habitat, and spawning periods. Stream dwellers and spawners usually show the darkest and most vivid colors and markings. River or stream residents normally display the most intense pink stripe coloration and the heaviest spotting, followed by rainbows from lake and lake-stream systems.

Size/Age. In general, stream-dwelling rainbows commonly weigh a pound or so, whereas fish from larger rivers and lakes commonly weigh between 2 and 4 pounds. Rainbows that have migrated to a large inland lake, such as one of the Great Lakes, may attain double-digit weights, although most weigh 7 to 10 pounds, and sea-run fish likewise become heavyweights. The largest nonanadromous rainbow trout in North America presently come from Alaska and British Columbia waters. World records are kept for all varieties of rainbow trout as one species, meaning that the anadromous form dominates the record books, including specimens from 20 to more than 30 pounds. They can live for 11 years but typically have a 4- to 6-year life span.

Life history/Behavior. Most varieties of rainbow trout spawn in the spring in small tributaries of rivers or in inlets or outlets of lakes. Spawning frequency ranges from annually to once every 3 years. Rainbow trout usually return to the streams where they hatched.

During the late winter or the early spring, when water temperatures are on the rise, maturing adult rainbows usually seek out shallow gravel riffles in their stream or a suitable clear-water stream that enters their lake. Spawning takes place from the late winter or the early spring through the early summer. The female uses her tail to prepare a nest (redd) 4 to 12 inches deep and 10 to 15 inches in diameter. Eggs are deposited in the redd, fertilized by a male, and covered with gravel. Hatching normally occurs from a few weeks to 4 months after spawning, depending on the water temperature.

Small trout assemble in groups and seek shelter along the stream margins or protected lakeshore, feeding on crustaceans, plant material, and aquatic insects and their larvae. They rear in similar habitats for the first 2 or 3 years, then move into the larger water of lakes and streams and turn more to a diet of fish, salmon carcasses, eggs, and even small mammals.

Food. Rainbows feed on a variety of food, mainly insects, crustaceans, snails, leeches, and other fish, if available.

the western United States easterly to western Texas, and sporadically in the central United States south of the Great Lakes.

Habitat. Although rainbows do well in large lakes with cool, deep waters, they prefer moderately flowing streams with abundant cover and deep pools. In most streams they are found in stretches of swift-flowing water, at the edge of strong currents, and at the head of rapids or strong riffles. They prefer water temperatures of 55° to 64°F but can tolerate water to 70°F.

Trout, Sunapee

Salvelinus alpinus oquassa

This member of the charr family was once classified as a separate species with the scientific name *Salvelinus aureolus*. A landlocked, or nonanadromous, charr, it was reclassified as a subspecies of the arctic charr *(S. alpinus oquassa; see: Charr, Arctic),* along with its close relatives the blueback trout and the Quebec red trout. The common name is derived from a native population of Sunapee Lake in New Hampshire; Sunapee trout there hybridized with lake trout and are no longer believed to exist, and the species is not currently documented in that state. Sunapees do exist in Maine, where there is a remnant population in Flood's Pond, and reintroductions have been made into some other waters.

Trout-Perch
Percopsis omiscomaycus

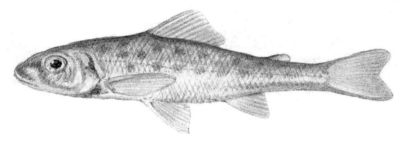

A member of the small Percopsidae family, the confusingly named trout-perch is neither a trout nor a perch, nor is it of angling significance, although it is an important forage species for predators.

Identification. The trout-perch derives its name from a superficial resemblance to a trout, by virtue of having an adipose fin, and to a yellow perch or a juvenile walleye by its body configuration. It has a fairly deep cylindrical body with a narrow caudal peduncle, large eyes, and a large unscaled head that is flattened on the underside. Its color is transparent yellow olive with silver flecks above, and rows of dusky spots appear along the back and the sides. A related species, the sandroller *(P. transmontana)*, is smaller and slightly darker, with a more arched back.

Size. This species reaches a maximum length of 6 to 8 inches; 3 to 5 inches is common.

Spawning behavior. This species spawns in the late spring, usually on sand and gravel sections of tributaries and occasionally on lake sandbars. Most trout-perch die after spawning, although a few fish live to spawn twice.

Food and feeding habits. Trout-perch feed on aquatic insects and small crustaceans and generally move from deeper water to shallower near-shore areas at night to feed.

OTHER NAMES
troutperch, silver chub; French: *omisco.*

Distribution. The trout-perch ranges from Hudson Bay to the Yukon Territory and from the Potomac River west to Kansas. The sandroller is found in the Columbia River drainage.

Habitat. The trout-perch occurs in lakes, and in the backwaters and the pool margins of midsize to large streams. It is primarily a deep-water resident.

Walleye

Stizostedion vitreum

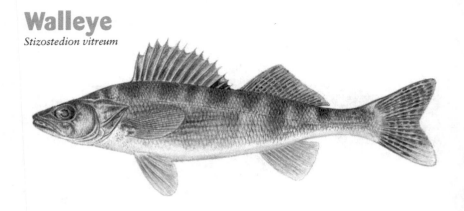

OTHER NAMES

pickerel, yellow pickerel, walleyed pike, yellow walleye, jack salmon, jack, pike-perch, walleyed pike-perch, pike, gray pike, green pike, 'eye, marbleye, glass-eye; French: *doré*.

Distribution. *The walleye is widely distributed in North America. Its native range in the north extended from Great Bear Lake in the Northwest Territories easterly to James Bay and the Gulf of St. Lawrence. In the east it extended southward along the Allegheny Mountains to Georgia and Gulf Coast drainages in Mississippi and Alabama. In the west it extended from Saskatchewan throughout the Dakotas to Arkansas. Through some natural expansion and extensive introduction, the range has been extended eastward to Atlantic coast drainages from Vermont to South Carolina and westward to all western states except California, as well as to southern Alberta and British Columbia.*

The walleye is the largest member of the Percidae family of perch in North America and a close relative of the sauger. A popular freshwater sportfish, the walleye is relatively abundant in many waters, grows to large sizes, and is renowned for its delicious, sweet, and fine-textured meat.

Identification. The walleye has a slender and cylindrical body with a tapered head. Its first dorsal fin has needle-sharp spiny rays and is separated from the soft-rayed second dorsal fin. The cheeks are sparsely scaled, the gill covers are sharp, and the teeth are sharp. When handling the fish, anglers must take care around the teeth, the gill covers, and the spiny dorsal fin to avoid cuts and stab wounds.

The walleye has a dark green back, golden yellow sides, and a white belly. The lower lobe of the caudal fin is white, and there is a large black blotch at the rear base of the spinous first dorsal fin. Color is highly variable, depending on habitat, with golden color characteristics in many populations. Typically, fish in turbid or off-color waters are paler, with less obvious black markings; clear waters produce more definitively marked specimens.

Perhaps the most prominent feature of a walleye is its large, white, glossy eyes. The special reflective layer in the retina of the eye is a characteristic known as tapetum lucidum; it gathers light that enters the eye, making it extremely sensitive to bright daylight intensities but conducive to nocturnal vision.

Size. The size of walleye varies with their environment, but anglers commonly encounter fish in the 10- to 18-inch range and weighing about 1 to 3 pounds. Some waters support fish that are larger on average, and it is not uncommon to catch walleye exceeding 5 pounds in many places. The all-tackle world record is a 25-pounder caught in Old Hickory Lake, Tennessee, in 1960.

Walleye (continued)

Life history/Behavior. Spawning occurs in the spring or the early summer, depending on latitude and water temperature. Normally, spawning begins shortly after the ice breaks up in lakes that freeze; water temperature is usually in the mid-40s, but spawning may occur at a range between 38° and 50°F.

The males move to the spawning grounds first. These are usually rocky areas in flowing water below impassable falls and dams in rivers and streams, coarse-gravel shoals, or (least common) along rubble shores of lakes at depths of less than 6 feet. Spawning takes place at night, in groups of one large female and one or two smaller males or two females and numerous males. The male walleye is not territorial and does not build a nest.

In clear lakes, walleye often lie in contact with the bottom during the daytime, seemingly resting. In these lakes, they usually feed from top to bottom at night. In turbid water, they are more active during the day, swimming slowly in schools close to the bottom. Walleye frequently are associated with other species, such as yellow perch, northern pike, white suckers, and smallmouth bass. During the winter, walleye do not change their habitat except to avoid strong currents. In large water bodies, they will orient to open water in schools that coincide with the presence of baitfish, especially alewives, but also shad and perch.

Food and feeding habits. The walleye can be a voracious feeder and primarily consumes other fish. The wide diet includes alewives, smelt, shad, cisco, shiners, sculpin, suckers, minnows, darters, perch, and crayfish, as well as many other items. Their diet shifts rapidly from invertebrates to fish as walleye increase in size. Some populations, even as adults, feed almost exclusively on emerging larval or adult mayflies for part of the year. The relative amounts of the various species of fish that walleye feed on apparently are determined by their availability. Yellow perch and cyprinids are particularly favored when these species are present.

Habitat. Walleye are tolerant of a great range of environmental situations but seem to do best in the open water of large lakes and reservoirs, as well as the pools of large rivers. They inhabit many smaller bodies of water but are not typically prolific in the most turbid environs, preferring somewhat clearer water than their sauger cousins. Gravel, rock, and firm sand bottoms are preferred, and they may associate with various weed cover; they will also use sunken trees, standing timber, boulder shoals, and reefs as cover and foraging sites. Although they can survive temperature extremes from 32° to 90°F, they prefer waters with a maximum temperature of roughly 77° and are commonly associated with 65° to 75° water in summer.

Warmouth

Lepomis gulosus

goggle-eye, openmouth, perch.

Distribution. *Originally found in the Great Lakes and Mississippi River basins from western Pennsylvania to Minnesota and south to the Gulf of Mexico, warmouth occur in Atlantic and Gulf drainages from the Rappahannock River, Virginia, to the Rio Grande in Texas and New Mexico. They are abundant in lowland areas and less common in the uplands, and they have been introduced in many places, including the lower Colorado River drainage, where they are common.*

Habitat. *Warmouth inhabit relatively shallow, vegetated, slow-flowing, mud-bottom creeks, ponds, lakes, swamps, and reservoirs. They are often found around weedbeds, snags, hollow trees, or stumps, and under the banks of streams and ponds.*

The warmouth is a member of the Centrarchidae family of sunfish and has white, flaky flesh.

Identification. The warmouth has a deep, stout body and is olive brown above and cream to bright yellow below, often with an overall purple luster and a dark brown chain-like mottling on the back and the upper sides. Dark, red brown lines extend from the back of each eye. On a breeding male, there is a red orange spot on the yellow edge of each short ear flap, and there are dark brown spots and wavy bands on the fins. The warmouth has a large mouth and a patch of teeth on the tongue, and the upper jaw extends under or past the pupils of the eyes. It also has short, rounded pectoral fins and stiff rear edges on its gill covers.

Size/Age. The warmouth can reach a weight of 1 pound and a length of 12 inches. It is capable of living for 6 to 8 years. The all-tackle world record is a 2-pound, 7-ounce fish taken in Florida in 1985.

Spawning behavior. Warmouth begin spawning from April through August when they are 3 to 4 inches long and from 1 to 3 years old. Spawning peaks in early June, when waters warm to about 70°F. The male builds a shallow, bowl-shaped nest in water less than 5 feet deep, often in the company of others, so that a small colony of nests is formed. Preferred nesting sites are in a sand or a rubble bottom with a thin covering of silt, near patches of lily pads, cattails, and grasses, or at the base of trees standing in shallow water.

Food. Warmouth feed on invertebrates, small sunfish, darters, mosquitofish, crayfish, snails, freshwater shrimp, dragonflies, and other insects.

Whitefish, Lake

Coregonus clupeaformis

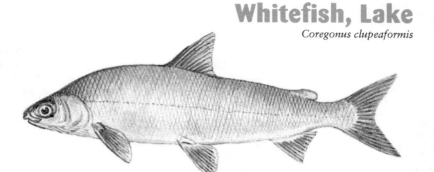

The lake whitefish is a larger and more widespread fish than are the mountain and the round whitefish, and it is more highly regarded among anglers. A member of the Salmonidae family, the lake whitefish is a valuable commercial freshwater fish in Canada, although its numbers have declined due to environmental factors and overfishing, especially in the Great Lakes. The flesh—prepared fresh, smoked, and frozen—is considered superb in flavor, and its roe is made into an excellent caviar.

Identification. A slender, elongated species, the lake whitefish is silvery to white with an olive to pale greenish-brown back that is dark brown to midnight blue or black in some inland lake specimens; it also has white fins and a dark-edged tail. The mouth is subterminal and the snout protrudes beyond it, with a double flap of skin between the nostrils. The tail is deeply forked, and an adipose fin is present. The lake whitefish is occasionally referred to as "humpback" because the head is small in relation to the length of the body, and older specimens may develop a hump behind the head. It has 10 to 14 anal rays, 70 to 97 scales down the lateral line, and 19 to 33 gill rakers. The body is more laterally compressed than that of the round or the mountain whitefish, which belong to a separate genus of "round whitefish."

Size/Age. The lake whitefish is commonly 18 inches long and weighs 2 to 4 pounds. Some are said to reach as much as 31 inches, and the all-tackle world record is a 14-pound, 6-ounce fish caught in Ontario, Canada, in 1984. The average whitefish caught by anglers is in the 1- to 2-pound range. Fish of 4 or 5 pounds, and even larger, are sometimes caught. This species can live for 18 years.

Life history/Behavior. Spawning occurs in the late fall, when fish migrate into shallow areas over sandy bottoms or

OTHER NAMES

high back, bow back, buffalo back, or humpback whitefish; common whitefish; eastern whitefish; Great Lakes whitefish; inland whitefish; Sault whitefish; gizzard fish; Cree: *atekamek;* French: *grand corégone.*

Distribution. *Lake whitefish occur throughout Alaska and Canada; in the mainland United States, they occur throughout central Minnesota and the Great Lakes and from New York to Maine. Transplanted populations exist in Washington, Idaho, and Montana. They have been stocked into high Andean lakes in a few countries in South America.*

Habitat. *Lake whitefish are named for their primary habitat of large, deep lakes, but they are also residents of large rivers. They prefer water temperatures of 50° to 55°F and will enter brackish water.*

shoals in large lakes or tributary streams. Eggs are randomly deposited over the bottom by females laying up to 12,000 eggs per pound of body weight. These fish do not build nests, and parents return to deep water after spawning, leaving eggs unprotected on spawning grounds until they hatch the following spring. By early summer, the young move from shallow inshore areas to deeper water.

Food and feeding habits. Mainly bottom feeders, adult lake whitefish feed primarily on aquatic insect larvae, mollusks, and amphipods, but also on other small fish and fish eggs, including their own. Young fish feed on plankton.

Whitefish, Mountain

Prosopium williamsoni

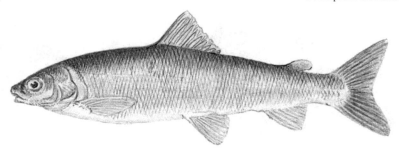

A member of the Salmonidae family, the mountain whitefish provides an important winter fishery in certain areas, especially where steelhead are absent.

Identification. Possessing an adipose fin and an axillary process, the mountain whitefish is long, slender, and nearly cylindrical, although not quite as cylindrical as the round whitefish. It is nevertheless among the species referred to as "round whitefish" and can be distinguished from the lake whitefish, which is more laterally compressed than is the mountain whitefish. Silvery overall, it is dark brownish to olive or greenish to blue-gray above, with scales that often have dark borders and ventral and pectoral fins that may have an amber shade in adults. The small mouth is slightly subterminal, and the snout extends clearly beyond it. The caudal fin is forked, and there are 74 to 90 scales down the lateral line and 19 to 26 gill rakers.

Size/Age. The mountain whitefish can grow to 22½ inches and 5 pounds. The all-tackle world record is a 1988 5½-pound fish from Saskatchewan. The mountain whitefish can live for 18 years.

Spawning behavior. Spawning takes place from October through December in shallow, gravelly streams or occasionally in lakes at water temperatures of 42°F or less. Parents do not guard the eggs, which incubate over the winter to hatch in the spring.

Food and feeding habits. Mountain whitefish feed primarily on benthic organisms like aquatic insect larvae, mollusks, fish, and fish eggs (including their own), as well as on plankton and surface insects when primary food sources are unavailable.

OTHER NAMES

Rocky mountain whitefish, Williamson's whitefish, grayling; French: *ménomini des montagnes.*

Distribution. The mountain whitefish is endemic to the lakes and the streams of the northwestern United States and southwestern Canada. It occurs inland into Alberta and Wyoming, overlapping the range of the lake whitefish and slightly overlapping that of the round whitefish.

Habitat. Generally inhabiting rivers and fast, clear, or silty areas of larger streams, as well as lakes, mountain whitefish usually occur in stream riffles during the summer and in large pools in the winter. They prefer temperatures of 46° to 52°F and are found in the deep water of some lakes, although in northern lakes they usually hold no deeper than 30 feet.

Whitefish, Round

Prosopium cylindraceum

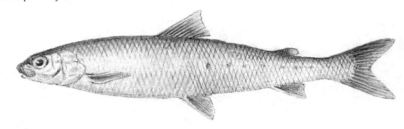

OTHER NAMES

menominee, round fish, frost fish, pilot fish, grayback; French: *ménomini rond.*

Distribution. *The round whitefish occurs in arctic drainages and is a wide-ranging species in the northern portions of North America. It has disjunct populations, one of which is found through the St. Lawrence-Great Lakes basin (with the exception of Lake Erie), north to the Arctic Ocean east of Hudson Bay; the other is found through-out the northern Canadian provinces and Alaska west of Hudson Bay. It also occurs in limited areas directly south of Hudson Bay and in East Twin Lake in Connecticut.*

Habitat. *Occurring in the shallow areas of lakes and streams, round whitefish may also inhabit rivers with swift currents and stony bottoms. They rarely enter brackish water or water more than 150 feet deep.*

A member of the Salmonidae family, the round whitefish seldom exceeds 2 pounds and is sought to a limited degree by anglers.

Identification. The round whitefish is mostly silvery and has a dark brown to almost bronze coloring, with a greenish tint on the back. It has black-edged scales, particularly on the back. The lower fins are an amber color, becoming slightly more orange during spawning, and the adipose fin is usually brown spotted. Young fish have two or more rows of black spots on the sides that may merge with a row of black spots on the back. The round whitefish has a small head, a fairly pointed snout, and a single flap of skin between its nostrils. It also has a forked caudal fin, 74 to 108 scales down the lateral line, and 14 to 21 gill rakers. The round and the lake whitefish can be easily distinguished from each other because the round whitefish has a very cylindrical body, whereas the body of the lake whitefish is laterally compressed.

Size. Usually about 8 to 12 inches long and weighing ½ pound or less, the round whitefish can grow to more than 20 inches long and weigh several pounds. The all-tackle world record is a 6-pounder taken in Manitoba in 1984.

Spawning behavior. Spawning takes place during the fall in lakes, in tributary mouths, and occasionally in rivers over gravelly shallow areas. Fish spawn in pairs; their eggs hatch in the early spring.

Food. Round whitefish feed on benthic invertebrates and occasionally on fish and fish eggs.

Glossary

ADIPOSE EYELID
A translucent tissue partially covering the eyeballs of some species of fish.

ADIPOSE FIN
A small fleshy fin without rays found on the backs of some fish, behind the dorsal fin and ahead of the caudal fin. Only a small percentage of fish have an adipose fin; among gamefish, these include various trout, salmon, grayling, whitefish, and piranhas.

ALGAE
The term "algae" refers to a large, heterogenous group of primitive aquatic plants whose members lack roots, stems, or leaf systems and range from unicellular organisms to large networks of kelp. Algae exist in both freshwater and saltwater. They can be blue-green, yellow, green, brown, and red; there are more than 15,000 species of green algae alone. All species of algae photosynthesize.

As the primary or lowest plant forms, algae are important in sustaining marine and freshwater food chains. In freshwater, algae occur in three different types often encountered by anglers: plankton, filamentous, and muskgrass. Plankton is a diverse community made up of suspended algae (phytoplankton), combined with great numbers of minute suspended animals (zooplankton). Filamentous algae consist of stringy, hairlike filaments, often erroneously described as moss or slime because of their appearance when they form a mat or a furlike coat on objects. Muskgrass, or stonewort, algae are a more advanced form that has no roots but attaches to lake or stream bottoms.

ALIEN SPECIES
A species occurring in an area outside of its historically known natural range as a result of intentional or accidental dispersal by human activities. These are also known as exotic or introduced species.

AMPHIPODS
A large group of crustaceans, most of which are small, compressed creatures (such as sand fleas and freshwater shrimp). These may be of food importance to juvenile fish.

ANADROMOUS
Fish that migrate from saltwater to freshwater in order to spawn. Fish that do the opposite are called catadromous.

Literally meaning "up running," anadromous refers to fish that spend part of their lives in the ocean and move into freshwater rivers or streams to spawn. Anadromous fish hatch in freshwater, move to saltwater to grow to adulthood or sexual maturity, and then return to freshwater to reproduce. Salmon are the best-known anadromous fish, but there are many others, including such prominent species as steelhead trout, sturgeon, striped bass, and shad, and many lesser-known or less highly regarded species. Around the world there are approximately 100 species of anadromous fish.

Complicating an understanding of anadromy is the fact that some anadromous species have adapted, either naturally or by introduction, to a complete life in freshwater environments. These species, which include salmon, striped bass, and steelhead, make spawning migrations from lakes, where they live most of their lives, into rivers to spawn.

In such instances, these fish are originally saltwater in origin. They remain anadromous when moved into purely freshwater, although they use the lake as they would the ocean. There are also species of freshwater fish that are native to freshwater and that migrate from lake to stream or river to spawn. These are not technically anadromous but adfluvial.

Fish that originate in saltwater but have freshwater forms are often called "landlocked," whether or not they have a clear path to and from the sea. Sometimes these fish are physically blocked from reaching the ocean. Fish in a reservoir or a lake may be unable to leave. Fish in some streams, like those in high-mountain areas, have a clear passageway to the sea but no means of returning because of waterfalls. Coldwater species may be effectively landlocked in the colder headwaters of a stream because temperatures are too high for them in the lowland parts of that stream or in the ocean in that area. Dolly Varden, for example, are landlocked in the southern tip of their range, but anadromous forms are common farther north.

ANAL FIN
The median, unpaired, ventrally located fin that lies behind the anus, usually on the posterior half of the fish.

AXILLARY PROCESS
A fleshy flap, which is usually narrow and extends to the rear, situated just above the pectoral or the pelvic fins on some fish.

BAITFISH
A generic term used by anglers for any fish species that are forage for predators, although it often specifically pertains to smaller fish; this term also references fish that are used in live bait angling.

BARBEL
A whiskerlike feeler on the snouts of some fish that contains taste buds and is used for touching and tasting food before ingesting it. One or more barbels

may be present on either side of the mouth of a fish that is primarily a bottom feeder and is attracted by food odor. Catfish, carp, and sturgeon are among the species with such appendages.

BASS
Many species of fish, in both freshwater and saltwater, are referred to as "bass." Some are truly bass and some are not, but all have a physique and a profile that are generally similar. Three of the most prominent freshwater sportfish with this name include the largemouth bass and the smallmouth bass, both of which are actually sunfish, and the peacock bass, which is actually a cichlid.

True bass are members of the Serranidae family of sea bass,, which in freshwater includes the white bass and the yellow bass, and in saltwater includes the black sea bass, the striped bass, the giant sea bass, the kelp bass, and many other species that do not carry the name "bass."

BASS, BLACK
"Black bass" is a common name for all species and subspecies of the genus *Micropterus,* which belong to the Centrarchidae family of sunfish. These include largemouth bass, smallmouth bass, redeye bass, spotted bass, Suwannee bass, and Guadalupe bass. Black bass are strictly freshwater species, and they are more elongated and generally larger than their family relatives.

The term should not be confused with the various sea bass that are members of the Serranidae family of saltwater fish, some of which have a physique similar to that of species in the genus *Micropterus.*

BENTHIC
The bottom layer of the marine environment and the fish or the animals that live on or near the bottom.

BONY FISH
Fish that have a bony skeleton and belong to the class *Osteichthyes.* Basically, this includes all fish except sharks, rays, skates, hagfish, and lampreys.

BREAM

Many species of both freshwater and saltwater fish around the world are referred to as bream, particularly in Australia, the United Kingdom, and the United States. In the United States, "bream" (pronounced "brim") is a colloquial expression for various freshwater panfish species, particularly sunfish and especially bluegills.

In Europe, the bream pursued by anglers are members of the Cyprinidae family and are relatives of carp, barbel, and tench. These primarily small or mid-size fish (less than 8 pounds) are bottom feeders and are widely distributed. They are also a popular coarse (non-gamefish) species. The primary quarry is the bronze bream, which is also known as the common bream or the carp bream.

In saltwater, various members of the Sparidae family are known as sea bream and are related to porgies. Sea bream occur in temperate and tropical waters worldwide.

CANINE TEETH

Pointed canine teeth are found in some carnivorous fish; they are usually larger than the surrounding teeth.

CATADROMOUS

Fish that migrate from freshwater to saltwater in order to spawn. Fish that do the opposite are called anadromous and are more numerous. Freshwater eels are typical of catadromous fish; they are born at sea, migrate upstream to live and grow to adulthood, and then return to the sea to migrate to their spawning grounds.

CAUDAL FIN

The tail fin, or the fin at the rear of the fish. The fleshy section connecting the caudal fin to the end of the body is called the caudal peduncle (see).

CAUDAL PEDUNCLE

The fleshy tail end of the body of a fish between the anal and the caudal fins. On some fish, the caudal peduncle is rigid and provides a convenient "handle" of sorts for holding the fish.

COLDWATER FISH

A term for freshwater species whose optimum environment contains cold and well-oxygenated water, usually under 60°F, throughout the season; trout, salmon, grayling, whitefish, and cisco are among this group. They inhabit coldwater streams and generally infertile lakes; in lakes, their deep environs must have cold, well-oxygenated water through the summer.

COOLWATER FISH

An occasional term for freshwater species whose optimum environment is water of intermediate temperature, approximately from 60° to 70°F; northern pike, muskellunge, yellow perch, walleye, and smallmouth bass are among this group. They inhabit cool to moderately warm rivers and lakes of moderate fertility, often existing in waters that also accommodate species preferring colder and warmer temperatures.

CRUSTACEAN

A group of freshwater and saltwater animals having no backbone, with jointed legs and a hard shell made of chitin. In saltwater this group includes shrimp, crabs, lobsters, and crayfish, all of which may be used as bait when angling but are not targeted by anglers or deliberately sought with sporting equipment. Freshwater crustaceans also include crayfish, as well as scuds, sowbugs, and shrimp.

DEMERSAL

A term used for fish or animals that live on or near the seabed or the water bottom. Examples include flounder and croaker. Demersal is often used synonymously with groundfish.

DETRITUS

Waste from decomposing organisms, which provides food for many other organisms.

DIADROMOUS

Fish that migrate between freshwater and saltwater.

DINOFLAGELLATE

Unicellular microscopic organisms, classified as plants or animals, depending on the presence of chlorophyll or the ingestion of food, respectively. Found in two main groups, armored and naked, dinoflagellates have flagella (whiplike extensions) that provide locomotion, and they move vertically in response to light. Many dinoflagellates are phosphorescent, and some greatly increase in number periodically, occasionally resulting in toxic red tides. Some dinoflagellate blooms are toxic to shellfish and can cause gastroenteritis in the organisms that feed on them, including humans. As a component of phytoplankton (microscopic organisms that photosynthesize), dinoflagellates are an important basis for marine life.

DORSAL FIN

A median fin along the back, which is supported by rays. There may be two or more dorsal fins, in which case they are numbered, with the fin closest to the head called the first dorsal fin.

ENDANGERED SPECIES

In the United States, a species is classified as endangered if it is in danger of extinction throughout all or a significant portion of its range. Elsewhere, a species is classified as endangered if the factors causing its vulnerability or decline continue to operate, as defined by the International Union for the Conservation of Nature and Natural Resources.

EXOTIC SPECIES

Organisms introduced into habitats where they are not native are called exotic species. They are often the agents of severe worldwide, regional, and local habitat alteration. Also referred to as nonindigenous, nonnative, alien, transplant, foreign, and introduced species, they can be the cause of biological diversity loss and can greatly upset the balance of ecosystems.

Exotic species have been introduced around the world both intentionally and accidentally; occasionally, exotic species occur in new places through natural means, but usually the agent is some action of humans. That includes transportation of fish or larvae via the ballast of ocean freighters and the bait buckets of small-boat anglers, passage of new species via newly constructed canals, the introduction of plants by using them in packing shellfish that are shipped transcontinentally, the dumping of aquarium plants and fish into local waterways, the experimental stocking of predator and prey species by scientists and nonscientists, and many other means. Exotic species can be transported by animals, vehicles, commercial goods, produce, and even clothing.

While some exotic introductions are ecologically harmless, many are very harmful and have even caused the extinction of native species, especially those of confined habitats. Freed from the predators, the pathogens, and the competitors that have kept their numbers in check in their native environs, species introduced into new habitats often overrun their new home and crowd out native species. In the presence of enough food and a favorable environment, their numbers explode. Once established, exotics rarely can be eliminated.

FIN

An organ on different parts of a fish's body that may be used for propulsion, balance, and steering.

FINFISH

An alternative collective term for all species of fish, used to separate true fish from crustaceans and mollusks, which are collectively termed shellfish. The term is rarely used in reference to freshwater species but is commonly used to refer to saltwater and anadromous fish, particularly by fisheries managers.

FINGERLING

A young fish about 2 to 4 inches long.

FISHERY

In a biological sense, all the activities involved in catching a species of fish or a group of species; the place where a species or a group of species is caught. In common usage by the general public, fishery also refers to fishing opportunity or species availability in either a recreational or a commercial sense, as in "the fishery for coho salmon does not commence until the annual migration run." This term is used interchangeably with fisheries.

FISHKILL
The die-off of fish, usually in numbers. Fishkills may occur as the result of chemical pollution, especially from pesticides in agricultural runoff, but most often happen as a result of insufficient oxygen in the water.

A winter fishkill occurs when ice and snow cut off the transfer of oxygen from the air to the water; the oxygen in the water gets used up, and fish die. This does not happen if there is enough oxygen in the water to last throughout the winter until the ice and snow melt.

A summer fishkill usually occurs when inadequate amounts of oxygen exist in the water during extended periods of hot, calm, and cloudy days. Warm summer water temperatures, high demands for oxygen, and days with no sunlight or wind to mix the surface water may lead to oxygen demands exceeding oxygen production. When this happens, distressed fish may be seen as they rise to the surface and gasp for oxygen, and dead fish may be seen floating on the surface.

FRESHWATER
Water with less than 0.5 gram per liter of total dissolved mineral salts.

GILL
A breathing organ with much-divided thin-walled filaments for extracting oxygen from the water. In a living fish, the gills are bright red feathery organs that are located on bony arches and are prominent when the gill covers of the fish are lifted.

GILL RAKERS
Toothlike extensions, located along the anterior margin of the gill arch, that project over the throat opening and strain water that is passed over the gills. These protect the gill filaments and, in some fish, are used to sieve out tiny food organisms. The number of gill rakers on the first gill arch is sometimes used as an aid in identifying or separating species that closely resemble one another.

GRILSE
A salmon, usually male, that returns to freshwater rivers after 1 year at sea. These are small fish, generally weighing from 2 to 4 pounds.

GROUNDFISH
A species or a group of fish that lives most of its life on or near the seabed. The term may be used synonymously with demersal. Groundfish refers to Atlantic cod, haddock, pollock, American plaice, white hake, redfish, and various flounders.

HYBRID
The offspring of two individuals of different species. The offspring of two individuals belonging to different subspecies of the same species are not hybrids.

Hybridization may occur in the wild or under artificial conditions. Some species that have been known to crossbreed naturally, although not frequently, include lake trout and brook trout (splake), northern pike and muskellunge (tiger muskie), and walleye and sauger (saugeye). Hybrid fish have been cultivated in hatcheries by fisheries managers for stocking purposes; hybrid striped bass (known as whiterock bass, wiper, and sunshine bass), which result from a cross of pure-strain striped bass and white bass, have been extremely popular for stocking and are widely spread in freshwater lakes and reservoirs. Most hybrid fish are sterile (although some, like whiterock bass, are not), so the stocking of these fish is attractive because they can be controlled fairly well; if the initial stocking experiment does not achieve the desired results, the population of hybrids can be extinguished by discontinuing stocking.

INSHORE

The waters from the shallower part of the continental shelf toward shore. In saltwater fishing parlance, inshore is a loose and variable term referring to that portion of the water from which land is visible or is nearly visible, usually on the shoreward side of major currents or shelves, and is populated by nonpelagic species. This term is seldom used by freshwater lake anglers.

LACUSTRINE

Having to do with, or living in, a lake.

LANDLOCKED

A term for anadromous fish that have adapted to a completely freshwater existence, spending the greater portion of their lives in a lake and returning to natal rivers or streams to spawn. Any fish—usually salmon but also striped bass—with such behavior and without access to saltwater is landlocked.

LARVAE

The early life forms of a fish or other animal between the time of hatching and transforming to a juvenile.

LATERAL LINE

A series of sensory cells, usually running the length of both sides of the fish's body, that performs an important function in receiving low-frequency vibrations.

LITTORAL

Living in or related to nearshore waters; the intertidal zone of the marine environment that is exposed at low tide and covered at high tide.

LUNATE

Used to describe a caudal fin that is shaped like a crescent moon.

MARINE

Pertaining to the sea and saltwater environs, from the open oceans to the high-water mark and into estuaries; also used to refer to seawater or saltwater.

MIDWATER

In or near the middle layer of water. This term is generally used by biologists to describe the habitat of fish that are not surface or bottom (benthic or demersal, respectively) dwellers.

MIGRATION

A regular journey made by a particular species of fish, on an annual or a lifetime basis, usually associated with propagation patterns but also associated with the seasonal availability of food. Most migrations are mass movements and involve travel over a particular route, usually at the same time annually. Migration is not to be confused with the relocation of fish because of pollution, sedimentation, storms, or the temporary relocation of food sources. Anglers, for example, often refer to fish as making migrations from deep water to shallow water to feed, an action that is really a localized movement. The periodic movement of fish in a water body is not necessarily a migration, although the movement of a fish species to and from breeding grounds (such as walleye in the spring moving from a spawning river back to the main lake) is a migration.

Migrations occur in various species and in both freshwater and saltwater. All freshwater fish that move from lake or river environs to a tributary in order to spawn will migrate to and from the spawning grounds at or around the same time each year. All anadromous and catadromous fish undertake spawning migrations, the former from saltwater to freshwater and the latter from freshwater to saltwater, also around the same time annually. Pelagic ocean species migrate from winter to summer grounds, both for spawning and for food procurement, also around the same time annually.

Migrations occur in north-south, south-north, offshore-inshore, and inshore-offshore patterns, and in combinations of these (some sea organisms migrate up and down in the water column). Some fish migrations cover great distances, even thousands of miles, and some are extremely short, perhaps just a short distance up a river.

MOLLUSK

A group of freshwater and saltwater animals with no skeleton and usually one or two hard shells made of calcium carbonate. This group includes the oyster, the clam, the mussel, the snail, the conch, the scallop, the squid, and the octopus. Mollusks may be used as bait when angling, but they are not targeted by anglers or deliberately sought with sporting equipment.

NATIVE
A species of fish that is endemic to a region, a watershed, or a specific body of water. A native species is distinguished from an introduced or exotic species, which occurs outside its endemic range and has been placed there by unnatural means (usually deliberate but sometimes accidental planting by humans). The term "native" is particularly applied in North America to endemic trout, especially brook trout.

NEARSHORE
The shallow portion of inshore saltwaters adjacent to the shoreline. In fishing parlance, inshore is a more common term than nearshore, and they are generally interchangeable, although nearshore is more specific.

NEST
A visible bed, often circular, made by egg-laying fish on the bottom of a body of water for spawning. Eggs are laid in the nest, and sometimes they are guarded by one or more of the parents.

NURSERY
The part of a fish's or an animal's habitat where the young grow up.

OFFSHORE
Although this term practically signifies the direction away from land, in fishing parlance it generally means that portion of the water from which land is not visible, and to most saltwater anglers it pertains to deep-water areas, on the edge of ocean currents or shelves, where big-game species, particularly billfish and tuna, are pursued.

ONSHORE
Waters abutting a coastline. This word is also used synonymously with ashore, meaning physically on the land adjacent to water, but is even more specific than nearshore. It is not the opposite of offshore in common angling usage.

OPERCULUM
The largest and uppermost bone that forms the gill cover of a fish.

PALATINE TEETH
Teeth located on the palatine bones inside the upper jawbone, usually behind the vomerine tooth patch.

PANFISH
This term is used widely by anglers and fisheries managers to collectively describe a variety of small fish of several species. There is no individual species called a panfish. The term is used almost universally in freshwater, seldom in saltwater; although common to anglers, it may be unfamiliar or even confusing to nonanglers.

The term "panfish" often refers to fish that, when fried whole, can fit into a pan, but it is also frequently understood to mean species that are not technically classified as gamefish and that are usually abundant and as valued for their tasty flesh as for the enjoyment of catching them.

Although panfish are commonly linked by these factors, the species that fit under this umbrella are not all linked biologically. Many "panfish" are members of the sunfish family, perch family, bass family, catfish family, and sucker family. These include, but are not limited to, such sunfish as green, longear, orangespotted, spotted, and redear varieties; plus bluegill, Sacramento perch, rock bass, warmouth bass, black crappie, white crappie, yellow bass, white bass, yellow perch, and white perch. In some areas, people include suckers, bullhead, pickerel, and even carp in this category.

PARR
Small, young anadromous fish, particularly salmon and trout, living in freshwater prior to migrating out to sea. During this life stage, parr develop large vertical or oval rounded spots (sometimes called bars) on the sides. Called parr marks,

these help camouflage the fish and also identify it; they will gradually disappear as the fish becomes silvery, regardless of whether the fish goes to sea (some do not). In the silvery phase, the fish is known as a smolt. Migration to sea occurs between 2 and 8 years.

PECTORAL FIN
The fin usually found on each side of the body, directly behind the gill opening.

PELAGIC FISH
Free-swimming fish that inhabit the open sea and are independent of the seabed or the water bottom.

PELVIC FIN
The pair of adjoining fins ventrally located beneath the belly and in front of the anus; also called ventral fins.

PHARYNGEAL
Bones in the throat of certain fish that are used like teeth to crush food. These bones are hard and strong and will crush such objects as clams, mussels, and snails. Carp have pharyngeal teeth, which play an important role in their forage habits.

PHYTOPLANKTON
Microscopic suspended algae in the surface waters of seas and lakes, where there is enough light for photosynthesis to occur.

PISCIVOROUS
Fish eating. Most predatory fish, and most of those considered sportfish, are piscivorous.

PLANKTON
Passively floating or weakly swimming organisms in a body of water. Planktonic organisms may drift and float freely, range widely in size, and include the larval stages of many fishes. Some are invisible without magnification, and others are visible to the unaided eye.

POD
A small, tight group of fish swimming together.

POTAMADROMOUS
Fish that migrate within rivers or streams to spawn.

PREDATOR
A species that feeds on other species. Most of the fish species that are pursued by anglers are predators at or near the top of the food chain.

PREY
A species that is fed upon by other species.

REDD
A pit or a trough made by female salmon and trout in the gravel bottom of rivers or streams for spawning. Eggs are laid in the redd, which is sometimes also called a nest.

RIVERINE
Of or living in a river or flowing water.

ROE
The eggs of a female fish; also a term for a female fish with eggs.

SALTWATER/SEAWATER
Commonly used terms for water with many dissolved salts in or from the ocean, as well as in connected seas, bays, sounds, estuaries, marshes, and the lower portion of tidal rivers.

SCHOOL
A closely spaced collection of fish whose members swim in association with each other. Fish in a school are often of the same species and of similar size, but species may intermingle and may vary in size. Some species are noted for their tendency to school, while other species are more solitary.

SCHOOLING
(1) The behavioral grouping of fish, usually of the same or related species, which move together as a unit and exhibit a specific geometrical relationship. Similar to herding, schooling may be a natural means of reducing predation and ensuring the survival of some individuals. Many species of fish school throughout their lives, and young fish, as well as prey species, are especially likely to school.

Fish of different species seldom intermingle, although related species (such as white bass and striped bass, for example) may do so.

Schools are composed of many fish of the same species moving in more or less harmonious patterns throughout the oceans. A very prevalent behavior, schooling is exhibited by almost 80 percent of all fish species during some phase of their life cycles. Many of the world's commercial fishing industries rely on this behavior pattern to produce their catch, especially for species like cod, tuna, mackerel, and menhaden.

SEA-RUN
Another term for anadromous, referring to fish that move from the sea to freshwater to spawn.

SHOAL
A school of fish, usually at the surface or in shallow water (a term used in Europe and sometimes in South America).

SMOLT
A young silvery salmon migrating from freshwater to the sea.

THREATENED SPECIES
In the United States, a species is classified as threatened if it is likely to become endangered within the foreseeable future throughout all or a significant portion of its range. Elsewhere, a species is classified as vulnerable rather than threatened, according to the International Union for the Conservation of Nature and Natural Resources.

TUBERCLE
A small hard knob on the skin that appears seasonally on some breeding male fish.

VERMICULATIONS
Short, wavy, wormlike lines on the backs and sides of some fish.

VOMERINE TEETH
Teeth located on the vomer, a median bone in the front of the roof of the mouth of a fish.

WARMWATER FISH
A term for freshwater species whose optimum environment contains warm water, usually over 70°F, and that can tolerate warm and even turbid or poorly oxygenated water during summer; largemouth bass, various sunfish, crappie, bullhead, and catfish are among this group. They primarily inhabit warm rivers and streams and very fertile lakes and ponds, many of which are shallow.

ZOOPLANKTON
Minute suspended animals in the water column of seas and lakes.

CPSIA information can be obtained
at www.ICGtesting.com
Printed in the USA
JSHW021408111220
10121JS00005B/182

9 781620 458433